The Anatomy of Fake News

The publisher and the University of California Press Foundation gratefully acknowledge the generous support of the Anne G. Lipow Endowment Fund in Social Justice and Human Rights.

The Anatomy of Fake News

A CRITICAL NEWS LITERACY EDUCATION

Nolan Higdon

 UNIVERSITY OF CALIFORNIA PRESS

University of California Press
Oakland, California

© 2020 by Nolan Higdon

Cataloging-in-Publication Data is on file at the Library of Congress.

ISBN 978-0-520-34786-1 (cloth : alk. paper)
ISBN 978-0-520-34787-8 (pbk. : alk. paper)
ISBN 978-0-520-97584-2 (ebook)

Manufactured in the United States of America

28 27 26 25 24 23 22 21 20
10 9 8 7 6 5 4 3 2 1

Contents

Acknowledgments   *vii*

Introduction   *1*

1   The Fourth Estate: Democracy and the Press   *15*

2   The Faux Estate: A Brief History of Fake News
in America   *26*

3   Satirical News and Political Party Propaganda
Apparatuses   *49*

4   The Roots of State-Sponsored Propaganda   *67*

5   Fake News and the Internet Economy   *92*

6   Fighting Fake News: Solutions and Discontent   *125*

7   The Fake News Detection Kit: The Ten-Point Process
to Save Our Democracy   *144*

Notes   *159*
Bibliography   *207*
Index   *229*

Acknowledgments

The origins of this book date back to my childhood, when my mother, Brenda Higdon, explained that the advertisements I was watching on television ranged from misleading to false. This early media literacy lesson engendered a healthy skepticism of media texts and curiosity about the purpose, function, and influence of media. I am forever grateful to my mother for fostering and encouraging my critical view of media.

My interest in fake news was piqued by my undergraduate history instructor Mickey Huff. Mickey's contemporaneous analysis of the news media's coverage of the 2003 US invasion of Iraq nurtured a lifelong curiosity and cynicism about the power of news media. Mickey and I would go on to have a fifteen-year-long professional relationship, which still persists, where he acted as my mentor, colleague, coauthor, and friend. Mickey has worked tirelessly to encourage my research and construct a platform for my success. His support, intellect, and wit were pivotal to the completion of this project.

The idea for this book germinated from a 2012 meeting with Kathryn Olmsted, where she proposed news media propaganda as a doctoral dissertation topic. Although I did not choose the topic, I continually confronted fake news in my research and courses. Finally, in 2017 my department chair Mary Cardaras encouraged me to teach a special topics course on fake news. I shaped the course around the dissertation proposal I discussed with Dr. Olmsted. The research I performed for that course, and the feedback I received from the students who completed it, served as the basis for this book. Thank you to Dr. Cardaras, Dr. Olmsted, and the students enrolled in the 2018 spring quarter "Fighting Fake News" course at California State University, East Bay, for making this book possible: Amber Abadia, Ethan Alonzo, Liam Beyerle, Vanessa Cardenas, Yasmine Castaneda, Alex Chacala, Hannah Childress, Monique Contreras, Gabriel Cox, Juan Cuatlatl Grande, Jayakrishna Dasappan, Selena DeSanto, Juan Manuel Diaz, Keanu Estrada, Christopher George, Kevin Gichuru, Emmanuel Godinez-Jimenez, Matthew Granados, Joseph Guarnero, Shyra Gums, Tanaya Landry, Christian Martinez, Daniel McGuire, Marvin Mendoza, Lidia Montiel, Justin Casey Mutch, Eric Lee Parker, Sierra Perales, Alexis Perez, Timothy Lee Salinas Piper, Mitchell Scorza, Justin Danile Tatum, Evelyn Tijero, Allison Weseman, Joshua Williams, and Niara Williams.

In addition to those who completed the course, I have been privileged to work with a multitude of dedicated research assistants that painstakingly polished this book: Matthew Aldea, Chelsea Corby, David Dube, Ryan Edmonson, Katherine Epps, Alexis Figuera, Ashkoon Iravani, Jessica Irrera, Logan Key, Lucas Martin, Allison Pelland, Monika Richards, Jake Romero, Fortunata Sparnauskaite, Shanice Thomas, Shante Thomas, Josine Torres, Ryan Wilson, and Aaron Wood. Not only did they demonstrate intellect and talent, but their writing, editing, and commentary shaped my manuscript into a solid publication. They are an incredible bunch and an honor to work with.

Much gratitude is owed to my partner Kacey VanderVorst, whose deconstruction of fake news over numerous phone calls and meals served as some of the earliest analysis for this study. Kacey remains my earliest and most valuable critic, working arduously to transform my ideas into completed projects. In addition to Kacey, I could not have completed this manuscript without Robin Andersen and Allison Butler. They acted as mentors throughout the publishing process, offering crucial feedback and guidance that strengthened this project and improved my scholarly acumen. Thank you to both of you for your contributions, guidance, and friendship. Similarly, I am eternally grateful to the University of California Press's Lyn Uhl, Lisa Moore, Enrique Ochoa-Kaup, Dore Brown, and Elisabeth Magnus for fostering careful scholarship through a well-executed publication process. Last, I am privileged to collaborate with numerous organizations (Action Coalition for Media Education, Media Freedom Foundation, Project Censored and its *Along the Line* podcast, the Mount Diablo Peace and Justice Center, and Union for Democratic Communication) and thought-provoking individuals that left an indelible mark on this book: Adam Armstrong, Margli Auclair, Phil Auclair, Jorge Ayala, Kate Bell, Lori Bindig-Yousman, John Boyer, Lony Brooks, Kenn Burrows, Allison Butler, Mary Cardaras, Aimee Casey, Jamal Cooks, Ian Davis, Lindsay DeFranco, Brian Dolber, Janice Domingo, Anthony Fest, Julie Frechette, Andrea Goldfien, Doug Hecker, David Hemphill, Barbara Henderson, Linda Ivey, Dorothy Kidd, Grant Kien, Dylan Lyzaga, Steve Macek, Susan Maret, Emil Marmol, Abby Martin, Desiree McSwain, Michael Niman, Sangha Niyogi, Chase Palmieri, Peter Phillips, Albert Ponce, Susan Rahman, Andy Lee Roth, Danuta Sawka, Mitch Scorza, T.M. Scruggs, Jeff Share, Obed Vasquez, Wanda Washington, Rob Williams, and William Yousman.

As any author knows, the catharsis derived from the love and laughter of friends and family is as vital to the completion of a project as anything else. Thank you to Grandpa Cannon for showing me the value of reading at a very young age; Grandma Cannon for making history interesting; Mickey Huff for an invaluable friendship made up of great memories from Diablo Valley College to City Lights; Abby Martin and Emil Marmol for the music and spirits in Chicago; Allison

Butler for the beach walks in Bodega Bay, World Series–watching party in Marin County, and display of unapologetic joy as my vegetarianism was compromised in Savannah; Robin Andersen for her mentorship and making conferences just as much about food, friendship, and fun as about scholarly pursuits; Monet Diaz-Huth for the Giants' games and complex excursions; my podcast cohosts Nicholas Baham III, Dylan Lazaga, and Janice Domingo for transforming drab Friday mornings into hours of intellectually engaging laughter and social justice discourse on *Along the Line;* Ben Boyington for making sure we never wasted one minute of our travels on sleep; Vangl for the hundreds of hikes throughout California; the weekend wolf pack of the Jarretts (Chris, Dana, Elvin, Holiday, Monnette, and Pieter), McDaniels (Dominic "Pudge," Katie, Leiana, and Ray), and Dudleys (Dan, Jessica, and Xavier) for the Sunday fundays, bucket list travels, and ridiculous text chains; the Lopez family (Christopher, Matthew, Monicia, and Roy) for the Sunday barbeques and guitar jam sessions; the California VanderVorsts (Hailey, Kirsten, and Marilyn) for the Sunday dinners, Disneyland trips, and garage sales; the nomadic VanderVorsts (Carla and Pieter) for the tour of Fort Collins, engaging conversations, and camping and road trips; and Kacey VanderVorst for draping the whole process and every moment of our lives in an exciting combination of laughs and love.

Introduction

"Not you. Your [news] organization is terrible," shouted president-elect Donald Trump at White House reporter Jim Acosta of CNN during a press conference, to which Acosta replied, "Since you're attacking us, can you give us a question? Mr. President-elect, since you're attacking our news organization, can you give us a chance?" Trump shot back, "I'm not going to give you a question. You are fake news."[1] Ever since that January 2017 morning, *fake news* has become an omnipresent idiom in American discourse. In fact, during his first year in office, Trump used the phrase over four hundred times.[2] The phrase became a cultural phenomenon, frequently appearing in entertainment media such as *Comedy Central's The Fake News Hour with Ted Nelms,* where "Ted Nelms" is played by actor Ed Helms; Britain's *The Fake News Show,* where participants compete to see who can most often discern a false news story from a real one; and the 2018 reboot of the journalism sitcom *Murphy Brown,* with the premiere focused on fake news.[3]

The popularity of the phrase saw media scholars, political scientists, and news analysts began investigating the influence of fake news on American democracy.[4] They argued that regardless of the medium, fake news was dangerous to democracy and public safety when it was optimized by politicians (such as President Trump), television news personalities (such as Sean Hannity), and online news outlets (such as InfoWars).[5] In addition to assessing the problems associated with fake news, critics and scholars have offered a series of solutions to diminish the threat posed by fake news, including industry- and government-imposed regulations, as well as legal action against individuals and nations known to engage in the production and dissemination of fake news.[6] However, all of these solutions have showed little promise because they do not address the central factor enabling the legitimization of fake news: news users cannot distinguish between fake news and journalism.

The Need for Media Literacy

In response, scholars argued for the adoption of a media literacy component in American schooling.[7] National media literacy initiatives were implemented in Canada, Great Britain, Australia, and several Asian countries some decades ago,[8] but not in the US. However, fears that fake news had circulated widely on social media and influenced the 2016 election created a sense of public urgency for media literacy in the United States. Only after the post-2016 fear of fake news took root did half of US states pass legislation encouraging media literacy.[9] Media literacy organizations such as the National Association for Media Literacy Education (NAMLE), one of the biggest media literacy organizations in the United States, define media literacy as "the ability to access, analyze, evaluate, create, and act using all forms of communication."[10] Proponents of media literacy argued that the news literacy component of media literacy education would provide students with the tools and perspectives to mitigate the negative influences of fake news.[11]

Media scholars who study critical media literacy contend that media education will be ineffective at producing effective news literacy unless it contains a critical framework.[12] A critical approach to media understands that power dynamics are embedded within the presentation of content, and therefore, meaningful analysis of media content interrogates "the ways media tend to position viewers, users, and audiences to read and negotiate meanings about race, class, gender, and the multiple identity markers that privilege dominant groups."[13] Furthermore, a critical analysis not only accounts for the power inequities of media content but explores pathways to liberation through self-actualization and democracy.[14] They argue that acritical media literacy normalizes and empowers the very actors and tools that produce and disseminate fake news.[15] Although they advocate for a critical framework to be applied to news literacy pedagogy, the lack of comprehensive research on fake news has left critical media literacy scholars unable to conceptualize a critical news literacy pedagogy.[16] This book provides the comprehensive research required to develop effective critical media literacy pedagogy.

What Is Fake News?

It is impossible to develop effective news literacy pedagogy, critical or acritical, that mitigates the influence of fake news without a comprehensive understanding of fake news. Despite the phrase's ubiquity, scholars contend that fake news is difficult to define.[17] A 2018 study of fake news by Edson C. Tandoc Jr., Zheng Wei Lim, and Richard Ling concludes that "there is no agreed upon definition of the term 'fake news.'"[18] In fact, in 2017 Merriam-Webster argued that it "sees no need to even consider it for entry in the dictionary as a separate term" because it is "self-explanatory and straightforward."[19] However, fake news is anything but self-explanatory. It extends far beyond news itself and exists in numerous formats such as rumors, lies, hoaxes, bunk, satire, parody, misleading content, impostor content, fabricated content, and manipulated content.[20]

Fake news has been around for ages. As far back as 1475, the Christian city of Trent was so outraged by the false story of a Jewish man killing a two-year-old boy that they imprisoned and tortured the local Jewish population as punishment.[21] In eighteenth-century Portugal, a fake news story distributed in a pamphlet recounted how the Virgin Mary had rescued survivors from the 1755 Lisbon Earthquake.[22] Fake news is not new. What is new is the amount of fake news being consumed and legitimized. In fact, about two-thirds of Americans report encountering fake news on a regular basis.[23] However, a century of varying definitions and applications of the term *fake news* has complicated its study.

From a historical perspective, the expression was invoked fairly regularly starting in the 1890s, appearing in newspapers such as an 1891 edition of the *Buffalo Commercial* in Buffalo, New York, and across the continent in an 1899 edition of the *San Francisco Call*.[24] Newspapers were employing the phrase, as it would come to be used for a century, to denounce false stories packaged and sold as legitimate news content. By 1992, the phrase appeared again, this time in a *TV Guide* cover story by David Lieberman that rebuked content providers for putting out video news releases (VNRs). Lieberman referred to VNRs as "fake news" because they were public relations content presented to the public as objective journalism.[25] A decade after VNRs, the term *fake news* appeared consistently in academic studies analyzing satirical news programs such as the *Daily Show*.[26] In the early twenty-first century, scholars used the phrase to denounce news content that acted as propaganda.[27]

In 2016, the phrase reemerged in political discourses concerning that year's presidential election. A month after the election, the defeated Democratic Party candidate Hillary Clinton argued that "the epidemic of malicious fake news and false propaganda that flooded social media over the past year, . . . [has] real-world consequences."[28] Clinton echoed the increasingly popular sentiment that fake news was a threat to democracy. For his part, Trump exploited the actual threat posed by fake news for his own purposes. Trump weaponized the phrase to dismiss inconvenient or uncomfortable facts illuminated by the news media, whom he referred to as an "enemy of the people."[29]

Trump's use of the phrase was undoubtedly bolstered by the press's low public opinion rating. In fact, a 2018 Knight Foundation-Gallup poll found a 69 percent decrease in the public's faith in journalism since 2008.[30] When people have no faith in the press, they have no universally trusted source to determine falsehood from fact. Oddly, it was the press that primed audiences to conflate Trump's political narratives with truth, and reporting with fake news. Scholars contend that by consistently privileging political narratives over facts, the press has conditioned audiences to view truth as subjective.[31] This creates space for politicians to lie with impunity. For example, Trump lied nearly five times per day when he first took office, but after spending a year and a half in office, this number had increased to eight times per day for a total of 4,229 false or misleading statements.[32] Nonetheless, journalists failed to convince Trump supporters that the president lied consistently. A year and half into Trump's presidency, 91 percent of his supporters relied on Trump as their most accurate form of news and information.[33] Trump's use of the term *fake news* effectively tapped into citizens' existing mistrust of the press.

With regard to fake news, to focus on Trump is to miss a larger problem: most Americans are unable to distinguish objective journalism from fake news. By 2016, less than one-fifth of middle school students could distinguish a news story from a sponsored story, and less than one-third could identify the implicit bias in a news article.[34] In 2018, Stanford University professor Sam Wineburg and his colleagues found that "students struggled to effectively evaluate online claims, sources, and evidence."[35] Older citizens fared worse than youth at detecting fake news. A 2019 study by Andrew Guess,

Jonathan Nagler, and Joshua Tucker revealed that people over sixty-five years of age "were seven times more likely to share fake news articles than those aged between 18 and 29."[36] Similarly, a 2019 Stanford History Education Group national survey of nearly 3,500 people found that

> fifty-two percent of students believed a grainy video claiming to show ballot stuffing in the 2016 Democratic primaries (the video was actually shot in Russia) constituted "strong evidence" of voter fraud in the U.S. Among more than 3,000 responses, only three students tracked down the source of the video, even though a quick search turns up a variety of articles exposing the ruse.
>
> Two-thirds of students couldn't tell the difference between news stories and ads (set off by the words "Sponsored Content") on Slate's homepage.
>
> Ninety-six percent of students did not consider why ties between a climate change website and the fossil fuel industry might lessen that website's credibility. Instead of investigating who was behind the site, students focused on superficial markers of credibility: the site's aesthetics, its top-level domain, or how it portrayed itself on the About page.[37]

Scholars' attempts to study and offer remedies for fake news have also suffered from the lack of an agreed-upon definition and comprehensive understanding of fake news. Much of the scholarship on fake news focuses on narrow forms of news communication, such as print and broadcast media, while ignoring the other ways in which fake news is communicated, such as oral transmission and online videos. In 2018, David M. J. Lazer and his colleagues defined fake news as any "fabricated information that mimics news media content in form but not in organizational process or intent."[38] Yet this ignores the long tradition of news dissemination via oral communication, which is not media but can be false news.[39] Similarly, in 2017, Hunt Allcott and Matthew Gentzkow defined fake news as "news articles that are intentionally and verifiably false, and could mislead readers."[40] However, fake news content exists in formats beyond articles such as oral communication, online videos, and broadcast news media.[41]

Other scholars have looked at the intended purpose of the content as a determining factor in whether to categorize it as a form of fake news.[42] Gillian Bolsover of the Computational Propaganda Research Project argued in 2018 that "fake news is propaganda."[43] In fact, scholars have used the terms interchangeably, including media literacy researcher Renee Hobbs, who wrote, "Often, the true funder of fake news or propaganda is disguised or hidden."[44] Much of the scholarship on falsified news content focuses on how it acts as propaganda.[45] However, other forms of fake news are not propaganda: for example, some journalists misreport in error, fabricate stories to further their career, or publish false stories as April Fools' pranks, such as making up a story about beach towns prohibiting surfing.[46]

Although scholars disagree on a definition of fake news, they tend to agree that fake news poses an existential threat to democracy. Citizens' agency in a democracy is dependent upon accurate information; ultimately, media manipulation prevents meaningful participation.[47] Furthermore, the ubiquitous consumption of fake news not only weakens democracies but promotes totalitarian regimes.[48] Despite the numerous studies on fake news, scholars have yet to synthesize the various elements into a comprehensive understanding of fake news.

To truly address the threat of fake news and to educate students to discern it, we must develop a critical news pedagogy and implement it in US schools. But that effort will require a broad scholarly understanding of the phenomenon's definition, producers, themes, purposes, and influence. This book, to further that end, offers the first comprehensive study of fake news. It employs a critical-historical media ecosystems approach, dissecting fake news to identify and analyze the structure of its contents and illuminating how it is used, by whom, and why. The findings act as the scaffolding for the effective critical news literacy pedagogy proposed in the final chapter. This study is the first attempt to anatomize fake news for critical media literacy educators.

Methodology: A Critical Media Ecology Approach

Like any other message, fake news is given power and meaning through the communicative process.[49] Media ecology theory argues that we can understand that process through an examination of the relationship between technology, communication, media, and their impact on the human environment.[50] Media ecology scholars value "networks of relations (ecosystems) rather than individual essences and processes rather than entities."[51] Throughout this book, I examine the network of relations and processes by which fake news is produced, disseminated, and legitimized. Media ecology scholars argue that the complex and changing relationships and processes that make up a media ecosystem are best understood through a historical approach to the media environment.[52] As a result, I take such an approach to analyze the technological, communication, media, and human influences associated with fake news.

My analysis follows the tradition of media ecology scholars who integrated the critical framework of the Frankfurt school into their analysis.[53] The critical theory of the Frankfurt school posits that dominant ideologies result from power inequities that are strengthened and fortified through media and communication.[54] They contend that liberation from dominant ideologies is possible through a critical examination of media and power.[55] As a result, this study critically analyzes the power dynamics associated with the production, purpose, and themes of fake news in an effort to synthesize them into a pedagogy of resistance and liberation.

The data in this book came from three areas. First, I performed an extensive review of scholarship in the communication, history, media studies, and media education disciplines. I used key word searches to identify scholarship on journalism, propaganda, news, and media. This enabled access to primary and secondary sources of fake news. Next, I combed through the newspaper and congressional archives for key terms such as "fake news," "false news," and "propaganda" to locate primary news media content about fake news. Finally, via internet searches of corporate and independent news outlets, I examined contemporary news stories from 2016 to 2019 that were false or misleading. I collected both national and international fake news content. This enabled my research to have a global perspective. All of this research was augmented by secondary sources about the influence and outcome of fake news consumption.

Each piece of data was scrutinized to determine if it was in accordance with a baseline definition of fake news: false or misleading content presented as news and communicated in formats spanning spoken, written, printed, electronic, and digital communication.[56] Each of the hundreds of pieces of content underwent three cycles of process coding to determine the producer, purpose, themes, and influence of the fake news.[57] During the initial cycle of coding, I summarized fake news content with words and phrases.[58] During the second cycle of coding, I categorized the codes on the basis of producer, purpose, themes, and consequences. During the final cycle of coding, I looked for reappearing terms and concepts within each category.

The data revealed the producers of fake news; the purpose behind the production of fake news; the themes found in fake news content; and the consequences associated with the consumption of fake news. The producers of fake news are the press; governments both foreign and domestic; satirists; self-interested actors; and political parties and politicians. A series of recurring themes are found in fake news content: nationalism, fear, hate, and celebrity gossip. I also examined the consequences of fake news. It serves to engender moral panic and outrage; radicalize supporters; marginalize the press; sow division; manipulate democracy; and implement an authoritarian regime.

Throughout the text I classify press outlets on the basis of their funding, ideological underpinnings, and party affiliation. A critical framework understands that economic incentives, ideology, and political affiliation influence the ways in which news, including fake news, is produced and disseminated. Thus, rather than use terms such as *mainstream media,* which assumes that the six corporations who own 90 percent of the news media that America's 330 million people consume are representative of mainstream culture, I refer to them as the corporate press to highlight their corporate funding model.[59] Similarly, rather than use the term *alternative media,* I label the media outlets who are funded by independent sources, such as donors, nonprofits, and foundations, as the independent media. In addition, I use the term *public media* to describe news media that are funded by the government; *liberal* and *conservative media* to illustrate the ideological underpinnings of news media outlets; and *Democratic* and *Republican Party media* to illustrate a media outlet's party affiliation. These terms help the reader better examine the power dynamics that shape and explain fake news.

Layout of This Book

The Anatomy of Fake News offers the first comprehensive examination of fake news for the purpose of creating effective critical news literacy. To understand fake news, we must understand news itself. As a result, chapter 1 examines the concept and functionality of news. It outlines the history of news production and consumption, paying special attention to the news industry, journalistic theory, and the terms essential for understanding the remainder of the book.

The second, third, and fourth chapters provide a historical analysis of the various motives, consumption patterns, and technologies that enabled the pervasive spread of fake news in the predigital age. Chapter 2 begins the examination of fake news through an analysis of the content created and disseminated by press outlets and journalists prior to the digital age. The press began as a disorganized bunch of individuals, with varying degrees of ethics, publishing news stories, which ranged from true to absolutely false. Eventually, they developed into a well-organized structure of reporters with standardized ethics and professional practices. Ironically, it was this homogeneity of practices that led to national fake news stories regarding large events such as the war in Vietnam. By the late twentieth century, the press was again transformed, largely by economic and political factors, into a tiny club of corporate-owned and sensationalistic news outlets that came to rely on fake news over fact-based content.

The third chapter analyzes the fake news produced and disseminated by satirical news programs and political propaganda apparatuses. A political party propaganda apparatus is the loosely connected group of actors and institutions who, sometimes through coordination and other times through overlapping interests and actions, strive to influence public opinion. Over the course of the twentieth century, modern public relations firms working on behalf of political parties built upon the techniques of propaganda and persuasion and became embedded within corporate-structured news organizations that merged marketing with content and blurred the lines between promotion and fact-based reporting. The result was an impotent press, incapable of holding leaders accountable. This transformation resulted from the increased popularity of satirical news and the creation of political propaganda apparatuses. Out of a desire to expand their revenue and audience size, the corporate news media adopted the satirical news practice of privileging divisive content over facts. Much of the corporate news content originated from political party propaganda apparatuses. The press's pursuit of increased profit through hyperpolarized content weakened their ability to hold leaders accountable. Their ineptitude derived from their repeated conflation of truth and political ideology.

The fourth chapter offers an analysis of the fake news produced by twentieth-century state-sponsored propaganda machines. These propaganda machines organized people and resources in an effort to construct and circulate a dominant message that would control and influence human behavior and attitudes. Originally, they were created for a temporary purpose, such as increasing troop enrollment for the military, but the demands of the Cold War made propaganda machines a permanent component of nation-states. They not only produced and disseminated fake news but worked to construct an environment where that fake news was more likely to be believed by large portions of the public.

The fifth chapter examines the rise of the technology economy and the relationship it cultivated between data collection and fake news in the digital age. The advent of the internet ushered in a new era of fake news. In the preinternet years, governments, political parties, press outlets, and individuals had to rely on conventional wisdom and anecdotal evidence to determine if the design of fake news content would resonate with target audiences. The internet provided fake news producers with something more effective: predictive analytic products. These products exploit user data to predict with precision and some cases direct human behavior. The internet's political economy privileged massive data collection on a scale unrivaled in human history. Suddenly, fake news producers had a road map of users' thought processes. This enabled the construction of effective fake news content with targeted precision. The chapter discusses the platforms and actors that generate and disseminate fake news. It ends with an analysis of how the digitizing of propaganda and persuasion machines discussed in chapters 3 and 4 created a global information war that spreads fake news across international boundaries.

The sixth chapter assesses news users' media literacy skills while analyzing contemporary discourses on the solutions to combat fake news. Looking through a historical and educational lens, the chapter argues that the proposed solutions to fake news since the 2016 election have failed because they do not address the central factor legitimizing fake news: news users cannot distinguish between fake news and journalism. As previous chapters will illustrate, the only cure for fake news is a media-literate citizenry. However, few media literacy courses are offered in the United States, and the majority of those offered serve to empower fake news producers. The chapter concludes that critical news literacy education is the most effective solution for mitigating the pernicious influence of fake news.

The final chapter is a fake news detection kit that explains how to achieve the learning outcomes of effective critical news literacy pedagogy. It maps out the ten components of an effective critical news literacy pedagogy for addressing fake news. The chapter revisits the main findings of the text, introducing them as a guide for how readers can better distinguish fake news from journalism. The goal of critical news literacy education is to produce intelligent media users through a pedagogy of critical thinking, critical theory, journalism, democratic theory, and an anatomy of fake news.

Throughout history, fake news has been an influential and dangerous force, especially on democratic societies. As this study will illustrate, many of the twenty-first-century proposals for mitigating fake news derive from the very individuals and institutions that have historically produced and disseminated fake news: governments, private industry, technology companies, and political parties. Rather than trust fake news producers to solve our twenty-first-century information problem, we need to develop a solution that empowers the citizenry to distinguish fake news from journalism. As an educator, I believe that effective critical education is that solution.

This study is the first attempt to anatomize fake news for critical media literacy educators. Armed with a comprehensive understanding of fake news, critical media literacy scholars can incorporate this study's findings into a curriculum with lesson plans, resources, and teacher training workshops that educate students on fake news. The final chapter of this study utilizes its findings to propose effective critical news literacy pedagogy. The presumed impact of this pedagogy will be to diminish the power of fake news machines and/or fake news propagators.

1   *The Fourth Estate*

Democracy and the Press

Legendary reporter Walter Cronkite purportedly declared that "freedom of the press is not just important to democracy, it is democracy." Cronkite's emphasis on the centrality of the press to a democracy was reminiscent of Enlightenment thinkers such as John Milton and John Locke, who argued that a free and vibrant press was essential for democratic self-government.[1] In fact, in 1787, American democracy was entrusted to American newspapers such as the *New York Packet,* which informed the public about the content and implications of the US Constitution.[2] By the late eighteenth and early nineteenth centuries, Enlightenment philosophy had produced numerous democratic revolutions: the United States had declared its independence from Great Britain; France had undergone a bloody democratic revolution; a slave uprising in Haiti had morphed into an anticolonial war for independence; and throughout Latin America, revolutionary figures such as Simón Bolívar had promoted democracy by liberating colonial subjects.[3]

Many of the late eighteenth- and early nineteenth-century democracies viewed the press as an essential pillar of democracy. After his famous tour of the United States in the 1830s, the French political observer Alexis de Tocqueville argued in his classic analysis *Democracy in America* that the press was "the chiefest democratic instrument of freedom."[4] To understand why fake news is "fake," it is critical to understand news. This chapter examines the history and theoretical underpinnings of news and news dissemination as they relate to democracy.

Democracy and the Press

The concept of "the press" derives from the 1440 advent of the printing press, which enabled written content to spread further and faster than previously thought possible.[5] However, the printing press was neither the original nor the last form of news dissemination. The printing press was preceded by spoken and written news. News began as an oral transfer of information. Spoken news was, and remains, a reflection of the human impulse to both share and hear information. Because spoken news was a much more central part of Asian, African, and Native American societies, known for their rich traditions of oral history, Westerners often forget that it was also an important part of Western civilization, especially during the Middle Ages (ca. fifth to fifteenth centuries). The Middle Ages refers to a pre-printing press era in Europe where the slowness of information transfer made the spread of knowledge difficult.[6] Given that their communication network spanned Europe, priests were some of the biggest disseminators of news during the Middle Ages. For example, in the fourteenth and fifteenth centuries, English citizens were informed about the Hundred Years' War, raging in France at the time, largely from priests.[7] Today, the spoken word remains a dominant mode of communicating news in traditional settings such as bars, coffeehouses, and restaurants.[8]

The advent of the written word engendered written news as a concept. Early incarnations of written news, largely in the form of letters, did not move as fast as the spoken word of the time. However, by the fourth century, monarchs and other leaders depended upon written news to maintain their empires. For example, Alexander the Great's military decisions were informed by written and oral accounts of his enemies. He then collated the various reports he received into written news that he disseminated to his subjects about the purpose, strategy, and need for war.[9]

The influence of written news would be intensified by the invention of the printing press, which allowed for the dissemination of the written word to vast portions of the globe. In the fifteenth century, Johann Gutenberg created the letterpress, which allowed multiple copies to be made of a written document. His creation was highly influenced by the Chinese and Korean invention of movable type nearly four hundred years earlier.[10] Eventually, these inventions would result in the printing press. The printing press allowed for the printing of replica documents at unprecedented speed. This meant that written news content could be replicated and then disseminated around the world.

The printing press made the newspaper possible. The same century the printing press was invented, Columbus landed in the Americas. The news story of him and his crew was sent throughout Europe.[11] Centuries later, in Boston, Massachusetts, America published its first newspaper, *Publick Occurrences, Both Foreign and Domestick.* By then, newspapers had existed in Europe for decades. In fact, in 1605 the world's first newspaper was published in Germany, and fifteen years later the first English newspaper was produced.[12] Newspapers resulted from individuals and businesses aggregating various news articles into publications. American colonists showed appreciation for the labor performed by journalists, offering legal protections to the industry. For example, in 1733 colonial courts protected John Peter Zenger, editor of the *New York Weekly Journal,* who had printed unflattering (if true) stories about colonial officials. He was charged with libel, but his defense was that journalists could not be convicted for libel simply because those in power disapproved of what they were reporting. The jury agreed, declaring Zenger innocent of all charges.[13]

By the time of the American Revolution, the press had established itself as an effective tool for public information and mobilization.[14] By the late eighteenth century, newspapers had developed a more frequent and predictable publication schedule. The first daily newspapers in the United States, the *Pennsylvania Evening Post* and the *Pennsylvania Daily Advertiser,* were published in 1783.[15] The founding fathers recognized the powerful impact newspapers had on the development of the United States. They credited newspapers with uniting colonial Americans to resist Great Britain's monarchical rule.[16] Thomas Jefferson remarked, "Were it left to me to decide whether we should have a government without newspapers, or newspapers without a government . . . I should not hesitate a moment to prefer the latter."[17] In fact, democracy and the press became so indivisible in the minds of Enlightenment thinkers that they referred to the press as "the fourth estate," because it was just as important to democracy as the traditional three branches of Western governments.[18]

Although democratic nations have almost universally recognized the essential role the press plays in their style of government, they have offered varying degrees of protection to journalists and new outlets. The US offers some of the most expansive protections to the press and journalists under the First Amendment to the US Constitution, which guarantees "freedom of the press." This protection was originally limited to the printing press. However, in the 1970s, the US courts began interpreting the First Amendment as a protection for journalists.[19] The United States' constitutional protection of the press is unique. Great Britain has no constitutional freedom of the press but has awarded protections through the courts in the form of licenses.[20] Other nations such as Denmark, Norway, Italy, Canada, and India offer some legal protections to the press, but in these countries, unlike in the US, protections are accompanied by clear restrictions.[21] However, written law is not enough to ensure the protection of the press. Even nations with protections such as the US can see their freedom of the press compromised. In fact, in 2019 the US ranked 48th on the Press Freedom Index, behind Chile and South Korea.[22]

In addition to legal protections, the US has offered economic incentives for the press. During the term of America's first president, George Washington, the federal government offered subsidies to the press, including discounted postage and tax breaks.[23] The economic incentives were viewed, not as a handout to the press, but as an investment in democracy. Although the amount of subsidies would fluctuate, they would remain in place into the twenty-first century. For example, as of 2010, the amount of federal subsidies for the press was $2 billion per year, which was less than half of the value received by the press in 1970, when adjusted for inflation.[24] The reduction in subsidies illustrates the fading public commitment to the press.

What Is News? Five Functions of the Press

With its protections and influence, the press holds a massive amount of power in a democracy. As former Federal Communications Commission (FCC) commissioner Nicholas Johnson (who served 1966–73) once observed, "Whatever is your first priority . . . your second priority has to be media reform. With it you at least have a chance of accomplishing your first priority. Without it, you don't have a prayer."[25] Johnson was arguing that the news media, in their decision to cover or ignore a certain story or issues, have unmatched influence over political discourses in a democracy. This is known as agenda setting, which is one of the five functions that the press performs in a democracy.

The press is tasked with five critical functions for maintaining democracy:[26]

1. **Marketplace of Ideas.** Former congressman Lee Hamilton once noted that democracy is "virtually impossible without a solid base of information and analysis."[27] The press offers a diverse set of facts, perspectives, and ideas for voters to consider when making their democratic decisions.

2. **Agenda Setter:** The press has a unique role to inform the public about what they should be paying attention to in order to maintain their democracy.

3. **Watchdog:** The press is tasked with finding and searching every avenue of corruption and oppression that threatens the sustainability of a democracy.

4. **Information Disseminator:** Without the press, the public has little hope for knowing fact-based information about the places, people, and items it does not come into contact with. In fact, there is a long history of marginalized groups creating or relying on the press to disseminate their message. Conversely, the press works with politicians to share information between representatives and leaders about policy.[28]

5. **Public Mobilizer:** It is up to the press to convince the public that the important issues of the day are important.

The five functions of the press exist to serve American democracy. Regardless of their stated function, news outlets cannot serve the public unless they seek, access, and report on the content that will best serve the democratic process. That is achieved if the reported stories are newsworthy and reported in a responsible way.

What Is Newsworthy? Reporters, Journalists, and the Spin Room

The degree to which the news media are effective at fulfilling their democratic function depends upon which content they decide to cover or ignore. If they ignore a story or issue, it will die in obscurity. However, if they focus on that issue or story, it can dominate American political discourse. Their decision-making process about whether to ignore or report on each piece of content has huge implications for strengthening or weakening democratic self-government. For example, to ignore a story that potentially exposes malfeasance in the democratic process enables that malfeasance to continue without public knowledge. However, sometimes even when they report on a story, journalists empower what media scholar Carl Jensen referred to as "junk food news" to dominate American political discourses. A junk food news story is a story irrelevant to the citizenry that is reported by news outlets at the expense of newsworthy content.[29] As a result, the public is aware of what is irrelevant but remains ignorant of the stories that are essential to strengthening the democratic process.

To uphold their democratic duty, journalists have developed a methodology for determining whether a news story or issue is worthy of reporting. They have five criteria to determine if something is newsworthy:

Is it new?
Is it unusual?
Is it interesting?
Is it significant?
Is it about people?[30]

Even after they effectively identify a potential piece of news, journalists face a conflict in how they report that news to the public. Commentators and critics have long made a distinction between stories from journalists and those from reporters. American media commentator George Snell argues that someone who is reporting is explaining what happened on a time line of events. This is well suited for stories such as a plane crash, a hurricane, or a terrorist act. Journalism, in contrast, goes beneath the reporting, providing investigative analysis and thoughtful commentary that contextualize the time line. For example, explains Snell, a reporter would say that "a 747 aircraft crashed in the middle of the Atlantic Ocean yesterday," but a journalist would bring to light that a "review of maintenance reports of the 747 aircraft that crashed last month revealed that the airplane had faulty engine parts. Reports indicate that airline management ignored warnings that the parts were malfunctioning."[31]

Journalists face multiple dilemmas regarding how they frame the news story they are planning to disseminate. *Framing* refers to journalists' interpretation of an event in the context of larger concepts and theoretical perspectives[32] For example, an individual can frame the story of a hurricane as a story about climate change or a story about government preparedness in how it responds to the hurricane.

Editors are supposed to check for potential abuses in framing by identifying and mitigating the bias, spin, or slant of a journalist. *Bias* refers to an individual's preference or prejudice. Editors have historically seen their job as identifying and mitigating the journalists' bias. *Spin* refers to a twist put on a story so that it controls a consumer's interpretation. Spin is such a problem that there are "spin rooms" at events such as campaign speeches and debates where public relations firms inform members of the press how a real fact or event confirms journalists' political or economic ideology. *Slant* refers to the practice of introducing a story in a narrow fashion that conforms to a certain bias. Slant has become increasingly problematic as news outlets become politically homogenized. For example, given that Fox News Channel has branded itself as the bastion of conservative media, it functions to introduce actual reporting in a way that conforms to a conservative bias regardless of contradictory facts or opinions.

The New News: Digital Outlets

Television and print have been succeeded by electronic and digital news, complicating the work of editors and journalists. The accessibility of the internet has transformed America into the most media-saturated society in history. On average, American adults spend about ten and a half hours per day consuming media (TV, video games, radio, tablet, smartphone, and computer).[33] A majority of American adults own a combination of laptop or desktop computer, tablet, or smartphone.[34] As a result, individuals are confronted with news, almost without interruption, through various channels including word of mouth, written word, radio, TV, computers, laptops, and handheld devices. About 75 percent of Americans take in some form of news at least once a day.[35] It is almost too much to handle when you consider that there are local, national, domestic, and international news agencies. The news they offer can be political, social, cultural, economic, or entertainment based. Individuals under fifty years of age receive their news mostly from these digital devices. Conversely, those over fifty continue to consume primarily television news. About 76 percent of US adults go to the same news sources daily without straying to another news outlet. Surveys show that individuals loyal to their news organizations check the news at a much higher rate than those willing to examine multiple news outlets.[36]

In the internet age, journalists also have to consider how early they want to submit a story. A submission too early may mean relying upon impulse rather than the facts, but waiting too long may mean getting scooped by a competitor. A journalist is scooped when a second journalist working on the same topic publishes the first's story before the first journalist can complete that story. Journalists used to have twenty-four hours before they decided whether to publish their story because that was how long it took to publish the next edition of the newspaper.

However, with both the twenty-four-hour broadcast news cycle and the internet, a journalist can be scooped at any moment. This battle over speed versus accuracy has led to numerous errors in reporting. For example, in 2017, the *Washington Post* quickly published a story "Russian Hackers Penetrated U.S. Electricity Grid through a Utility In Vermont, U.S. Officials Say," but a few hours later they retracted the story, admitting it had been discredited.[37]

Technological, Economic, and Political Threats to Journalism

The ubiquity of the internet has forced many journalists to evaluate content based on its potential to go viral rather than its contribution to democratic discourse. When a story is widely shared and discussed online it is considered a viral story. Shifting technological and revenue models have altered the way journalists envision their content. Internet algorithms privilege "viral" content.[38] Increasingly, news outlets are measuring the success of a story by whether it goes viral.[39] This has resulted in the conflation of viral and newsworthy when journalists are deciding what to report or ignore. Journalists have to consider if their piece will go viral or if it will be viewed as a boring piece of information, in which case they risk their job by reporting it.

Technological changes and economic hardships are hardly the only threats facing journalists. The threat journalists pose to those in power is illustrated by the response they receive from authoritarian regimes. Autocrats tend to rely on imprisonment and murder as means to prevent journalism. In fact, from 1992 to 2018, 1,285 journalists around the world were killed while doing their job. Many of them were murdered in response to stories they had published exposing abuses of power. The 2018 murder in the Saudi Arabian embassy in Istanbul, Turkey, of Jamal Khashoggi, a *Washington Post* columnist and critic of the Saudi regime, is one of the most prominent examples of the political threat journalists face.[40] Nations such as Turkey, China, and Egypt are some of the largest offenders imprisoning journalists for doing their job.[41] A 2018 report from Reporters without Borders, an investigative press freedom group, found that "more and more democratically-elected leaders no longer see the media as part of democracy's essential underpinning, but as an adversary to which they openly display their aversion."[42]

Journalists are the individuals tasked with confronting threats to democracy and self-determination. The cost of a press failure is high not just for the journalists but also for democracy. The strength of democracy is rooted in a well-informed electorate. The press is entrusted with finding and spreading critical fact-based stories to the voters. When the press fails to equip citizens with the facts and perspectives to execute their civic duty, democracy ceases to exist. That is why the press is entrusted with protecting democracy.

If citizens are expected to understand and act as equal participants in a democracy, they must be familiar with its fourth estate: the press. Citizens cannot be expected to properly evaluate the news content that informs their electoral decision-making unless they can differentiate journalism from nefarious content. A democratic nation can mitigate the negative influence of fake news if its citizenry is educated about the criteria and practices behind news production. The next chapter shows that citizens must be familiar with press practices in order to determine when and if the press is distributing fake news. If citizens are ignorant of press practices, they are more likely to conflate fake news with journalism.

2　The Faux Estate

A Brief History of Fake News in America

"I waited all Tuesday and dear Jesus did not come;—I waited all the forenoon of Wednesday, and was well in body as I ever was, but after 12 o'clock I began to feel faint, and before dark I needed someone to help me up to my chamber, as my natural strength was leaving me very fast, and I lay prostrate for 2 days without any pain—sick with disappointment," Henry Emmons wrote as he relived the anticlimactic moment that he and thousands of others shared in October of 1844.[1] They had gathered for what they expected to be the end of the world, but as the day ended and the next began, the world remained. This day would forever be known as the Great Disappointment.

Emmons and the others who gathered were followers of William Miller, a Baptist preacher, who had predicted the end of the world would occur on October 22, 1844. In the 1820s, Miller began a series of calculations about the end of the world based on the stories in the Christian Bible. Those calculations, according to Miller, proved that the world would end between March 21, 1843, and March 21, 1844.[2] In 1832, Miller could no longer stay silent about the earth's demise. He began to publish stories about his prediction in newspapers, such as the *Vermont Telegraph*. The news scared some readers and attracted others. Until 1840, those attracted to his publications, known as Millerites, remained a small regional movement. However, that changed after Joshua Vaughan Himes, a Boston preacher who remained skeptical of Miller's predictions until 1842, began spreading Miller's forecasts to a larger audience through his newspaper *Signs of the Times*. Soon other newspapers copied Himes's news stories into their publications.[3]

The expanded press coverage transformed Millerism from an obscure belief into a national movement. Nearly fifty periodicals from New York, Pennsylvania, Ohio, Canada, and Great Britain published stories about Miller's predictions.[4] As March 21, 1844, passed without incident, Miller admitted that his calculation was incorrect, but he remained convinced that the end of the world was near.[5] The press continued to report Miller's new rapture dates such as April 18, 1844, and eventually October 22, 1844, the day that left Emmons with feelings of emptiness and dejection. On each of the proposed dates, thousands of people turned out cheering for the end of the world. The Millerites continued in their belief that the world would end, creating the Seventh Day Adventist religion, which is still in existence. The story of Miller illustrates the powerful influence of the press to spread fake news. It is doubtful that Miller's predictions would have resulted in a mass movement that became a religion that exists two centuries after his death without the coverage they received from the press.

Colonial-Era Fake News: Moral Panic

The fake news of the colonial era, roughly the fifteenth through the eighteenth century, was typically composed of rumors that had been passed orally or documented by colonial and religious leaders. The era saw the continued development and dissemination of fake news content that dehumanized individuals as way to legitimize acts of violence and control. Dehumanization is a reoccurring form of hate in fake news stories. Mount Allison University's Erin Steuter and Deborah

Wills argue that dehumanization can be a powerful weapon of violence and genocide because it "allows us to re-cast cruelty and violence as something else; after all, if an enemy is so far down the evolutionary ladder that it cannot feel pain, then how can inflicting pain be cruel?"[6] In the colonial era, Native Americans were one of the largest groups victimized and dehumanized by fake news. In fact, it contributed to a 90 percent decline in their population between 1500 and 1890.[7] For example, newspapers consistently fabricated lone survivor witnesses that they referenced as sources for news stories about famous battles such as Custer's Last Stand and the Fort Buford Massacre. The stories portrayed Native Americans as cowardly savages, thereby serving to justify future aggression against Native Americans.[8]

One of the earliest examples of fake news from this era is Christopher Columbus's journey. Columbus was America's earliest European settler. He sent reports of his journey, written in Spanish, to the Spanish monarchy, which sent them to Rome, where they were republished in Latin.[9] The reports were sent throughout Europe, where they shaped news consumers' conception of his travels and eventually of the Americas. However, the reports were untrue. First, Columbus claimed to have arrived, not on a new continent, but in "the Indes" (as China, Japan, and India were then known in Europe); he believed he had accomplished his mission to discover maritime access to the spices and silk trade of the Eastern Hemisphere. Furthermore, he claimed to have found a considerable amount of gold, when in reality he had found next to nothing. He also falsely reported that only a small number of people existed in the Americas; there were in fact one hundred million people.[10] He incorrectly reported that Native Americans were "ignorant" people who "willingly traded everything they owned" and defended themselves with "spears," when they were actually a diverse group of societies that included massive empires such as the Aztec and Inca, who were some of the most effective warriors in human history.[11]

Columbus's account demonstrates the widespread violence and hate that fake news narratives can engender and justify. Columbus fabricated his tales in order to justify the expenses paid by the Spanish monarchy for his journey. However, these tales had the effect of inspiring genocide in the Americas. Columbus reported that the indigenous peoples he had found "would make fine servants. . . . With fifty men we could subjugate them all and make them do whatever we want." At the time, few knew of the lands he had discovered and even fewer wanted to travel there. However, Columbus's fake news reports portrayed these new lands as begging to be exploited. This resulted in a horde of conquistadors coming to the Americas in search of gold. These violent extremists committed mass genocide in the name of religion and profit.[12]

Columbus was hardly the only person to spur violence through the spread of fake news about the indigenous peoples of America. Much of the fake news during the seventeenth century served to validate the genocide of Native Americans. At that time, New England colonists were hungry for additional land. As historian Howard Zinn explains, "The Puritans lived in uneasy truce with the Pequot Indians, who occupied what is now southern Connecticut and Rhode Island. But they wanted them out of the way; they wanted their land."[13] They concluded that they could expand their settlement only if the neighboring Native American tribe, the Pequots, were removed from the land they occupied. In order to mobilize the colonists to remove the Pequots, colonial leaders falsely attributed the murder of two colonists to the Pequots.[14]

In response to the murders, a group of American colonists were sent to murder the Pequots. The governor explained that "they had commission to put to death the men of Block Island, but to spare the women and children, and to bring them away, and to take possession of the island."[15] Once they arrived, colonist William Bradford recalls that they set the villagers' living quarters on fire. "Those that escaped the fire were slain with the sword; some hewed to pieces, others rune throw with their rapiers, so as they were quickly dispatched, and very few escaped. It was conceived they thus destroyed about 400. At this time. It was a fearful sight to see them thus frying in the fire, and the streams of blood quenching the same, and horrible was the stink and scent thereof; but the victory seemed a sweet sacrifice, and they gave the prayers thereof to God."[16] The Pequots' murder serves as an example of how fake news is often used as a justification and source of motivation for a particular goal, in this case land seizure. To achieve that goal, fake news content offered a justifiable reason for news consumers to engage in or support the mass murder of between four hundred and seven hundred people.[17]

A century after the slaughter of the Pequots, on the eve of the American War for Independence, colonists worried that Native American attacks during the war might hinder the colonists' success against Great Britain. Benjamin Franklin convinced colonists to preemptively attack Native Americans by publishing a fake news story that Native Americans were scalping colonists at the behest of the British.[18] This provided colonists and militias with the pretext for attacking and murdering an unknown number of Native Americans.

The Moral Panic of Colonial-Era Fake News

In addition to dehumanization, fake news content that is designed to spread fear can cause a moral panic, in which, according to Stanley Cohen's 1972 *Folk Devils and Moral Panics,* "a condition, episode, person or group of persons emerges to become defined as a threat to societal values and interests; its nature is presented in a stylized and stereotypical fashion by the mass media; the moral barricades are manned by editors, bishops, politicians and other right-thinking people."[19] Scholars have long argued that anxiety can result in a moral panic.[20] Fake news has often played the catalyst for spreading fear that turns into mass anxiety, moral panic, and eventually violence and murder.

The Salem witch trials illustrate the degree to which the consumption of fear-laden fake news content can produce and intensify moral panic to the point of murder. By 1669, the advent of the printing press led to the dissemination of thirty-six editions of the *Malleus Malefi-carum* (Hammer of the witches), a treatise on how to exterminate witches that had been written in 1484 by two Dominican priests.[21] The publication gave the impression that witches were everywhere. Where the printed word informed the literate, a vast number of wood-carved art and silhouette illustrations communicated about witchcraft to the illiterate.[22] All of the fake news content swirling around the Western world about witches and witchcraft influenced Cotton Mather, a Puritan minister whose publications that related childhood illnesses in Boston to witchcraft were influential in the Salem witch trials.[23] Mather's most famous work, the 1688 *Memorable Providences,* was a fake news soliloquy about witchcraft in the colonies. It served as the rationale for two years of trials that saw the imprisonment of hundreds of individuals as well as the execution of fourteen women, five men, and two dogs suspected of witchcraft.[24] Mather defended the trials and executions— and the "spectral evidence" (dreams or visions that a person was a witch, itself a form of fake news), that was used to convict.[25] But some of Mather's contemporaries, such as Robert Calef, criticized the witch trials and their supporters, particularly Mather, whom Calef described as "the most active and forward of any Minister in the Country in those matters."[26] Calef rejected "Spectral Accusations" and fears of witchcraft founded on "fables"; he described the proceedings as driven by "a Biggotted Zeal, stirring up a Blind and most Bloody rage."[27] The trials are an example of how fake news from multiple sources, in multiple forms, can cause a murderous hysteria as people conflate repetition of a message with its accuracy.

In addition to witch hunts, fake news inspired violent moral panic about African Americans. The mass murder of African Americans in eighteenth-century New York shows how anxiety over real tragedies can produce fake news in the form of rumors. In 1741, a series of fires erupted in New York that burned numerous locations including the governor's mansion. Soon the city's residents were gripped with anxiety about the prospects of another fire. During that same period of time, there had been slave rebellions in Antigua, Barbados, Jamaica, and South Carolina. New York was one of the largest slaveholding colonies at the time. The fear over slave rebellions and anxiety over the fires led to rumors that African Americans had conspired to start the fires. The so-called New York Conspiracy of 1741 resulted in colonists torturing and murdering New York's black population as retribution for the fires. Over 150 black men were arrested, imprisoned, and interrogated, while nearly twenty others were executed.[28]

Fake News in the Early Republic: Partisan Narratives

The establishment of the United States did nothing to mitigate the harms of fake news. The fake news of the Early Republic era was mostly inflammatory and divisive content that spread through newspapers. As discussed in the next chapter, divisive content that incites violence would remain a theme of fake news content into the twenty-first century.[29] One of the most divisive forms of fake news content in the US is partisan narratives. Leonie Huddy, Alexa Bankert, and Caitlin Davies, writing in *Political Psychology*, found that partisanship, in both the US and Europe, was influenced more by identity than by stances on issues and ideology and was characterized by strong emotions in defense of one's party against that of others.[30] Partisan narratives seek to create division among the political parties with inflammatory false stories that polarize party adherents to take extreme action against their opponents. Such divisive fake news content dominated reporting in the Early Republic.

During George Washington's first presidential term, fake news fueled a polarized debate over a federal tax on whiskey known as the

Whiskey Rebellion. The rebellion began as a seemingly innocent political debate carried by numerous newspapers. Tom the Tinker was an anonymous writer who used emotional language to argue that a proposed tax on whiskey by Secretary of the Treasury Alexander Hamilton was a form of tyranny.[31] Tom claimed in numerous newspapers to have organized individuals to pursue those who supported the tax. He promised that those were "deemed as enemies" would receive a "punishment according to the nature of the offense."[32] There was no evidence of this organized rebellion, but in response, groups in Pennsylvania and Virginia organized rallies to denounce the tax. Meanwhile, another anonymous writer by the pen-name of Tully defended Hamilton and the whiskey tax. As it turned out, Tully was a pseudonym used by Hamilton.[33] Just like Tom the Tinker, Hamilton's fake persona Tully had given citizens the false impression that there was already organized populist support for the tax under way. The inflammatory rhetoric of Tom and Tully sowed the seeds of division to the point of violence. Thousands rose up against the tax, and the state governments responded by calling up thousands of militia men, leading to violent clashes between 1791 and 1794.[34]

Partisan fake news dogged Washington's successor, John Adams. The Adams presidency illuminates how fake news can hinder the legislative and elective success of a president. During his presidency, news writers reported in 1797 that Adams had cut diplomatic ties with France in an effort to instigate a war between the two nations.[35] In actuality, France had demanded an absurd amount of money to open talks with the US, which Adams refused to pay.[36] Two years of hostilities with the French at sea in what was called "the Quasi-War" ensued. Adams's political rival Thomas Jefferson, a supporter of French democracy, hired James Callender, a newspaper editor, to publish fake news stories claiming that Adams had provoked France into war, not the other way around as Adams had stated.[37] Other journalists repeated and expanded upon Callender's stories. For example, one journalist implied that Adams wanted war with France as an excuse to expand the US military, claiming that the president was spending "millions for defense, but not one cent for tribute."[38] The press reports, both true and false, became so detrimental to Adams's presidency and he began to view the freedom of the press as such a hindrance to his administration that he passed the Sedition Act of 1798. The law empowered the government to jail and silence journalists who criticized the president.[39] Callender was jailed under the act until the next president, Jefferson, pardoned him.[40]

The Nineteenth Century: Fake News and the Penny Press

As the US population grew in the nineteenth century, the press began to coalesce into a set of profit-seeking organizations. The world was changing. The cotton gin had revolutionized agriculture in the South, which in turn led to expanded textile operations in the North, and these in turn relied on transportation innovations like railroads, steamships, and the Erie Canal to bring goods to wider national markets. All this also made communication faster. Where once word had traveled by horse or by foot, transportation innovations linked the Pacific West to the Atlantic Seaboard, and postal offices along these routes proliferated. The advent of the telegraph, invented by Samuel Morse in 1844, enabled press outlets to share stories and bring national news to local audiences. An underwater telegraph cable across the Atlantic Ocean brought news from Europe. A period of prosperity for the country also included the social ills of labor exploitation in new factories and a revitalized slave system in the cotton states. Wage labor and the so-called American system of manufacturing, which involved the use of interchangeable parts and the assembly line, brought rural populations (and immigrants) to cities, and these dense city populations enabled newspapers to reach a wider audience with less travel time and expense than ever before.[41] Some entrepreneurs believed that newspapers could produce vast profits, but that required building an audience. It was at that point in history, the early nineteenth century, that news outlets became obsessed with identifying the perfect content for maximizing their revenue and audience size. This obsession would still be with us in the twenty-first century.

In the nineteenth century, the average cost of a newspaper was six cents, which covered the cost of journalists' labor, production, and distribution and left a little extra profit for the newspaper owner.[42] These newspapers soon had competition from the penny press newspapers, which charged one cent for each newspaper they sold. They were able to reduce their costs and increase their profits by selling space to advertisers, adopting new technologies for mass printing, and replacing real journalism with fake news stories that drew the attention of larger audiences. After 1830, penny press fake news dominated the news industry. The Millerite movement discussed at the beginning of this chapter illustrates how newspapers were instrumental in the spread of fake news in this period.

The penny press found exquisite writers such as Edgar Allan Poe to draft fake news stories for their readers.[43] Poe's work for the *Sun*, for example, included a fake news story about a trans-Atlantic balloon trip.[44] This fictional trip had never occurred. Another hoax in the *Sun*, commonly referred to as the Moon Hoax, included a series of stories about a moon colony that had supposedly been sighted through a telescope.[45] The *Sun* was one of the first penny press papers to maximize profits from fake news. The Penny Press Wars began when New York's *Morning Herald* attempted to offer more sensationalistic and violent news, including trash-talking that relied on the theme of division.[46] In their war for fake news supremacy, the newspapers relied on having local reporters fabricate letters from overseas so they could claim to be providing international coverage.[47]

The penny press identified fake news with themes of racism and fear as effective for expanding their audience size and revenues. For example, much of the penny press exploited America's racist attitudes by publishing fabricated tales of planned slave rebellions.[48] They also exaggerated real rebellions, such as Nat Turner's 1831 Virginia rebellion, by inflating the number of associates and lending credence to the rumors that other rebellions were being planned.[49] The fear and panic prompted individuals to continue buying papers to keep up with the latest news about the rebellions and their organizers. These stories sometimes, in the case of Turner, resulted in whites hunting and killing suspected rebellion organizers who often had nothing to do with a real or imagined rebellion. They also mixed mysticism with fear and racism in a series of stories about African Americans suddenly turning white.[50] This played into whites' racist fears that even the white person sitting next to them could be black.

War, War, and Rumors of War

Despite attempts to distinguish actual journalists from the penny press, the news industry continued to peddle fake news. In the nineteenth century, the newspaper industry discovered not only that war was profitable but that fake news about war was equally profitable. Commentator Chris Hedges argues that "war is a force that gives us [citizens] meaning," providing purpose and reason for celebration, real or imagined.[51] War attracts news consumers through the spread of fear about an impending attack; stories of bravery in war; and concepts of moral superiority over one's enemy. The events leading to a war and the discussions by the political class about the impending war build an audience and thus revenue. The same can be said for the concerns that families have for their loved ones at war, battle outcomes, and results of the war.

The US-Mexico War illuminated how fake news can lead a nation to war. In 1845, President James K. Polk and his surrogates sent US forces to the border and then falsely claimed that those forces had been attacked by Mexico. The ruse was a way of starting a war with Mexico in order to justify stealing their land.[52] At the time, no news outlet had the resources to offer accurate reporting from the border. Instead, journalists regurgitated lies from war-hungry politicians in the form of news stories and opinion editorials.[53] The bias and unsubstantiated fake news content from these journalists helped galvanize the American public into approving our entry into a war with Mexico in 1845. Historian Tom Reilly, a premier scholar on the press during the US-Mexico War, explains that during the war "many of the articles were romantically written and filled with unsubstantiated facts and opinions."[54] The ensuing warfare cost the lives of 13,200 Americans and 25,000 Mexican civilians and troops.[55]

A "paranoid style of politics," as historian David Brion Davis refers to it, was a major contributing factor to the American Civil War, which cost over six hundred thousand lives.[56] Northern anxiety was heightened by fake news stories about an alleged "slave power" plot by southern individuals, in collaboration with northern Democrats, to promote and protect slavery within the US legal and judicial systems.[57] Southern anxiety was heighted by stories that northerners were the ones organizing slave rebellions in the South.[58] Photography, a relatively new technology during the war, was used to provide sensationalistic images for the accompanying newspaper story,[59] and photographers such as Alexander Gardner often repositioned the bodies of the dead for dramatic effect. Thus began a fake news tradition of altering real people in photos to sensationalize the image.

New technologies and the popularity of news during the Civil War resulted in the development of newspaper empires with wealth and influence unparalleled at the time. Just as the efforts of Andrew Carnegie, John D. Rockefeller, J. P. Morgan, and Cornelius Vanderbilt had led to virtual monopolies on steel, oil, banking, and railroads after the Civil War, the tactics of publishers like Jay Gould, William Randolph Hearst, and Joseph Pulitzer would lead to a virtual monopoly on the national press during the period between the 1870s and 1890s. These men recognized the demand for news the Civil War had created,[60] and they were dedicated to making news profitable, even going as far as cutting costs by relying on child labor,[61] and even at the expense of good reporting. For example, the Hearst newspapers, recognizing the economic opportunity that war coverage offered, published false stories, known as "yellow journalism," about the brutal treatment of the Cubans, particularly Cuban prisoners, by their colonizer, the Spanish. Journalists who never actually traveled to Cuba falsely reported that they had witnessed Cubans die in front of them.[62] In 1897, a Hearst employee and famed illustrator, Frederic Remington, wrote back to Hearst about his boredom covering Cuba, noting, "Everything quiet. There is no trouble here. There will be no war. Wish to return." Hearst reportedly replied, "Please remain. You furnish the pictures and I'll furnish the war."[63] The baseless claim that an explosion inside a US naval ship, the USS *Maine*, at the time in Havana's harbor, was caused by a Spanish torpedo was successful in leading US citizens to support US involvement in what would be known as the Spanish American War.[64] In total, the war killed over three hundred thousand people from battle and disease.[65]

Celebrities, Self-Interest, and Scapegoating

Newspapers during this period, which was sometimes referred to as the Gilded Age for its tremendous concentration of wealth among a handful of tycoons, introduced the theme of celebrity gossip to fake news. Annie Oakley was a beloved star of the traveling Buffalo Bill Cody's Wild West show. In 1901, she retired from her career as an entertainer. Then in 1903, newspapers across the nation began reporting that she was addicted to cocaine. The story was based on interviews with a burlesque dancer who claimed to be Oakley. The real Oakley ended up traveling from city to city waging fifty-five libel lawsuits against local papers for reporting the fake news.[66] For over a century, celebrity gossip fake news would remain a profit-making tradition, with future incarnations including tabloids such as the *National Enquirer* and online blogs such as *Gawker*.[67]

The Gilded Age era began the practice of entrepreneurs using their news outlets as a means to protect their economic interests. This would continue into the twenty-first century with Jeff Bezos, owner of Amazon and Whole Foods, buying the *Washington Post* and limiting its coverage to content that was favorable to his business interests.[68] During the Gilded Age, Jay Gould's *World* furthered his economic interest by publishing fake stories about his critics and his allies. He made false allegations against then New York State representative Teddy Roosevelt because Roosevelt had brought impeachment charges against a Gould ally.[69] The divisive use of fake news to denounce enemies and protect economic interests would become a continuing phenomenon of the American press. For example, in 2016 Michael Ferro, then chief news executive for the *Los Angeles Times,* the *Chicago Tribune,* and the *Baltimore Sun,* "urged his editors to devote negative coverage to people he saw as obstacles in business, including competitors and even fellow investors." According to his employees, Ferro was motivated, not by journalistic integrity, but by a desire to increase revenue.[70]

Gilded Age newspaper owners also started the practice of using xenophobic fake news to deflect readers' anger against the business practices of the wealthy. Xenophobia is the hatred or fear a person holds toward others because of their origin in a foreign country.[71] In 1873, the stock market crashed, causing the Panic of 1873, also known as the Long Depression.[72] The economic downturn that left thousands poor and unemployed was caused by a series of reckless speculative investments by the wealthy and major financial losses in the Chicago and Boston fires of 1871 and 1872.[73] To redirect working-class anger against the wealthy elite's economic mismanagement, the Gilded Age newspapers blamed the Chinese for the economic crash.[74] The Chinese had already been a longtime favorite scapegoat of American journalists: mid-nineteenth-century newspapers described them as "unnatural and filthy" and as "a dependent, ignorant, animal machine."[75] During the Gilded Age, newspapers, especially those owned by William Randolph Hearst, popularized the phrase "yellow peril" to depict the peoples of East Asia as a danger to the Western world.[76] The reporting resulted in violent attacks on the Chinese in places like Seattle, Washington, as well as legislation to ban Chinese immigrants, such as the Chinese Exclusion Act of 1882.[77] Such deflection of blame from economic elites to immigrants and ethnic minorities through fake news content is still occurring in the twenty-first century. For example, politicians and news outlets used fake news stories about immigrants to deflect blame from Wall Street and the banking class for the 2008 recession.[78]

The Twentieth Century: Radio

In the early twentieth century, radio became the first battleground for a struggle between commercial and public interests regarding news and information. The Federal Radio Commission, a predecessor to the Federal Communications Commission (FCC), was created through the Federal Radio Act of 1927 to regulate the use of airwaves for commercial and public communication. The act limited the number of radio stations a company could own in a market. Progressives had lobbied for the act to prevent media consolidation and media monopolies. The concept behind the bill was that diversity of views and news strengthened democracy.

The legislation and activism put extreme pressure on radio stations such as CBS and NBC. To silence their critics, the public relations innovator Edward Bernays developed a plan: radio stations could transform their image from one of commercialism to one of public service if they offered news programming. The stations would rely on newspaper journalists' reporting for their radio news broadcast content and would insert advertising to increase the stations' profits. The stations agreed, and radio news broadcasts were born.[79]

Just as newspapers had learned a century earlier, radio companies would come to realize that fake news and war news were conducive to maximizing revenue and audience size. World War II would be the first global story that the radio news industry covered. The rise of Adolf Hitler, Francisco Franco, and Benito Mussolini in Europe offered radio news programs their first long-running international news stories. Radio broadcast stations offered on-the-ground reporting from Europe. Reporters such as twenty-nine-year-old Edward R. Murrow were hired to synthesize the reports from a series of journalists to the American public.[80]

However, because of the wartime "press codes" imposed by the federal government, journalists were largely limited to reporting rumors and official statements from military leaders.[81] The War Department would not allow radio personalities to say, "And now for some good news." Nor could reporters in the field describe their location.[82] Some of the content was false because it was misleading. The press was allowed to offer news reports that benefited US policy, but contradictory evidence and facts were forbidden and hidden. For example, they were not allowed to describe what US bombing had done overseas. In addition, Murrow and other radio operators depended upon journalists embedded with the soldiers for their content. Often these journalists wore officer uniforms and held in-camp meetings with leaders of the military such as Dwight D. Eisenhower. This created a conflict of interest, as reporters were limited to reporting hero myths about the great personality and leadership of Eisenhower in exchange for access. In fact, General Douglas MacArthur was known to aggressively pressure journalists to publish stories that lauded his leadership.[83] Furthermore, the camps were rife with false news in the form of rumors. Soldiers had such a bad habit of spreading rumors that in 1943 the federal government paid Theodor Geisel (aka Dr. Seuss) to create a short film called *Rumors* for the "Private Snafu" series, which humorously depicted the negative consequences of not observing proper military conduct. In this cartoon, a chance remark made by one soldier leads another to jump to the conclusion that a bombing is imminent and eventually to cause a widespread panic throughout camp.[84] Rumors spread so quickly that in one actual instance two soldiers lied to another claiming that the local water was contaminated just to see how long it took to get back to them. The next day, their headquarters informed them the water was contaminated. The liveliness of rumor-mongering among the troops meant that journalists reported and radio stations broadcast numerous false stories, such as tales that Germany was in revolt or Hitler was dead.[85]

During World War II, radio became a source of fake news that inflamed divisions among the American people. Father Charles Coughlin went from being a progressive champion of Franklin Delano Roosevelt (FDR) to becoming a fake news peddler and FDR opponent. His weekly broadcast, which reached tens of millions of people, by 1936 began to include support and sympathy for the fascist governments of Hitler and Mussolini as an antidote to what Coughlin perceived as the real problem: communism.[86] Coughlin disseminated hate-filled anti-Semitic fake news such as the claim that a secret cabal of Jewish bankers had funded and orchestrated the communists' Russian Revolution.[87] His unsubstantiated claims were so toxic that the FCC, the federal regulatory body that oversaw both television and radio at the time, introduced the Fairness Doctrine in 1949. The doctrine mandated honest, fair, and balanced treatment of controversial issues and prevented a media outlet from offering political views without equal time for countering views.[88] Throughout the 1970s and 1980s, conservatives spearheaded a series of court cases and personal changes that hindered the enforcement of the Fairness Doctrine.[89] The removal of the Fairness Doctrine revived the spirit of Coughlin's vile and baseless broadcasts with radio personalities such as the hyperpartisan conservative Rush Limbaugh, whose fake news included reports that Austin, Texas, was "effectively" imposing "a ban on barbecue restaurants," that children coming across the southern US border had caused a measles outbreak in the US, and that then President Obama sought to "mandate circumcision."[90] Limbaugh's success gave rise to similar radio personalities, including Mark Levin, Rusty Humphries, Sean Hannity, and Glenn Beck[91]—several of whom have made the transition to television.

The Revolutionary Medium of Television

Fake news dissemination by radio was quickly eclipsed by that of the revolutionary medium of television. Early television news was dominated by the NBC, CBS, and ABC networks. Their news outlets relied upon newspaper journalists for the majority of their news content.[92] By the mid-1960s, nearly two-thirds of Americans relied on television and about half relied on newspapers for their news.[93] Television advertising spending quadrupled from $1.3 to $6 billion between 1950 and 1960.[94] Television revolutionized news with new programming such as prime time news and on-the-ground visual reporting. It also revolutionized fake news, bringing the sensational hoaxes of the penny press era to a visual broadcast. For example, on April 1, 1957, Britain's BBC broadcasting network aired a three-minute video segment that showed a family of Swiss farmers "harvesting" spaghetti from a grove of trees. The program known as the "spaghetti tree" hoax had viewers watching the scientifically impossible.[95] The BBC quickly noted it was an April Fool's Day prank.

Television fake news sowed division and fear to create a moral panic about communism, which culminated in attacks by Joseph

McCarthy (Republican senator from Wisconsin from 1947 to 1957) accusing everyone from actors to the military of communist subversion and Communist Party activity or sympathies. The news media participated in the moral panic by spreading fake news stories. For example, John Decker, a lawyer and World War II veteran, colluded with the military veterans' organization the American Legion and local newspapers to stage a mock communist takeover of Mosinee, Wisconsin, on May 1, 1950.[96] Sixty reporters, many with video recording devices, were attracted to the event thanks to Decker's public relations campaign. The mayor and the editor of the *Mosinee Times* were "arrested," prices were inflated, religious leaders were taken to a mock concentration camp, the library was closed, the local Boy Scout troop was turned into a Communist Youth group, and restaurants even added Russian rye bread and borscht to their menus. The town paper put out a "Red Star" edition with a photo of Stalin on the front page, and the nearest town's *Wassau Herald* trumpeted the headline, "Mosinee Seized by Reds!"[97]

Although McCarthy was eventually discredited, his anticommunist campaign and the wave of imprisonments, firings, blacklisting, and harassment that his fake news caused had a chilling effect on the news media for decades to follow. Researchers Nancy Berlinger and Rachel L. Zacharias have defined *chilling effect* as "the behavioral effect of policy that interferes with a person's ability to use a legal right that this person technically holds, often by inducing fear."[98] In fact, during the Cold War not even the FCC mandate for honest, fair, and balanced reporting could alter the homogeneity of reporting styles and narrow framing of limited topics in news media.[99]

The war in Vietnam was a case in point. The war began with fake news when the press reported the federal government's false claim about an "unprovoked" attack on a US destroyer by the North Vietnamese military on August 2, 1964, and, a few days later, a second attack.[100] The *Washington Post* headline claimed, "American Planes Hit

North Vietnam after Second Attack on Our Destroyer," and the *New York Times* reported "renewed attacks against American destroyers in the Gulf of Tonkin,"[101] Media outlets knew at the time only what the government had told them. Nevertheless, as formerly classified government documents released in 2005 and 2006 would reveal, the first attack was not unprovoked: the US Navy boats were gathering intelligence for South Vietnamese forces that were raiding the North Vietnamese coast. The second attack was what Cronkite called in retrospect a "phantom attack": it never actually occurred.[102]

The Vietnam War revealed how fake news can be used to support the initiation and continuation of a futile war. For nearly a decade, the US press failed to critique the government's claim that the war was nearing its end with a US victory, despite evidence to the contrary.[103] Since the late 1940s, each president, but especially Lyndon Johnson, knew the war was unwinnable but kept sending troops into combat while lying to the public about the military realities of Vietnam.[104] Eventually, the falsehoods became impossible to maintain, leading some reporters, including Cronkite, to report that the war was a "stalemate."[105] Still, other outlets continued to support the war: the *Washington Post,* one of the last cheerleaders, did so until 1969.[106] The mirroring narratives of the press and the federal government about the Vietnam War illustrate the danger of fake news narratives. The war resulted in the casualties of 58,220 Americans and over one million Vietnamese.[107]

Diminishment of the Press

The Vietnam War was a transformative event for American news media that revealed to news consumers the positive and negative aspects of a free press in the age of television. On the one hand, because it brought the American people closer to seeing war than ever before, video documentation and press reports seemed to be contributing to a more well informed electorate. However, the gate-keeper mentality of the press enabled media outlets and politicians to narrowly frame the war in ways that hid crucial realities such as the resolve of the Vietnamese people. In 1971, military analyst-turned-whistleblower Daniel Ellsberg leaked the Pentagon Papers, which revealed decades of presidents from both parties covering up America's operations, purpose, role, and inevitable loss in Vietnam. In response, the public's faith in both the federal government, which had lied about crucial aspects of the war, and the news media, which had failed for over two decades to inform the electorate about government's lies, began to wane.[108] In response to the declining faith in government, the Fairness Doctrine and Communication Act were repealed in 1987 and 1996 respectively.[109] Without a Fairness Doctrine, hyperpartisan fake news narratives from figures such as Rush Limbaugh were broadcast unchallenged. Furthermore, the removal of the Communication Act saw the fifty corporations that controlled news media in the 1980s reduced to six by the start of the twenty-first century.[110]

The corporations that monopolized American news media quickly demonstrated a commitment to profit over quality journalism. In fact, a fifth of newspaper journalists lost their jobs between 2001 and 2009, and similar cuts were made to editorial staffs.[111] The reduction in news companies, editors, and journalists left journalists scrambling for ways to solidify their position in the news industry. Some, such as Jayson Blair, disseminated fake news to maintain employment. Blair, a reporter for the *New York Times,* the *Boston Globe,* and the *Washington Post,* plagiarized and falsified stories for his entire career, including many about a gripping series of murders on Washington, D.C., highways known as the D.C. Sniper case.[112] On May 11, 2003, the *New York Times* released a 7,239-word front-page story with his retractions.[113] Similarly, for over three years, Stephen Glass, a young and upcoming writer for the *New Republic,* published a series of fake news stories about a Monica Lewinsky memorabilia convention, racist cab drivers, and psychic hotline scams.[114] Broadcasters such as Brian Williams and Bill O'Reilly also solidified their position in the industry with fake news. During his career as an on-air reporter, MSNBC's Williams falsely claimed to have traveled with SEAL Team Six, witnessed a suicide during Hurricane Katrina, and survived a missile attack while aboard a helicopter in Iraq.[115] Similarly, Fox News Channel's O'Reilly falsely claimed that he had been present while a friend of John F. Kennedy's never-before-revealed assassin committed suicide and that he had been active in fighting to save journalists' lives during the Falklands' War.[116]

Regardless of their outlet's economic modeling, ethical code, or organization, members of the press have historically confused and misled consumers by conflating fake news with journalism. In pre-press America, fake news often took the form of unsubstantiated rumors and malicious or fear-based accusations, as was the case in the infamous Salem witch trials in the late 1600s, where at least two hundred people went to trial and twenty were executed. The modern newspaper emerged in the mid-1800s, but in the early days the press was largely a disorganized group of for-profit journalists who often spread sensationalistic fake news tales, especially regarding war, to build their audience. The Millerite movement described at the beginning of this chapter is just one of the sensational stories that brought in readers. War, however, was the proving ground for readership, and in the 1800s, false stories about Mexico contributed to the Mexican-American War, just as false stories about Spanish plots to sink American ships enticed readers to buy newspapers and led to the Spanish American War. Wars in Vietnam and Iraq are more recent examples of the same fake news role.

The power of the press to influence public opinion remains strong. However, there are two sides to this power. The press's ability to simultaneously serve and weaken democracy puts news consumers in a precarious position. News consumers rely on the press for fact-based reporting. After all, journalists are tasked with protecting democracy by dispelling falsehoods, especially those from people in power, while illuminating truths that enable a democracy to function. It is worth noting that at the same time that the penny press was printing hoaxes and fiction, muckrakers were uncovering abuses and corruption through what would become investigative journalism.[117] When done properly, journalism equips citizens with the knowledge to control their system of government. When done poorly, journalism results in fake news content that is so divisive, hateful, and inflammatory that it engenders fear, anxiety, moral panic, and war.

In order to responsibly consume news content, citizens must be aware of the vested interests of the news media producers. Citizens who are unaware of these interests run the risk of conflating fake news with journalism. Conversely, when aware of these competing interests, news consumers are empowered to make more informed decisions about the veracity of news outlets and content. The public backlash against the news media during the Cold War, specifically with regard to the Vietnam War, led to a dismantling of the twentieth-century regulations. At the same time another iteration of the press emerged: the twenty-four-hour news cycle. As discussed in the next chapter, the avaricious capitalist model and political allegiances of the for-profit news industry incentivized fake news.

3 Satirical News and Political Party Propaganda Apparatuses

"By the way, all those people in the back are fake news," shouted Fox News Channel's Sean Hannity as he pointed at the journalists corralled in the back of the Missouri Arena.[1] They had arrived at the November 5, 2018, rally to report on the man standing next to Hannity: President Donald Trump. Hannity's use of the term *fake news* outraged journalists, who had witnessed Trump repeatedly invoke it to deride the press.[2] Trump's use of the term exemplified George Orwell's concept of "doublespeak," which Rutgers University linguist William Lutz defined as "language which pretends to communicate but really doesn't. It is language which makes the bad seem good, the negative appear positive, the unpleasant appear attractive, or at least tolerable."[3] As a weaponized phrase, *fake news* pretends to expose lies but actually serves to normalize them while discrediting factual statements.

From the rally stage, Hannity and his Fox News Channel colleague Jeanine Pirro echoed Trump's use of the phrase as they castigated members of their profession with the *fake news* epithet. For their efforts, Trump lauded the Fox News Channel hosts as "special guest(s)," noting, "They're very special, they've done an incredible job for us. They've been with us from the beginning."[4] Trump said of Hannity's television program, "I never miss your opening monologue."[5] The rally illustrated the degree to which the line between objective journalism and political advocacy had been blurred in the twenty-first century.

But that line was being blurred long before Hannity got up on that Missouri stage. Partisan narratives characterized the divisive raggle-taggle press of the early Republic. Throughout the nineteenth century and into the twentieth, independent press organizations turned from partisan reporting toward sensationalized stories, often hoaxes or outright fiction, in the hope that these would attract a mass audience and thereby reap mass profits for newspaper owners. By the late twentieth century, the federal government's deregulatory policies and the public's waning support for the press enabled the creation of massive media monopolies owned by a handful of corporations. The corporate press developed into propaganda wings of America's political class. In the twenty-first century, the popularity of satirical news programs threatened the economic viability of the corporate news media. Out of a desire to expand their revenue and audience size, the corporate news media adopted the satirical news practice of privileging sensational and divisive content over journalism. Much of the corporate media's divisive content originated from political party propaganda apparatuses, which are loosely connected groups of actors and institutions who, sometimes through coordination and other times through overlapping interests and actions, strive to influence public opinion with fake news.

Infotainment

By the end of the twentieth century, the industry had become more consolidated as the fifty companies that had controlled 90 percent of news media in the 1980s were reduced to six : News Corp, Disney, Viacom, Time Warner, CBS, and Comcast.[6] The way that news was reported had dramatically changed with the advent of twenty-four-hour news. In June 1980, CNN became the first twenty-four-hour news channel, but in the 1990s it was joined by Fox News and MSNBC. Each outlet sought to build and maintain an ever growing loyal audience with news programming. In fact, their economic viability depended upon it. They faced an unexpected competitor in satirical fake news programs.

Satirical fake news is entertaining content and social commentary presented in a news format. Rather than appeal to the logical preponderance of evidence, as is the case with journalism, satirical fake news appeals to emotion through humor. Satirical news content such as *Saturday Night Live*'s "Weekend Update" segment, Conan O'Brien's "Not Necessarily the News," Stephen Colbert's *The Colbert Report,* the *Onion,* and the satirical website *Clickhole* parodied news content through impersonations, false stories, and fabricated on-the-spot reporting.[7] In the early twenty-first century, younger audiences were increasingly getting the majority of their news content from satirical news programs.[8] In fact, by 2008, the most popular satirical news programs, like Comedy Central's *The Daily Show,* hosted by Jon Stewart, garnered audiences comparable to Fox News Channel and PBS.[9] Rensselaer Polytechnic Institute's Benjamin D. Horne and Sibel Adali argued that satirical news was able to build an audience by exploiting "the widely-shared frustration and perception that the news media is failing democracy."[10]

By the early twenty-first century, the popularity of satirical fake news caught the attention of the corporate press. In an effort to engage with satirical fake news audiences, the corporate press began inviting satirical fake news personalities on their programming. However, as a consequence of this decision, the line between satirical fake news and journalism was blurred for audiences. For example, on a 2004 appearance of Jon Stewart on CNN's *Crossfire,* the *Daily Show* host chided *Crossfire* host Tucker Carlson for fostering partisan division rather than honest debate on his news program.

Carlson, in response, accused Stewart of being partisan, citing *The Daily Show*'s repeated lampooning of the George W. Bush administration and leniency toward Democratic politicians.[11] But Carlson was assuming that a satirical news program on Comedy Central should be judged by the same journalistic standards as traditional news organizations. This was not lost on Stewart, who told Carlson, "You're on CNN. The show that leads into me is puppets making crank phone calls. What is wrong with you?" Nonetheless, the corporate press was so impressed with these types of appearances that they began to replace traditional news programming with satirical personalities discussing news content.

The corporate press responded to the popularity of satirical news programming by emulating it. In 2007, Fox News Channel launched the satirical talk show *Red Eye*, originally hosted by comedian Greg Gutfeld.[12] *Red Eye* exemplifies the entertainment-based non-newsworthy programming that media scholar Neil Postman labeled as "infotainment."[13] *Red Eye*, which was for a time hosted by comedian Tom Shillue, offered humorous commentary on news stories such as "The Most Important Story of the Day" segment, which in fact introduced a sensational non-newsworthy story.[14] The same year that *Red Eye* launched, CNN's *Larry King Live* brought in comedian Joy Behar as a guest host.[15] Her performance resulted in the 2009 launch of the CNN program *The Joy Behar Show*, which featured comedian Joy Behar's witty commentary on news stories and personalities.[16]

Privileging Entertainment over Facts

Over time, the corporate press began to value the sensational content that drove the popularity of satirical news programming without much attention paid to the validity of what they were reporting. For example, in 2010, networks showed nonstop live video of a penny press–like story about a Toyota Prius that had driven itself for twenty-three minutes with a driver trapped inside. News consumers were glued to their television watching in horror as a car malfunction kept an individual trapped inside and racing up the highway. The twenty-four-hour news networks were thrilled that the sensational real-time video had helped build their audience. It was later shown that the story was fake news. The car was not a runaway. In fact, the driver had committed insurance scams previously. He was $700,000 in debt at the time, owing Toyota Financial more than $20,000.[17]

As famed journalist and author Matt Taibbi notes in *Hate Inc.*, the proliferation of cable television and the internet, coupled with the deregulation of news media in the 1990s, created a fragmented media landscape that valued an audience's attention more than performing sound journalism. Indeed, just as the satire news programs had discovered, sensational stories, such as that of the runaway Prius, framed in highly divisive ways, were the most effective content for building a loyal news audience.[18] As University of Pennsylvania's Matthew Levendusky points out, humans enjoy divisive content because they are "motivated reasoners. Humans have two broad classes of goals: accuracy goals (the desire to reach the correct conclusion) and directional goals (the desire to reach the preferred conclusion, i.e., the conclusion that supports our existing beliefs)."[19] When satirical news programs ridicule ideological enemies, they offer a simplistic view of the world that appeals to viewers' narcissism. Viewers are told that their ideological position is morally superior to that of their opponents.[20] It is reminiscent of pro wrestling, which for over half a century built a massive television audience by offering viewers sensationalistic and divisive story lines that simplified the world into "good guys" fighting "bad guys." Satirical fake news programs such as the *Daily Show* mirrored the story lines of pro wrestling but replaced wrestlers with political and media figures.[21] Stewart's popular *Daily Show* was grounded in polarizing critiques of Republicans and conservative news personalities, whom he targeted three times as often as members of the Democratic Party.[22] A decade later, Trevor Noah's *Daily Show,* Samantha Bee's *Full Frontal,* and John Oliver's *Last Week Tonight* utilized Stewart's divisive formula for their own success.[23]

From the 1990s on, the corporate news media increasingly mimicked the hyperpartisan formula of satirical news programs. By 2007, hyperpartisan commentary dominated the twenty-four-hour news industry, with Fox, CNN, and MSNBC each annually increasing the amount of commentary while decreasing the amount of news reporting in their programming.[24] The commentary-based programming has focused on attacking ideological opponents in the news media. For example, *Red Eye* had recurring conservative characters such as Pinch, a puppet made out of a folded-up newspaper and named after the *New York Times* former editor Arthur Hays "Pinch" Sulzberger, who was used to mock liberals.[25] However, the most illustrative example of the corporate news media's ideological entertainment war was between MSNBC's Keith Olbermann and Fox's News Channel's Bill O'Reilly. The war began with occasional critiques of each other in 2003 that transformed into frequent satirical attacks. In 2006, Olbermann began repeatedly referencing the workplace sexual assault allegations against O'Reilly on his program (allegations that would later get O'Reilly fired from his eponymous program at Fox). O'Reilly responded by banning the word "Olbermann" from his radio show and lobbying his listeners to put pressure on MSNBC to remove Olbermann from television.[26] Olbermann continued the attacks on his program, often as part of a daily segment titled "Worst Person in The World," which was Olbermann's attempt to humorously list the worst people in the world. The segment was reminiscent of satirical fake news in that it had funny and doctored images of the people Olbermann was lampooning.

The corporate news media's emphasis on entertainment and polarization set a series of events in motion that marginalized the influence of journalism. In the decade since *Red Eye* first broadcast, scholars have found that hyperpartisan content is privileged in traditional news media over journalism.[27] At the same time, news consumers have been conditioned to seek and accept hyperpartisan news programs over traditional journalism. As a result, the audience for hyperpartisan news has grown annually, while the audience for traditional journalism has declined.[28] According to a Pew Research study, the waning demand for traditional journalism resulted in 25 percent of newsroom positions vanishing between 2008 and 2018, with most of the loss driven by newspapers, where the job loss was 47 percent (digital news positions have actually increased).[29] Hyperpartisan entertaining content, especially on the internet, is a cost-saving substitute for journalism because it requires less resources than investigative journalism. However, the emphasis on party division is not simply a product of the market. Rather, the economic demands and hyperpartisan formula of news outlets have overlapping interests with some political parties. As a result, press outlets have been incentivized to transform into an extension of political propaganda apparatuses.

Political Propaganda Apparatuses

Political propaganda apparatuses are a group of connected individuals and resources loosely organized to achieve political domination through the manipulation of public opinion. There is scant evidence that news media outlets take direct orders from political parties. Nonetheless, their shared interests result in the production and dissemination of fake news.

Political propaganda apparatuses originated from political consulting firms. The world's first political consulting firm was the California-based Campaigns Inc., founded in 1933 by Clem Whitaker and Leone Baxter, which specialized in managing public perception through fake news. They optimized imagery and manipulated news reports to reframe negative press reports about monopolies, such as Standard Oil and Pacific Telephone Telegraph, in a positive fashion; published quotes by California gubernatorial candidate Upton Sinclair out of context in the historically antiunion *Los Angeles Times* in order to undermine his prounion labor agenda known as EPIC (End Poverty In California); and spread fake news to defeat then President Harry Truman's national health insurance plan in 1940.[30] Although numerous other firms were created after what Sinclair called the "Lie Factory," few used fake news as effectively as Campaign Inc. until Lee Atwater and Black, Manafort & Stone (BMS).

The modern political propaganda apparatuses are largely shaped by the work of Lee Atwater. Atwater was a Republican political strategist who went on to work for US presidents Ronald Reagan and George H. W. Bush. Although he would die at the young age of forty, he would leave a blueprint for modern-day political party propaganda apparatuses weaponizing fake news. For example, in the 1980 South Carolina House of Representatives contest, he employed push-polling, where political operatives approach voters under the auspices of collecting polling data but instead spread fake news about an opponent, to defeat the Democratic Party's candidate.[31] Atwater also planted reporters to ask loaded questions that insinuated that the Democratic Party's candidate was not mentally fit for office.[32] In 1985, Atwater was hired by BMS, a political lobbying firm started by Republican Party advisers Roger Stone, Paul Manafort, and Charlie Black.[33] Among its other contributions to the Republican Party propaganda apparatus was the "message of the day" which saw all Republicans repeat the same message throughout the day because they believed that citizens would conflate the message's frequency with authenticity.[34] BMS's aspirations for power were so far-reaching that they earned the name "the Torturers' Lobby" because of the conservative despots they represented in the Philippines, Dominican Republic, Nigeria, Kenya, and Somalia.[35]

BMS's most famous act of content manipulation was the famed "Willie Horton" advertisement. The Democratic Party candidate for president in 1988, Michael Dukakis, as governor of Massachusetts, had presided over a furlough program that allowed some inmates to leave prison grounds on weekends. While on a furlough, inmate William Horton did not return to prison and committed rape, assault, and theft.[36] During the election, Atwater, who was one of the many members of the BMS staff working on Republican presidential candidate George H.W. Bush's campaign, utilized focus groups to determine how they could exploit the Horton story. The focus groups revealed that the Republican Party propaganda apparatus could expect victory from the furlough issue if they framed it in a way that appealed to voters' racism.[37] Atwater said of Horton, "By the time we're finished, they're going to wonder whether Willie Horton is Dukakis' running mate."[38] Atwater and his team created an ad known as "Weekend Passes" which told the story of Horton's furlough and crimes. While flashing the words "stabbing," "raping," and "weekend pass" across the screen, they manipulated the content using the name "Willie" instead of "William"; they also chose photos that made Horton look taller and larger than the whites in juxtaposing images.[39] By insinuating that a Dukakis presidency would see the nation overridden with black crime and violence, the manipulated content aggressively appealed to voters' racism and helped deliver electoral victory to Bush.[40]

Despite BMS's closure in 1990, its founders and their protégées continued to influence electoral outcomes through the Republican political party apparatus for decades. During George H.W. Bush's presidency, Atwater's Republican Party propaganda apparatus sought to engender support for the drug war by having the Drug Enforcement Agency (DEA) set up a drug purchase from a nineteen-year-old African American drug dealer in front of the White House.[41] One of Atwater's associates, Karl Rove, shifted the 1986 Texas gubernatorial race to a Republican Party win by falsely reporting that the Democrats had planted listening devices in the Republican campaign office, when in fact it was Rove who planted them.[42] Rove successfully shifted the 2000 Republican Party presidential primary to George W. Bush by appealing to voters' racism with push-polling and stories that falsely claimed Bush's primary opponent Senator John McCain had fathered a black child out of wedlock.[43] However, the most influential fake news of the 2000 presidential election was the Brooks Brothers Riot or Docker's Rebellion, an event created by Roger Stone, who hired actors to stage a protest, known as astroturfing, against the recount of votes in Florida. The recount would have shown that Bush had lost the election.[44] However, it was superseded by a Supreme Court decision declaring that Bush won the election.[45]

In addition to shifting elections, the Republican Party propaganda apparatus has focused on destroying the careers of elected officials. For example, during Democratic president Bill Clinton's administration, the Republican political propaganda apparatus fabricated and legitimized a series of scandals about the president, including Whitewater, which claimed that the Clintons had collected illegal real estate funds; Travelgate, which insinuated that Bill had fired federal employees to hire cronies; Filegate, which asserted that Republicans were being illegally targeted by federal investigators; and a 1993 story that Bill and his wife Hillary had had White House lawyer Vince Foster murdered.[46] After Bill left office, the Republican Party propaganda apparatus smeared Hillary, during her time as US senator (2001–9) and as a 2008 and 2016 presidential candidate, by appealing to voters' homophobia with fake news stories of her being a lesbian.[47] During Barack Obama's presidency, the Republican Party propaganda apparatus sought to delegitimize Obama's electoral victory and policy agenda with racist and Islamophobic fake news stories such as the "birther conspiracy," which claimed that Obama had provided a fake birth certificate to the federal government in order to hide his true identity as a Muslim socialist born in Kenya.[48] One of the biggest funders and communicators of this conspiracy for the Republican political propaganda apparatus was Donald Trump. During Obama's first term, Trump offered to donate money if Obama would release his "real" birth certificate.[49]

The Fake News Press

Starting in the late twentieth century, members of the press were integrated into the political propaganda apparatuses. Initially, the press and the political class developed a codependent relationship of information and access to power: *New York Times* reporter Thomas Friedman, for example, was friends with US secretary of state James Baker, and dozens of reporters, including ABC White House correspondent Brit Hume, jogged and played tennis with President George H.W. Bush.[50] This interdependent relationship had emerged a few times previously in US history: President Theodore Roosevelt, for example, had close relationships with the press.[51] However, in the twenty-first century, the ideological relationship between the press and political parties became ensconced in American media.[52] The origins of that transformation are rooted in the 1990s, when these relationships were exploited by the political propaganda apparatuses.

In the 1990s, the political propaganda apparatuses began to include news outlets. Traditionally, the political parties had tried to control the news cycle by limiting access to critical journalists. However, this was not a foolproof plan because politicians' electability often depends on the press to communicate their message to the electorate.[53] As a result, politicians could not shun the press without risking their electability. Although it took a quarter century to achieve, in the 1970s the political propaganda apparatuses devised a method for politicians to simultaneously shun critical press outlets and disseminate their message: they would create their own ideologically driven media outlets.

Political propaganda apparatuses connected the economic interests of the corporations that owned the press with the electoral goals of the party. For example, the Gulf War was politically advantageous for the president's Republican Party, citizens historically support a president in a time of war, and the war was profitable for the corporations that owned the news media. In 1990, when Iraq invaded Kuwait, General Electric (GE), a defense company, that stood to profit from the US invasion of Iraq, owned NBC and shares of the *Washington Post*.[54] GE successfully convinced the public to support the Bush administration's invasion of Iraq with fake news stories such as that of Nayirah, a fifteen-year-old girl who falsely claimed she had witnessed the Iraqi Army launch babies out of incubators in Kuwait; in fact, she was no ordinary civilian but the daughter of Saud al-Sabah, the Kuwaiti ambassador to the United States.[55]

Political Propagandists Become the News Media

To better manage the shared interests of corporations and the party, political propaganda apparatuses began working with public relations firms to manage and spread information. The three largest in the US are Omnicom Public Relations Group, WPP, and the Interpublic Group of Companies. They each have hundreds of smaller propaganda firms that work under their corporate umbrella. They represent products and governments as well as specific wings of the government such as the Pentagon. They produce news stories and press releases that they give to the corporate press, who publish these as legitimate news stories. The prepackaged news stories serve the economic and political interests of these firms, which are hired by the same corporations that fund dominant political figures.[56]

To ensure that these stories would make it to the airwaves, the political propaganda apparatuses built their own news outlets. The Fox News Channel, founded in 1996 by conservative mogul Rupert Murdoch and run by Atwater protégé Roger Ailes was the first successful twenty-four-hour press outlet to act as an influential component of a political propaganda apparatus. Ailes had a background in television; most notably he worked on the *Mike Douglas Show,* where he met then vice president Richard Nixon during his 1968 presidential campaign. Ailes explained to Nixon that in order to popularize the conservative message and mitigate the influence of the counterculture, Republicans needed to harness the power of television. In fact, from that meeting until his 2017 removal from Fox News following a litany of sexual harassment and assault allegations, Ailes worked directly with the Republican Party as a political adviser and indirectly as a news producer to proliferate the party's message and shape their image through television broadcasts. For example, Ailes convinced Nixon and other Republican candidates that they could temper media scrutiny if they avoided the long-standing practice of depending upon press conferences for crucial media exposure. Instead of standing in front of journalists and answering their questions at press conferences, Ailes broadcast Republican candidates answering questions from party-approved individuals who were falsely portrayed to viewers as randomly selected audience members. Ailes's talents were recognized by influential party donors. In fact, in the 1970s, Ailes worked at the Coors Company's failed experiment to develop a hyperpartisan conservative news media network: Television News Inc. (TVN). Although TVN failed, it offered an influential experience for Ailes and a framework for what would become Fox News Channel. While at TVN, Ailes was running a political consulting firm, Ailes Communications Incorporated, which advised Ronald Reagan and George H.W. Bush among others. In the 1990s, after a three-year stint at NBC, where he oversaw CNBC, Ailes was approached by

Murdoch with an opportunity to combine his political consulting, television production, and twenty-four-hour news acumen to normalize conservative views nationally through the Fox News Channel.[57]

Under Ailes, the Fox News Channel acted as a megaphone for the Republican Party propaganda apparatus. The majority of the channel featured conservative personalities such as Sean Hannity, Bill O'Reilly, Glenn Beck, and Sarah Palin delivering long pasquinades about the Democrats. For example, their program *Special Report* had 89 percent Republican guests (out of those with a party affiliation) in the first nineteen weeks of 2001.[58] The slant was obfuscated by the channel's tagline "fair and balanced" and its slogan "We Report, You Decide." During George W. Bush's presidency, the Republican Party propaganda apparatuses also managed the news media by hiring an actor, Jeff Gannon, to pose as a reporter and ask easy or misleading questions that distracted the press from real scandals in the White House; paying journalists a quarter of a million dollars to write positive fake news stories about the president's Medicare reform and No Child Left Behind Act, which sought to alter health care and education policy respectively; and having twenty federal agencies, including the Defense Department, pay corporations to construct video news releases (VNRs), video segments that were constructed to look like news reports and sell their policies to the voters.[59]

The influence of the Republican Party propaganda apparatus over the news industry facilitated their ability to manage the American electoral system and government. For example, during the second Bush administration, Fox News falsely reported that Democratic presidential candidate John Edwards was lying when he said that two hundred thousand veterans were homeless because they perceived that the truth looked bad for Republican Party at a time of war.[60] During Obama's presidency, Fox News played a critical role in hindering the president's policy agenda with fake news such as their false claims that Obama's health care plan would "kill Granny" with "death panels."[61] In addition, Fox News undermined the Democratic Party's efforts at immigration legislation and buttressed up their own proposals for a wall along the United States-Mexico border in 2006 and 2016 with fake news that inflated the number of immigrants in the US, claimed that undocumented immigrants accounted for seven thousand leprosy cases in the US, and claimed that undocumented immigrants voted in and influenced the 2018 election.[62]

Nearly twenty years after the first war with Iraq, The Republican Party propaganda apparatus's fake news would propel the US to accept another war with Iraq under another president Bush. George W. Bush's administration wanted to go to war with Iraq under the pretense that Saddam Hussein, then president of Iraq, was procuring "weapons of mass destruction" (WMDs).[63] There was no evidence to substantiate the claim. The Republican Party propaganda apparatus manufactured fake news stories that claimed Britain, Italy, and the US had proof of Iraq's nuclear weapons program, while excluding from programming such antiwar voices as Bill Press, Bill Maher, Chris Hedges, Phil Donahue, and Jesse Ventura.[64] Others in the press were complicit with party officials in government, such as the *New York Times*'s Judith Miller, who falsely claimed that Hussein's regime was developing WMDs. Miller, like her sources in the Pentagon and the intelligence community, relied heavily on false reports provided by Iraqi defectors who had a special interest in Hussein being ousted.[65] Her articles were seen as critical to mobilizing liberal and Democratic Party support for the invasion of Iraq. A year after the war began the *New York Times* apologized for the stories. In a related development, the Republican Party propaganda apparatus actively worked to silence Joseph Wilson of the State Department and his wife Valerie Plame of the Central Intelligence Agency (CIA) for revealing that Iraq did not have WMDs. Veteran *Washington Post* reporter Bob Novak worked in collusion with the vice president's office to break federal law by exposing Plame's identity as an undercover CIA agent.[66].

With the fact-based critics silenced, the Republican Party propaganda apparatus was able to convince the public, through fake news about WMDs, that the US should invade Iraq. In the weeks leading up to the war, 71 percent of news program guests in the US supported the US invasion of Iraq, and only about 10 percent of news programming provided an antiwar critique. Viewers were six times more likely to encounter a prowar than an antiwar argument.[67] By the time the US Congress voted to invade Iraq, over two-thirds of US citizens supported the war that killed between half-million and a million Iraqis, under the false pretense that Iraq had WMDs.[68] The fake news had a long-term impact. By 2016, polls showed that 53 percent of Americans believed that the US had found WMDs in Iraq, despite denials from the Defense Department and Central Intelligence Agency (CIA).[69] The fake news reached global audiences after the Defense Department paid Iraqi journalists to publish pro-American stories in their newspapers.[70]

Compared to the Republican Party, the Democratic Party propaganda apparatus was disorganized and hampered by internal division. As a countermeasure to the spread of Republican Party propaganda, progressives launched Democracy Radio in 2002 and Air America in 2004. Their content often critiqued the party leadership and cultivated progressive media personalities such as Ed Shultz, Rachael Maddow, and Al Franken before Air America closed operations in 2010 on account of funding issues.[71] In 2007, MSNBC began testing liberal programming as a competitive alternative to Fox News. The experiment, which saw many of the Air America personalities employed by MSNBC, led to a rise in viewership in mid-2007.[72] Since then, MSNBC has largely acted as a political arm of the Democratic Party, with a majority of its coverage dedicated to critiquing conservatives and excusing the behavior and attitudes of Democrats.[73] For example, in order to defeat the Ohio Republican governor's state budget bill, which included changes to the state's abortion policies, MSNBC's Rachael Maddow falsely claimed that the bill included a "mandatory vaginal probe" when the ultrasound was actually specified to be transabdominal in the final version of the bill.[74]

To maintain its centrist position, the Democratic Party weaponized fake news to discredit both progressives and conservatives. For example, in addition to leaking debate questions, in 2016, the Democratic Party propaganda apparatus worked to shift the presidential primary to Hillary Clinton by attacking her rival on the left, Bernie Sanders, with fake news stories that Sanders supporters at the contentious Nevada Democratic convention had thrown chairs at party leaders (a chair had been raised but not thrown) and that male misogynist "Bernie bros" who harassed Sanders's critics and opponents online were representative of his supporters.[75] Similarly, much in the same way that Trump used "fake news" to stifle inquiry, the Democratic Party propaganda apparatus weaponized the phrase "Republican talking point." For example, in an August 2019 Democratic Party presidential debate, Elizabeth Warren dismissed questions about the budget for her health care plan as "Republican talking points."[76] The party has also adopted a message of the day that explains by naming: they frequently referred to Senate majority leader Mitch McConnell (R-KY) as "Moscow Mitch" as part of a three-year campaign by the Democratic Party propaganda apparatus to convince voters that the nation of Russia was responsible for the Republican Party's electoral victories.[77]

On November 6, 2018, Fox News Channel released a statement about the rally the previous night that read, "Fox News does not condone any talent participating in campaign events. We have an extraordinary team of journalists helming our coverage tonight and we are extremely proud of their work. This was an unfortunate distraction."[78] In fact, Hannity was missing from the network's election coverage on November 7, 2018.[79] The absence of such a popular figure gave the impression that Fox News Channel was taking action against the shameless political pandering performed by its network personalities. However, a day later, on November 8, 2018, Hannity was back on the air, this time doing his radio broadcast, peddling unsubstantiated stories that claimed the Democratic Party had performed election fraud the night before.[80] Soon Hannity was back on Fox News Channel and the Missouri appearance was another forgotten episode in the history of democracy's distortion by the political party system.

The political party propaganda apparatuses developed organically by capitalizing on the shared interests of corporations, news media outlets, advertisers, and political parties. Through coordination and collusion they worked to not only create but disseminate fake news to the American public. Their work reveals that American democracy can be managed by fake news if the electorate conflate political propaganda with journalism. Furthermore, American news consumers cannot depend on the press or the political class to behave in a manner that serves our democracy and exposes fake news. This points to the need for news consumers to develop the skills to distinguish journalism from fake news or risk becoming dependent upon political party narratives to inform their vote. However, political party propaganda apparatuses represent just one type of fake news producer threatening American democracy. In the next chapter we will examine another large-scale network of fake news producers: state-sponsored propaganda machines.

4   The Roots of State-Sponsored Propaganda

The Backstreet Boys blared through the Cleveland, Ohio, arena speakers as the audience shuffled toward the exit. The temperate-sounding lyrics of "I Want It That Way" were a big contrast to the energetic and emotional performance just given by candidate Donald Trump. During that October 22, 2016, evening speech, he falsely claimed that Secretary of State Hillary Clinton had sold "her office for personal enrichment" and that he had witnessed "the media colluding and conspiring directly with Clinton."[1] Unbeknownst to the crowd, in a few short weeks Trump would be president.

As the crowd was making their exit, one attendee, an unknown white man, shouted at the press standing nearby, "*Lügenpresse!* . . . You are all in bed with the Clintons, bought and paid for." As the man was filmed by BuzzFeed's Rosie Gray, he directed his antipathy toward the media and Hillary and Bill Clinton at Gray, noting, "You're [the press] all in bed with the Clintons." Occasionally, the man whispered to another white man wearing a hat with Trump's campaign slogan on it, "Make America Great Again."[2]

The attendees' use of the word *Lügenpresse* stood out because it was a centuries-old phrase popularized by Germany's Nazi Party. *Lügenpresse* is a German term that means "lying press." It had been used sparingly in late nineteenth-century Germany but had reemerged during World War I to denounce enemy propaganda.[3] During World War II, the Nazi Party weaponized the phrase to discredit journalists, silence critics, and spread hegemonic narratives. It is remembered by historians as a central weapon of the Nazi regime. The term lay dormant for decades until 2014, when its usage increased so much that Germany had to ban it the following year.[4] The reappearance of the Nazi term in US discourses in 2016 illustrates the long-lasting impact of state-sponsored propaganda machines.

A propaganda machine is a hegemonic force that organizes people and resources to construct and circulate dominant messages that seek to control and influence human behavior and attitudes. The term *propaganda* was coined by the Catholic Church in their 1622 *Sacra Congregatio de Propaganda Fide,* which sought to shift public opinion among Christians toward Catholicism and away from Protestant denominations.[5] Propaganda, according to Yochai Benkler, Robert Faris, and Hal Roberts, is a form of "communication designed to manipulate a target population by affecting its beliefs, attitudes, or preferences in order to obtain behavior compliance with political goals of the propagandist."[6] As writer and political commentator Walter Lippmann noted, propaganda is most effective when it saturates communication, leaving little to no space for contrary facts or evidence. He explained in his 1922 *Public Opinion* that "under the impact of propaganda, not necessarily in the sinister meaning of the word alone, the old constants of our thinking have become variables."[7]

Lippmann's entry elucidates how fake news is legitimized by state-sponsored propaganda machines: they create a social climate in which falsehoods are believed because they fit with the propagandistic narratives dominating national discourses. Communication scholars refer to this as priming.[8] The Nazi Party's ability to influence and control public opinion resulted from their state-sponsored propaganda machine, which relied on fake news to consolidate their power. Germany was hardly the only country to create and operate a propaganda machine. Since the early twentieth century, numerous nations have collectively spent trillions of dollars on the construction of fake news–peddling propaganda machines. The fake news they disseminate continues to appear in discourses long after the machine's architects and their regimes have disappeared. Originally, they were created for a temporary purpose, such as increasing troop enrollment for a war. However, the demands of the Cold War led to propaganda machines becoming a permanent component of nation-states. State-sponsored propaganda machines further complicate citizens' news consumption patterns by methodically priming the citizenry to accept fake news content as truth.

Nascent Propaganda Machines

In addition to costing tens of millions of lives, the First World War saw the birth of state-sponsored propaganda machines.[9] Where fake news from the press sensationalized war to build their audience, a state-sponsored campaign sought to build national support for war. In 1914, Germany had enlisted four million more troops in their military than Great Britain.[10] In order to close the enlistment gap with Germany, Great Britain's secretary of state, Lord Kitchener, was charged with increasing troop enrollment. To convince people to enlist, Kitchener developed the first state-sponsored propaganda machine to disseminate his messaging through posters, theatrical messages, advertisements, and fake news.[11] The fake news sought to prime audiences for war by dehumanizing the Germans and provoking moral outrage. Whereas a moral panic is a response to fear-laden content, Daniel Batson and his colleagues define moral outrage as the "anger provoked by the perception that a moral standard—usually a standard of fairness or justice—has been violated."[12] Great

Britain sought to cultivate moral outrage through fake news stories claiming that the Germans were impaling babies with bayonets, sexually assaulting nuns, enslaving and murdering priests, cutting off the hands of children, using civilians as human shields, turning cadavers into soap and margarine, crucifying soldiers, and cutting the breasts off nurses.[13] The grotesque nature of the stories had the dual effect of dehumanizing the enemy in British citizens' minds and creating moral outrage about the welfare of babies, fellow citizens, and priests. Kitchener's efforts were seen as a success, with Britain closing the troop gap.[14]

During World War I, US leaders emulated Britain's campaign. Although American public opinion favored isolationism when the war began, many US leaders felt that America should enter the war.[15] Thus they created a propaganda machine to transform US public opinion from isolationist to interventionist.[16] Their efforts were led by foundational figures in public relations and propaganda such as former journalist George Creel, who presided over 150,000 employees in the Committee on Public Information (CPI); Edward Bernays, who had helped devise the strategy for news coverage that would conform to FCC regulations; and the godfather of journalism, Walter Lippmann.[17] They worked to influence the American people and in some cases outright provide fake news content for journalists.[18]

The US entry into World War I exhibits how fake news content from domestic and international sources can stir up moral outrage to shift an isolationist public opinion toward intervention. On May 7, 1915, despite two warnings from Germany, the *Lusitania,* a British ocean liner carrying passengers and 173 tons of war munitions, was struck by a German submarine, killing three hundred people, twenty-five of whom were American.[19] The Germans claimed it was in response to the US trading weapons to their enemies via the ocean liner. A campaign of fake news swirled around the subsequent investigation. The British and US press largely maintained the narrative that the German attack was unjustified because the ship contained no employable weapons, only parts for creating weapons.[20] However, some in the press, such as the *Tucson Daily Citizen*, rightly denounced the government's fake news about the *Lusitania*, noting that there were indeed weapons onboard.[21] They were a minority voice, as most news outlets falsely reported that the Germans had murdered passengers without cause.[22] In fact, some news outlets included cartoons that dehumanized the Germans by showing them as hell-bent on attacking "civilization."[23]

The British also sought to increase Americans' support for entering World War I by disseminating fake news stories that would evoke feelings of national humiliation, such as a story that Germans were celebrating the sinking of the *Lusitania* with a holiday for all schoolchildren.[24] Populations often respond to events perceived as national humiliations with attempts to restore the nation's pride through war.[25] The American propaganda machine worked to turn shame over the *Lusitania* into support for the war with anti-German parades, posters, performances, speeches, and fake news.[26] National pride can become arrogance or a stance of moral superiority, where individuals become blind to context and reality because they feel justified on moral grounds.[27] For example, during World War I, Americans marginalized German Americans by expelling German clubs, nearly ending German-language courses in American schools, openly dehumanizing the Germans in newspapers that referred to them as "Huns," and renaming food with German origins, changing *hamburger* to *liberty sandwich*, *sauerkraut* to *freedom lettuce*, and *frankfurter* to *hot dog*.[28] Woodrow Wilson claimed that Americans should take pride in fighting the war because in the process they were going to deliver democracy to the world.[29] Appeals to national pride proved highly effective in garnering support for the US to join World War I.

Reporting during World War I demonstrated the recurring practice of state-sponsored propaganda machines censoring and colluding with the press to spread fake news content. The CPI recruited and managed journalists to report fake news for the federal government.[30] Some journalists joined the CPI out of patriotism, while others believed in Wilson's vision of the world.[31] Nonetheless, the CPI became what historian Stephen L. Vaughn calls a "a veritable magnet" for "intellectuals, muckrakers, socialists, and other reformers," with progressive journalists such as S.S. McClure and Ida Tarbell repeating CPI content as legitimate journalism.[32] The CPI's fake news targeted not only domestic audiences but, through its Foreign Language Newspaper Division, foreign audiences as well.[33] The journalists viewed themselves not as propagandists but as patriotic citizens. In fact, even if journalists wanted to print critical accounts, fact based or not, of the war, they were censored by the Espionage Act, which empowered the postmaster general to stop the distribution of materials deemed as, among other things, interfering with the war effort.[34]

The fake news stories continuously dehumanized Germans as a way to justify the continued war effort. For example, journalists falsely reported that Germans were selling court plaster (adhesive bandages) in the US that contained "leprosy germs," and that Germans ate the US soldiers they captured.[35] In fact, the *New York Tribune* mused about the health implications of the latter practice, predicting "an epidemic of stomach trouble if the German people were to indulge [in cannibalism]."[36] Another lie reported was that the Germans were fattening up prisoners before execution, then turning them over to the German Corpse Utilization Company (GCUP), where they could be turned into consumer goods. According to Virginia's *Clinch Valley News,* the GCUP was turning the fat from corpses "into lubricating oil and everything else is ground down in the bones mill into a powder which is used for mixing with pigs' food and as manure. Nothing can be permitted to go to waste."[37] The US would enter the war eighteen months before it ended, accounting for 110,000 of the nearly 30 million casualties during the war.[38]

Industrial Propaganda Machines

The incredible success of the World War I propaganda machines of the US and Great Britain caught the attention of a prisoner who described them as "marvelous."[39] His name was Adolf Hitler. In his book *Mein Kampf* he claimed that "the war propaganda of the English and Americans was psychologically sound. By representing the Germans to their own people as barbarians and Huns, they prepared the individual soldier for the terrors of war, and thus helped to preserve him from disappointments."[40] Hitler's Nazi regime would not only emulate but dramatically redefine the capabilities of state-sponsored propaganda machines. Eventually, Hitler's rhetoric and that of other aggressive nations would play a key role in mobilizing the Western war into World War II, which cost between sixty million and seventy-five million lives.[41]

The architect of the Nazi propaganda machine was Paul Joseph Goebbels. After reading *Mein Kampf*, Goebbels became an admirer of Hitler. In particular, he found himself agreeing with Hitler's argument that Marxism was a dangerous product of the Jews.[42] His approbation for Hitler and Nazi ideology gave him a direct role in constructing and operating the Nazi propaganda machine. As minister of propaganda for Nazi Germany from 1933 to 1945, Goebbels took supervisory control over the press and the arts. In addition, he incorporated new media such as film and radio into Nazi propaganda efforts.[43] Goebbels was familiar with Lippmann's belief that propaganda was most effective when consumed repeatedly. As a result, Goebbels ordered citizens to listen to the propaganda through radio transmissions. Citizens without radios in the home were forced into so-called Listening Rooms, such as meeting halls, courtrooms, and schoolrooms, where they were forced to consume Nazi propaganda. The messages reached 70 percent of German households, some fifty-six million people.[44]

Like the US authorities during World War I, the Nazis used censorship to strengthen the effects of their fake news. Under Nazi rule, journalists and press outlets that did not produce party propaganda were discontinued, silenced, and imprisoned.[45] The public was led to believe that the vast censorship was caused by enemy content that threatened the stability of Germany. The Nazis discredited the creators of this content with the term *Lügenpresse,* which equated fact-based reporting with treasonous lies.[46] The term was successful in convincing enough Germans to passively accept censorship of the press and the Nazi's totalitarian regime.

Nazis' fake news relied on fear to centralize the regime's power. English philosopher Thomas Hobbes argued that fear was an exploitable force, one that could promote an awesome concentration of state power and authority with popular consent.[47] The Nazis' message was that mismanagement by previous leaders and conspiracies by groups such as the Jews had caused cultural, economic, political, and social decay in Germany. The Nazis promised that removal of the "others" who were the source of social degeneracy, would restore Germany's glory in the form of the Third Reich, the heir to the Holy Roman and German Empires.[48] *Other* is a sociological term referring to an individual or group that is abused for being an outsider by the dominant group. In Nazi Germany, Jews were the main "other." They were blamed for crime, family dissolution, the poor economy, and defeat in World War I. In addition, the Nazis blamed Catholics, communists, the physically challenged, feminists, and liberals.[49] Fear of "others" was often stoked by fake news films that manufactured statistics about undocumented immigrant and Jewish crimes and exaggerated the prevalence of sexual relations between Jewish men and German women, with the implication that the supposed Aryan racial characteristics of the German people would be diluted, corrupted, or destroyed.[50] People whose fears were stirred up by these stories went along with measures that took away Jews' civil rights and eventually their lives. Those who were ambivalent about the treatment of Jews saw their own civil liberties diminished or taken away.[51] Hitler's propaganda would result in the deaths of eleven million civilians.[52]

As a means of cultivating public support for wars to expand the German Empire, the Nazis pioneered the fake news concept of the false flag operation. Jim Maddock and his colleagues at University of Washington define a false flag as "an attack designed to appear as if carried out by someone other than its perpetrators."[53] The Nazis frequently would orchestrate events and then blame them on someone else as a pretext to implement a policy.[54] The Nazis envisioned Germany as accomplishing vast infrastructure projects paid for by the exploitation of conquered nations.[55] A high degree of public faith in that vision was necessary, considering that it required millions to not only support but engage in war. As a result, the regime orchestrated false flag operations that they believed would engender public support for the war. For example, Henrich Himmler had the Nazis dress German soldiers in Polish military uniforms prior to staging an August 1939 attack on a German customs post.[56] The simulated attack was one of many reported by the press as an attack by Poland and thus served to convince the German public that an invasion of Poland was defensive rather than offensive.

The Nazis also pioneered the use of fake news as a distraction from and an outright denial of disturbing realities. As the Nazi military began to lose the war, fake news stories constructed narratives of German heroism and triumph. Despite massive losses at Stalingrad between 1942 and 1943, a battle that took nearly two million lives, the German press hid the number of dead Germans and reported victory.[57] One newspaper reported that "names like Stalingrad, Welikje-Luki, Rschew, Illmensee and others have become symbols of the unbelievable heroism of German soldiers. . . . Every day, positions held by a few troops must withstand steady attacks by enemy masses."[58] As late as 1944, when Germany was taking unsustainable losses of lives and resources, the German press reported that the US, not the Germans, were the ones taking unsustainable losses.[59] One newspaper reported that "recently the US military leadership admitted the loss of a 20,000-ton troop ship two years ago. That would not be possible with us."[60] Stories like these kept Germans feeling justified for engaging in the war and bolstered their faith that victory was both attainable and arriving soon while obscuring the reality on the ground.

The Nazi propaganda machine also worked on an international scale to spread fake news in enemy territory. "Lord Haw-Haw" was a nickname for a series of radio announcers, German, British, and American, who delivered pro-Nazi propaganda in English on a show called *Germany Calling* that was broadcast to Britain.[61] The content was aimed at demoralizing the British people and weakening their support for the war. In response, the British, who had earlier created the government-run British Broadcasting Corporation (BBC), began broadcasting a fake German-language program hosted by a fake person, code-named Gustav Siegfried Eins (GS1), supposedly a disaffected Prussian military officer, to undermine German support of the Nazi regime by delivering profanity-laced diatribes that spread unsubstantiated claims about Nazi corruption, immorality, and buffoonery.[62] The Nazis searched Germany to discover the illegal station and punish its evasion of censorship, but the show was actually being broadcast from England.

Fake News in Enemy Territory

The Nazi propaganda machine began the long-standing practice of regimes employing fake news as a tool to spread their ideology to other nations. During the war, the Nazis employed "Axis Sally" (real name Mildred Gillars), an American woman turned Nazi sympathizer, to broadcast defeatist propaganda to Canadian, US, and

British soldiers serving in Europe. Sally's content praised the Nazis, denounced the Allies, and attempted to sow fear and doubt among American soldiers that they would then spread to other Americans at war and on the home front. After the war, she was captured by the US and sent to prison for treason.[63]

In addition to this radio campaign, the Nazi propaganda machine encouraged Germans living abroad to spread "German virtues," which meant Nazi ideology, into the US. By the mid-1930s, it had successfully cultivated Nazi sympathizers in the US. In 1936, these sympathizers created the Amerikadeutscher Volksbund, or German American Bund, which included over twenty thousand members operating twenty youth camps led by Fritz Julius Kuhn. Until they fell apart in 1939, largely because of Kuhn's imprisonment for embezzlement, the organization spread Nazi fake news to American citizens. For example, on February 20, 1939, they held an "Americanization" rally of twenty thousand people in New York's Madison Square Garden.[64] The rally's rhetoric focused on repeating Hitler's fake news about a Jewish communist plot to take over the world. Kuhn warned the crowd of the "slimy conspirators who would change this glorious republic into the inferno of a Bolshevik Paradise" and "the grip of the palsied hand of Communism in our schools, our universities, our very homes." The rally was met by one hundred thousand counterprotesters, including one Isadore Greenbaum, who snuck on stage to attack Kuhn and was beaten half to death by attendees.[65]

The Nazi propaganda machine was hardly the only propaganda machine to spread fake news in the US during World War II. In 1922, Benito Mussolini and his thirty thousand supporters—known as Blackshirts—marched on Rome to seize power and install a fascist regime with Mussolini as their leader.[66] In response, the Italian monarch agreed to peacefully transfer power to Mussolini. Mussolini's fascist regime consolidated their authoritarian power through a propaganda machine that outlawed criticisms of the state, violently subdued and murdered the opposition, and destroyed rival newspapers, especially the socialist papers.[67] Meanwhile, the government funded and distributed fake news to press outlets, such as stories that Mussolini had saved and preserved Italy from communism and lawlessness.[68] Such stories obscured the fact that he had created an authoritarian regime and that in 1925 he declared himself Italy's lifelong leader.[69] US newspapers uncritically adopted this perspective. The *New York Tribune,* the *Cleveland Plain Dealer,* and the *Chicago Tribune* all claimed that Mussolini had stabilized Italy, and the *New York Times* repeatedly credited Mussolini's fascist "experiment" with returning Italy to "normalcy."[70] Historian Laylon Wayne Jordan writes that "the early Mussolini, who veritably personified Italy and Fascism to the outside world, enjoyed a cosmic reputation that was tailor-made to evoke admiration among Americans, whose basic criteria was [*sic*] pragmatic and materialistic."[71]

In Japan, the press, motivated by patriotism, worked with the state-sponsored propaganda machine to construct and disseminate fake news that emphasized heroism and reasons to support the Japanese war effort.[72] In addition, they, like Germany, spread fake news to create instability in enemy nations, including the US. For example, they broadcast into the US the radio program *Zero Hour,* which critiqued American culture, art, and society. One of the show's hosts was Iva Toguri, who would be dubbed "Tokyo Rose" by the US government. Toguri had originally lived in the US but had traveled to Japan to tend to her sick aunt. When Japan attacked the US at Pearl Harbor she was denied reentry to the US. When the war ended she was arrested for treason and spent ten years in prison before being pardoned by President Gerald Ford in 1977.[73]

Japan revealed that fake news is effective at creating division when it exaggerates a kernel of truth, such as America's long-standing racism. Although the *Zero Hour* program spread falsehoods about the US, it also discussed very real racial discontent among Americans as a way to exploit racial divisions in the US. The Japanese forced actual African American POWs to broadcast prescribed statements criticizing racial inequality in the US and surrendering their citizenship. The Japanese found these scripted messages to be so successful that they introduced them into other programs such as *Conversations about Real Black POW Experiences* and *Humanity Calls*. Although the content was scripted, the issue of racial inequality was real. In fact, the National Association for the Advancement of Colored People (NAACP) cited it to point out that racial inequality undermined the US war effort.[74]

The Second US Propaganda Machine

The success of enemy propaganda machines incentivized the US to update its propaganda machine. President Franklin Delano Roosevelt's propaganda machine was designed to stimulate American citizens' support for US entry into World War II. The operation, largely run by the US Office of War Information (OWI), distributed fake news through a series of government-run media such as the radio station Voice of America (VOA), which operated domestically and internationally on thirty-nine transmitters in over forty languages, and United Newsreel, which gave pro-US newsreels to US citizens.[75] Most of the content was misleading because of wartime regulations. Press codes censored various facts, allowing for only a narrow view of US operations and enemies, presenting a picture that benefited US war policy. If journalists had questions about the government codes, they were supposed to bring them to the Office of Censorship.[76]

Much of the fake news was a distraction from the contradiction of combating a hateful regime while practicing hate at home. During World War II, the public felt that US involvement in the war was justified because of the nature and actions of the fascists. However, at the same time, the US government arrested and interned innocent citizens and immigrants. The situation required a careful explanation, and the government relied on fake news to convince the public. After the December 7, 1941, attack by the Japanese at the US military base on Pearl Harbor, FDR signed Executive Order 9066 to intern seventy thousand Japanese and Japanese Americans in camps for the duration of the war out of fear that they would subvert the US war effort. Two-thirds of them were American citizens.[77] The government's Civilian Conservation Corps produced newspapers that offered fake news stories justifying internment to the internees, while providing a rosy image of their captivity to the rest of the public.[78] They also produced videos that showed internees smiling in a beautiful landscape and comfortable quarters. Such coverage hid the reality of the cramped quarters under military rule. At the same time, anti-Nazi and anti-Japanese films were being produced collaboratively by the OWI and the Bureau of Motion Pictures (BMP).[79] All together, the content justified Japanese internment and distinguished the US from enemy regimes.

Cold War Propaganda in the USSR

As World War II came to an end, the Union of Soviet Socialist Republics (USSR) and the US embarked upon a half century of Cold War, where the economic visions of capitalism and communism competed for world dominance. Each side used propaganda (as well as economic incentives and sometimes force) to win over other nations to their worldview. From 1945 to 1953, the USSR sought to turn eastern Europe into an ideological and politically homogeneous region, just as Germany had tried to do under the regime of Adolf Hitler. They invaded eight countries: Poland, Hungary, Czechoslovakia, eastern Germany, Romania, Bulgaria, Albania, and Yugoslavia. In each nation, the invaders would collaborate with local communist parties to immediately create a secret police force that relied on selective violence, precision targeting of political enemies, and other methods for maintaining Soviet influence.[80]

In a move reminiscent of previous regimes, the USSR relied on limiting news content in these regions to fake or approved news. The Soviet Union believed that eventually their propaganda machine, which limited radio and newspaper content to procommunist messages, would lead people to adopt and support communism. [81] Local communist groups, each with its own ministry of culture, were tasked with operating the media outlets.[82] The fake news they disseminated sought to maintain support for communism even by the most absurd claims. For example, when the weather reports revealed dark conditions for May 1, the very important communist celebration of Labor Day, fake news reports would predict and claim sunshine instead.[83]

Most of the USSR's domestic fake news was produced through government-controlled radio stations and newspapers such as *Pravda*. Soviet Party leaders controlled the flow of news in the USSR by censoring undesired information.[84] Individuals were jailed and murdered if they challenged the regime.[85] Just as Hitler had done with accusations of a *Lügenpresse*, the USSR claimed that any content critical of communism was false and had been planted by the US government.[86] Fake news stories buttressed citizens' morale under government-mandated labor programs such as the famous Glavnoye Upravleniye Lagerejare (Gulag), which from the 1920s through the 1950s forced tens of millions of Soviets to perform manual labor to industrialize the USSR through state-run projects.[87] These stories appealed to national pride and thereby gave workers a sense of accomplishment. They falsely reported that mandatory labor had produced the "overproduction of goods" that the capitalists had promised but never delivered. In actuality, the USSR was underproducing the amount of goods it had promised.[88]

Beyond its satellite states, the USSR's propaganda machine weaponized fake news to sow division in the US. One program called INFEKTION operated news outlets overseas such as the San Francisco-based publication the *Sun Reporter*. The USSR's publications tried to break up the North Atlantic Treaty Organization (NATO) by claiming that the US was planning to use nuclear weapons against its NATO allies. In the US, Soviet fake news attempted to intensify racial division through fake news stories that claimed Jimmy Carter supported apartheid in South Africa and that the US had invented the disease of AIDS as a weapon against black people.[89] The latter story had long-standing consequences, as in the twenty-first century 50 percent of African Americans either believed or did not discount the idea that the US government was behind the AIDS epidemic.[90]

US Cold War Propaganda

As World War II came to a close, the US was already seeking to update its propaganda machine for what would become the Cold War. During the Cold War, the US government sought to build national consensus against communism.[91] In January 1945, US congressman Karl E. Mundt (R-SD) introduced a bill, the US Information and Educational Exchange Act of 1948, popularly called the Smith-Mundt Act, and signed into law by President Harry S. Truman on January 27, 1948, that allowed Congress to fund media outlets, such as Voice of America and Radio Free Europe, to distribute propaganda that appeared as news content to international audiences. These outlets were banned from distributing their content domestically.

Despite the Smith-Mundt Act's intention to keep US propaganda from dominating domestic discourse, the US government weaponized television as a domestic fake news medium. During the Cold War, television news was dominated by Defense Department-scripted fake news programs such as *Battle Report Washington* and

The Armed Forces Hour.[92] Top government officials would appear on these shows, which were comfortable with the government-scripted content, but rarely on others. Because *Battle Report Washington* was broadcast in partnership with NBC, it had to placate advertisers, so the program's content often presented consumerism as an effective way to defeat communism. Rather than obtaining objective news, viewers were effectively treated to advertisements for capitalism, consumerism, and a Cold War military ideology of a world struggle between communism and freedom. By 1953, the Republican Party, fearing that the Democratic Party was using the show to their advantage, had funding for the scripted television shows canceled.[93]

The US Cold War–era propaganda machines employed hundreds of journalists who were working at private press outlets. The production of fake news reported by journalists was one of the multifaceted activities of the Central Intelligence Agency.[94] The CIA's Operation Mockingbird drafted content for journalists to publish in news outlets such as ABC, CBS, NBC, *Newsweek,* the *Miami Herald,* the *Saturday Evening Post,* and the *New York Herald-Tribune.* Journalists would engage in the common practice of copying and publishing content from these news outlets, not realizing that the content was CIA produced.[95] In fact, the CIA coordinated its operations closely with Arthur Hays Sulzberger, publisher of the *New York Times* from 1935 to 1961, and Joseph Alsop, the influential political columnist (from 1937 to 1971) and Washington insider who was the cousin of Franklin Delano Roosevelt.[96] The collective result of these journalists' efforts was that the CIA news stories were spread under the auspices of authentic journalism.

The extent to which Operation Mockingbird produced outright false stories or just misleading stories remains unknown. However, members of the press and the CIA were tightly connected. Veteran reporter Carl Bernstein wrote of Operation Mockingbird, "The general outlines of what happened are indisputable; the specifics are harder to come by." The content published has not been declassified. Out of the millions of stories published at the hundreds of outlets working with the CIA, it is hard to determine when the factually incorrect news was CIA propaganda and when it was journalistic error. However, Bernstein did determine that the *New York Times* reporting "provided cover for about ten CIA operatives between 1950 and 1966."[97] Furthermore, the known CIA content focused on favorable reporting for the politicians who were tough on communism, such as Dwight D. Eisenhower and Lyndon Baines Johnson,[98] effectively sidelining other political candidates and their positions.

Just as previous regimes had done, the US propaganda machine relied on censorship and intimidation to insulate their fake news narratives from facts or criticism. Some members of the press, such as Walter Cronkite, willingly worked with the government to manage news out of perceived patriotic duty.[99] Others had a vested economic interest, such as Henry Luce of *Time*, who became so close with then director of the CIA Allen Dulles that they shared the same mistress.[100] However, some journalists attempted to evade governmental news management. Robert S. Allen and Paul Scott, who wrote the popular syndicated column "The Allen-Scott Report," frequently cited anonymous top CIA officials in their articles to deliver information that had not been approved for public release. In their desperation to learn the sources' identities, the CIA spied on Allen and Scott by listening in on their phone calls.[101] The extent of these operations has not been declassified, so the American public remained ignorant about them. Nonetheless, they represent a clear attempt to limit news to the narrative offered and produced by the federal government.

The US Cold War–era propaganda machine started the practice, which had continued into the twenty-first century, of using fake news to produce regime change. The US, largely through the CIA, utilized fake news to motivate populations to overthrow their democratically elected leaders, such as Mohammad Mosaddegh of Iran in 1953,

Jacobo Árbenz Guzmán of Guatemala in 1954, and Salvador Allende of Chile in 1973.[102] In these cases, the propaganda machine followed the same pattern of action. First, the press would saturate the nation with fake smears of its leader. For example, in Iran, the CIA gave $45,000 to an Iranian press outlet in exchange for publishing CIA-generated fake news about Mosaddegh.[103]

Second, the CIA would spread fake news of a false flag operation to spark a rebellion and regime change.[104] For example, in Iran the CIA bombed the house of a prominent Muslim and then falsely reported the perpetrators to foster internal divsion in Iran.[105] In Guatemala, the CIA tried to blow up Guzmán's car to foster internal division.[106] In Chile, false flag operations were employed and reported in the local newspapers to prompt a rebellion.[107] Elsewhere, the CIA developed false flag proposals that never saw the light of day. For example, in Operation Northwoods the CIA discussed committing violent acts against civilian and military targets and blaming Cuba for them in such false flag operations as shooting down a civilian airliner, staging a fighter jet crash, hijacking a US ship, detonating bombs in the US, attacking a Cuban neighbor, and burning a ship in Guantanamo Bay Harbor.[108] Where the US was successful in fomenting rebellion and installing US-approved leaders, hundreds of thousands were killed and subjugated.[109]

The CIA even went so far as to use their control over the press to foster domestic support for regime change. The press evoked images of World War II dictators to justify coups overseas, such as the *New York Times* comparing Iran's Mohammad Mosaddegh to Hitler because he had sought to nationalize Iran's oil fields and use the wealth for the nation's social safety net.[110] *Newsweek,* the *New York Times,* and the *Washington Post* celebrated the ouster of Mosaddegh and the reentry of foreign oil companies into Iran.[111] Similarly, in efforts to justify the overthrow of a foreign leader, the US would distribute fake news claiming the leader was a communist despite evidence to contrary. For example, the *Christian Science Monitor* reported that Guzmán had become a communist despite conflicting reports. Numerous US press outlets celebrated his ouster as a victory for democracy even though he had been democratically elected.[112] This silenced critics and questions about the US participating in the overthrow of democratically elected leaders.

The War on Terror

In the waning days of the Cold War, there was a revolt against the federal government's fake news propaganda. During the 1970s, revelations of Richard Nixon's Watergate crimes inspired congressional investigations such as the Church Committee. The hearings' revelations were the first time that the American public was informed of how state-sponsored propaganda machines had dictated the media content that they consumed.[113] Critics like Carl Bernstein argued that the hearings did more to excuse and hide than to explain the extent of the CIA's operations involving journalists.[114]

Nonetheless, the hearings sparked discussions about reforming the CIA and making it more transparent regarding American propaganda. A reform effort supposedly began at the CIA that included ending their domestic propaganda operations.[115] After the revelations, some politicians focused on repealing the Smith-Mundt Act, which had legalized the activities of the US Cold War propaganda machine. Arkansas senator J. William Fulbright in the 1970s and Nebraska senator Edward Zorinsky in the 1980s argued that the Smith-Mundt Act was a relic of an era when propaganda had been viewed as acceptable.[116] They were not successful in repealing it, and in a grand twist of irony, the act would in fact be expanded and strengthened for the war on terror.

On September 11, 2001 (9/11), after the hijacking and crashing of four US commercial airliners in three American states, the US declared a war to find and capture individuals suspected of engaging in terrorism. Polls showed that the outpouring of patriotism after the event led a majority of Americans to support government spending on counterterrorism and national security.[117] However, maintaining that support would be difficult considering that it was an endless war with ever changing enemies and goals. The enemy was not a single terrorist or organization but rather a myriad of individuals and groups to be hunted down. The US would conceivably be fighting for years, decades, or maybe centuries as figures like Osama bin Laden and his al-Qaeda organization were replaced by Abu Bakr al-Baghdadi and the Islamic State of Iraq and Syria (ISIS).[118] The state-sponsored propaganda machine faced an arduous task: they would need to maintain public support for the war at home while maintaining costly support for our allies against the "terrorists" overseas.

Originally, the federal government was successful in manipulating public opinion with fake news stories that appealed to America's feelings of national pride. Americans felt shame after the events of September 11, 2001. The US propaganda machine attempted to remedy that shame with fake news that framed the US invasion of Iraq as an act of pride for citizens. In 2003, when the US invaded Iraq, over two-thirds of Americans supported the move.[119] Less than a month after the invasion, an unknown Marine colonel ordered that a statue of Saddam Hussein in Firdos Square in Baghdad, Iraq, be taken down. Members from army psychology operations used loudspeakers to direct Iraqi citizens to help take it down.[120] The image of Iraqis taking down a statue of Hussein, whom the US had just deposed, provoked pride in US news consumers by suggesting that Iraqis wholeheartedly backed the invasion and that the US had saved them from a tyrannical leader.

The US also manufactured fake news stories about the bravery of US soldiers to maintain domestic support for the war. Days after the war began, nineteen-year-old Private First Class Jessica Lynch was ambushed in her vehicle and arrested by the Iraqi army. Lynch was rescued from the Iraqi hospital where she was being held after the army and Navy SEALs created a diversion. After she was rescued, Pentagon sources told news outlets, such as the *Washington Post*, that Lynch had fought back bravely, firing at the Iraqis who had ambushed her, but ended up being captured.[121] It was actually a government fabrication meant to elicit support for the war by appealing to Americans' pride in their military and moral outrage over Lynch's treatment. The part of the story where Lynch fought back was invented by the Pentagon. Lynch stated, "I was captured, but then I was OK and I didn't go down fighting." Years later, she noted that people still believe the false story. Lynch said that "it was really hard to convince people that I didn't have to do any of that."[122]

Pat Tillman was another case where the government propaganda machine not only developed fake news about a soldier's death but also actively worked to maintain the charade in order to cultivate public sentiment for the war. Tillman had a National Football League (NFL) contract but was inspired by 9/11 to join the military. On April 22, 2004, Tillman, who had fought in Iraq, was killed in Afghanistan by what the military reported was enemy fire. Tillman's story made Americans feel proud that their nation was worth not only a lucrative NFL contract but a life. However, the story was false. Tillman did indeed die, but it was by three shots of friendly fire. Worse, the US Army knew the real story but hid it by burning Tillman's body armor so it could not be investigated.[123] It also mandated the enlisted men to lie about what they had seen,[124] and it posthumously awarded Tillman the Silver Star, which the army reserves for those "engaged in military operations involving conflict with an opposing foreign force" and has not traditionally given to people who die from friendly fire.[125]

During the war on terror, the federal government launched a program, reminiscent of Operation Mockingbird, that relied on the press to distribute state-sponsored fake news. The program, referred to as the Pentagon military analyst program, began in 2002 with the purpose of informing the public about the war on terror. It saw retired generals and active security agents using their employment by press outlets to shape the electorate's understanding of foreign policy. The *New York Times*'s David Barstow, who won a Pulitzer Prize for exposing the program in 2008, reported, "Some analysts stated that in later interviews that they echoed the Pentagon's talking points, even when they suspected the information was false or inflated."[126] The journalistic ineptitude exposed by Barstow went unreported by the twenty-four-hour news networks and received miniscule coverage in other outlets.[127] The government not only defended the program but used congressional legislation, the Smith-Mundt Modernization Act of 2012, a segment of the National Defense Authorization Act, to retroactively legalize their ability to propagandize the American public.[128] Prior to the Smith-Mundt Modernization Act of 2012 the federal government was forbidden from spreading propaganda domestically. Advocates of the bill argued that domestic propaganda was the most effective method for combatting terrorist propaganda.[129] In fact, in 2010, a scholar of conspiracy theories and the administrator of the White House Office of Information and Regulatory Affairs (OIRA), Cass Sunstein, had proposed "cognitive infiltration" of domestic Internet groups as way to combat terrorism.[130]

Nonetheless, the federal government continued to use the press as an extension of the propaganda machine. In 2014 former *Los Angeles Times,* Associated Press, and *Chicago Tribune* intelligence reporter Ken Dilanian stepped down after internal documents and emails confirmed that he had published CIA-approved reports and presented them as journalism. Dilanian not only sent the CIA advanced drafts and talking points for his articles but also introduced their talking points as his original and genuine reporting. Although it is not known if or how it influenced their reporting, other journalists from the *Washington Post,* the *New York Times,* NPR, and Fox

News's channel attended similar events with the CIA.[131] By 2019, the relationship between the corporate press and elements of the federal government was so strong that Pulitzer Prize–winning journalist Glenn Greenwald noted, "It's virtually impossible to turn on MSNBC or CNN without being bombarded with former Generals, CIA operatives, FBI agents and NSA officials who now work for those networks as commentators and, increasingly, as reporters." Greenwald's reporting was in response to an inspector general's report that revealed how the news media's relationship with the intelligence community had enabled the Federal Bureau of Investigation to falsify and conceal evidence regarding an opposition research study that was discredited by its author, the Steele Dossier, in order to secure a Foreign Intelligence Surveillance Act (FISA) warrant to spy on former Trump campaign adviser Carter Page during the 2016 US presidential election.[132] The episode revealed how the relationship between the federal government and corporate press not only results in the production of propaganda, but attempts to manage the democratic process.

In 2018, an internet video showed xenophobic Germans giving the Nazi salute and chanting *Lügenpresse*. Both of these actions are illegal in Germany. The men in the video were protesting what they viewed as their national government's complacent response to an immigrant who had allegedly murdered a German citizen.[133] However, their venting of frustration through a phrase and salute made popular seven decades earlier illustrated the enduring legacy of state-sponsored propaganda machines. In fact, although in English and an ocean away, at the same time Trump was regularly invoking the fake news epithet just as the Nazi regime had done, against enemies and truth-tellers. The history of state-sponsored propaganda machines illuminates the important function of fake news in international relations. Whether it be INFEKTION or Mockingbird, false flags or dubious reporting, fake news has been an influential weapon in global conflicts sparking world wars and regime change.

News consumers' civic agency depends upon an awareness of the complex organization and practices of state-sponsored propaganda machines. Just like political propaganda apparatuses, state-sponsored propaganda machines exploit citizens' tendency to conflate repetition with reliability. Furthermore, they take complex measures to censor and marginalize truthful content, especially if it discredits the government's narrative. Citizens cannot be full participants in a democracy unless they are aware of the warning signs of a state-sponsored epistemological crisis: censorship; shared narratives between the news media and government; and fear-laden stories that dehumanize enemies and elicit national feelings of arrogance, shame, pride, moral superiority, and moral outrage. However, to focus solely on fake news producers in government, the press, and political class risks missing the important ways that the internet has complicated the study of fake news. The next chapter analyzes the relationship between the internet and fake news.

5 Fake News and the Internet Economy

As Eric Tucker drove through his hometown of Austin, Texas, rain began battering his windshield. It was November 9, a day after the 2016 US presidential election, and the thirty-five-year-old cofounder of a marketing company had recently read internet stories about Democratic Party billionaires such as George Soros hiring busloads of actors to portray anti-Trump protesters in cities across America. As he drove through Austin, he noticed anti-Trump protesters on the sidewalk. At a nearby location, he noticed busloads of people arriving at a hotel. He had the fleeting thought, *What if these busloads of people are the Soros actors?* He searched for local conferences on Google but found nothing. Now convinced that he had discovered Soros's minions, he stopped his car, pulled out his phone, and began frantically taking photos of the people and buses. Within minutes he tweeted three of the images to his forty Twitter followers under the comment "Anti-Trump protestors in Austin today are not as organic as they seem. Here are the busses they came in. #fakeprotests #trump2016 #austin."[1]

Shortly after midnight, as the world was learning of Trump's victory in the Electoral College, Tucker's tweet was posted to the social news website Reddit under the headline "BREAKING: They found the buses! Dozens lined up just blocks away from the Austin protests." Over three hundred people commented on the story. By 9 a.m., less than a day after Tucker's original post, a user on the conservative internet website Free Republic spread his post to a massive swath of the online news reading community, including three hundred thousand Facebook users. The uproar over paid protesters drew attention to its source: Tucker. By the late afternoon, Tucker's initial tweet had been shared and liked over five thousand times; his forty Twitter followers had multiplied to nearly one thousand.[2]

It took fact checkers twenty-four hours to challenge the validity of Tucker's post. News reporters began to approach the bus company in Tucker's tweet, Coach U.S.A. North America, about its activity in the area. The bus company seemed unaware about its supposed connection to the protesters. Meanwhile, Tucker was replying to queries on Twitter about whether he had proof to support the claims made in his post. He confirmed in a post that he "did not see loading or unloading" but that the buses were "quite near protests."[3]

Tucker's transparency regarding his baseless claim did little to quell the growing hysteria among internet users. Around 6 p.m. on November 10, 2016, the conservative blog *Gateway Pundit* posted Tucker's image under the headline "Figures. Anti-Trump Protesters Were Bussed in to Austin #FakeProtests." It was shared forty-four thousand times. It became a prominent story throughout the conservative blogosphere—so much so that it reached president-elect Trump, who tweeted, "Just had a very open and successful presidential election. Now professional protesters, incited by the media, are protesting. Very unfair!"[4]

Two days after Tucker's post, a spokesperson for the software company Tableau announced that the buses had been hired by their company to drop off thirteen thousand individuals attending a conference in Austin. That same day, the conservative website American Statesman and the fact-checking website Snopes both posted evidence to debunk Tucker's claims. Tucker began to feel pressure about his news fabrication. He tweeted to his followers that it was a strong possibility he could have been "flat wrong" in his assertion about the buses.[5]

Three days after it was originally posted, Tucker's story was on popular conservative websites, discussed by the president-elect, and shared on social media over a half a million times on various platforms. However, the articles debunking the false claim did not receive nearly as much attention. The Snopes article debunking Tucker received a mere 5,800 shares, and Tucker's corrective was shared minimally. He eventually deleted his original tweet, replacing it with the same images covered by the word "False," illustrating that his previous claims were incorrect. However, after a week, the message had received a mere twenty-nine retweets and twenty-seven likes.[6]

Tucker's story exemplifies the global epistemological crisis brought about by the internet. The internet simultaneously offers access to endless truths and facts and provides a medium for creating fake news content that is easily disseminated and legitimized to audiences. This chapter delves into the political economy of the internet, not only to analyze fake news content and its producers, but to investigate why fake news is so pervasive and effective in the digital age. Like any other technology, the internet is not responsible for the production of fake news. However, the political economy of the internet incentivizes the spread of fake news. Data collection, machine intelligence, and the creation of algorithmically based predictive analytic products have maximized the effectiveness of fake news content. As a result, internet users are increasingly addicted to their screens, which results in more enclosure in a digital cave or bubble of fake news content that influences and directs their attitudes and behaviors. The fake news content derives partly from internet users and partly from digital propaganda machines that have all the hallmarks of twentieth-century state-sponsored propaganda machines, but with digital capabilities. Fake news predates the internet, but the internet certainly has enabled fake news to have a much more pervasive and powerful influence on news consumers than anything previous.

The Technomics of Data Collection

The influence of internet fake news is best understood through an examination of the internet's political economy. During the 1980s, as the internet entered the commercial sphere, there was great hope in its ability to deliver useful and boundless information to users. It was referred to as the "information superhighway" by then vice president Al Gore.[7] President Ronald Reagan promised that the internet would usher in freedom with his claim that "the Goliath of totalitarianism will be brought down by the David of the microchip."[8] The internet's attractiveness derived from its ability to give everyone who had access endless communication opportunities. Policy makers were so confident that the internet was a level playing field for users that the federal government absolved technology companies from liability for the content on their platforms with Section 230 of the 1996 Federal Communications Decency Act.[9]

For their part, technology companies extolled the opportunities afforded by the internet to potential users. In 1995, Apple CEO Steve Jobs proclaimed that the internet had transformed the economy, telling *Rolling Stone,* "We live in an information economy." A year later, Bill Gates of Microsoft promised that with the transition to an information economy, new tools, operating at record speeds, would become available at relatively low cost. "What we're saying to people," he told an interviewer, "is that every idea about ease-of-use, we can develop in software, for the PC, without asking them to buy new hardware, without asking them to throw away their old applications."[10] Google summed up the philosophy of the industry with its motto, "Don't be evil."[11]

The economic recession in 2000 and the terrorist attacks of September 11, 2001, saw technology companies shed principled commitments such as "Don't be evil." Since their inception, technology companies have been collecting users' data.[12] *Data* refers to the digital records of every action taken by an internet user.[13] Initially, companies such as Google and Amazon viewed their data-collecting activities as a necessary evil: companies would analyze the data to determine how to best design their platform to serve customers. Any data collected that was not directly related to these operations, known as behavior surplus data, was deemed expendable. Until 2000, most technology companies agreed that storing or sharing user data was unethical.[14] However in 2000, the US economy faced a recession that was largely due to over-speculation on the internet.[15] In less than a week, stocks on the NAS-DAQ exchange lost 25 percent of their value.[16] Promising new websites such as Pets.com, partially funded by Amazon, went out of business after losing 75 percent of their value.[17] The companies that remained in business began to search for new advertising strategies and revenue streams.[18] Their search would end with the new economic opportunities presented by the federal government after September 11, 2001.

The federal government's response to the terrorist attacks of September 11, 2001, reshaped the political economy of the internet. In the hope of preventing future attacks, US policy makers sought to expand the government's intelligence collection practices. Lawmakers quickly recognized that digital data collection would be a valuable resource in preventing future attacks. As a result, the federal government appealed to the technology industry to provide them with data. Soon the federal government became one of the technology industries' biggest clients, offering lucrative contracts for massive data collection.[19] Acting as one of (if not) the largest revenue providers on the internet, the US government has had massive influence in shaping the post-2000 recession internet economy toward data collection and analysis. In June 2015, the Freedom Act ended the federal government's bulk data collection but handed over those operations to private companies, whose data the government could then access.

The act represented a watershed moment repudiating the post-9/11 security framework. However, that framework had already shaped the internet economy to be dependent upon large-scale data collection and analysis.[20] Technology companies reeling from the 2000 recession were incentivized by the federal government to exploit the vast amount of user data, produced and posted free of charge by users, as the basis of the internet economy.[21] Harvard Business School professor Shoshana Zuboff refers to the economy that emerged as "Surveillance Capitalism," which she defines as

> A new economic order that claims human experience as free raw material for hidden commercial practices of extraction, prediction and sales; A parasitic economic logic in which the production of goods and services is subordinated to a new global architecture of behavioural modification; A rogue mutation of capitalism marked by concentrations of wealth, knowledge and power unprecedented in human history; The foundational framework of a surveillance economy; As significant a threat to human nature in the twenty-first century as industrial capitalism was to the natural world in the nineteenth and twentieth; The origin of a new instrumentarian power that asserts dominance over society and presents startling challenges to market democracy; A movement that aims to impose a new collective order based on total certainty; An expropriation of critical human rights that is best understood as a coup from above: an overthrow of the people's sovereignty.[22]

Surveillance capitalism's economy is dependent upon the vast collection and analysis of user data.

The Surveillance Capitalist Economy

Users' data includes their purchases, retina scans, DNA, statements, clicks, relationships, searches, travels, consumption patterns, and much more.[23] From product focus groups to Nielsen Set-Meter televisions, which monitored audiences' viewing habits, private industry has long believed that effective advertising derives from a deep analysis of consumer behavior.[24] Internet companies such as Facebook, Google, and Amazon amass enormous amounts of information about consumers' behavior in the form of data. They have achieved this by promising users that data collection will positively enhance their online experience. In reality, these companies have been building an infrastructure that collects data on every user twenty-four hours a day, not to enhance the user experience, but to provide critical insight into consumers' behaviors and attitudes.[25] To maximize their data collection, companies such as Facebook, Amazon, Apple, Microsoft, Netflix, Spotify, and Yahoo share their data with each other.[26]

The unfettered collection of data saw technology companies attain an unmatched trove of behavioral surplus data. In 2018, *Forbes* reported that humans create 2.5 quintillion bytes of data daily, with over 90 percent of that data generated in the last two years alone. Annually, 4.7 trillion photos are stored, and 9 billion people use email. Every day 1.5 billion people actively use Facebook; 5 billion search engine searches are made (3.5 billion on Google alone); 300 million photos are uploaded; 400 million Instagrammers are active. Every minute users send sixteen million text messages; perform 990,000 Tinder swipes; send 156 million emails; share fifteen thousand GIFs on Facebook Messenger; receive 103,447,520 spam emails; and make 154,200 calls on Skype. In that same minute, over half a million photos are taken on Snapchat; 120 people join LinkedIn; 4,146,600 YouTube videos are watched; 456,000 tweets are sent on Twitter; 46,740 photos are posted on Instagram; 510,000 comments are posted and 293,000 statuses are updated on Facebook; 18,055,556 forecast requests are sent to the Weather Channel; $51,892 in transactions are processed by Venmo; thirteen new songs are added to

Spotify; 45,788 trips are made on Uber; and six hundred new page edits are made to Wikipedia. Every second forty thousand searches occur on Google and five new Facebook profiles are created.[27] In addition to collecting data on their platform, companies such as Facebook buy troves of users' data from other companies.[28]

Predictive Analytic Products

In addition to collecting massive amounts of user data, technology companies such as Facebook and Google claim that they have the machine intelligence capabilities to create algorithm-based tools that can anticipate what a user will do at a particular moment, soon thereafter, and even much later. Algorithm-based predictive analytic products are lucrative features because they enable marketers and political campaigns, among others, to microtarget effectively.[29] Gutenberg University research associate Simon Kruschinski and University of Bamberg researcher Andre Haller describe microtargeting as "a commercial direct marketing practice" that refers to "the process of making strategic decisions at the individual level about which customer to target with what campaign message."[30] Predictive analytic products operationalize data so that companies can microtarget a particular individual or group with effective messaging. Predictive analytic products have proven so successful to the advertising industry that social media advertisement revenue jumped from $11 billion 2015 to $23.5 billion in 2018.[31] Predictive analytic products can serve various functions for various industries: health insurers would like to know what ailments their patients have searched for on Google and how active they are in order to calculate their patients' health insurance fees; car insurance companies seek Global Positioning System (GPS) data to analyze their customers' driving speed and frequency in order to calculate their customers' insurance premiums; law enforcement agencies seek DNA data from genealogy websites in order to solve crimes; and advertisers seek customers' data to create effective advertisements.[32] In fact, the field of computational journalism relies on data to popularize content. The perceived success of predictive analytic products has seen technology companies expand data collection to nonscreen activities such as retina scanning, facial recognition, and voice recognition software on cellphones and on in-home devices such as Samsung televisions and Amazon's Alexa.[33]

More recently, technology companies have begun experimenting with a more promising and thus more lucrative way to exploit behavioral surplus data: an economy of action. In an action economy, companies operationalize users' data to direct rather than predict their behavior. This behavioral modification is enabled by data analysis that offers a window into a user's thoughts and cognitive processes. Those with access to this data can construct content and situations where a user will act in a desired fashion. This redirection of behavior can be as subtle as a phrase found in a user's Facebook news feed or the particular timing and placement of a purchase button on a website. Zuboff concludes that technology companies' long-term goal is to triangulate data in an effort to direct or automate every human action.[34] One area where this appears to be true is social media.

Social Media, Repetition, Reinforcement, and the Privileging of Fake News

The economic incentives of social media have surrounded users in a digital version of Plato's cave. The Greek philosopher Plato's Allegory of the Cave tells the story of people who lived in a cave for so long that they could neither fathom nor trust any information from outside the cave. Social media repetitively reinforce fake news with little to no counterevidence, constructing an information cave around users.[35] There is a debate around when social media began, some dating it as far back as the telegraph in the 1840s, but most argue that its contemporary usage refers to platforms such as MySpace and Friendster in the early 2000s.[36] These companies are a result of Web 2.0, a term distinguishing post- from pre-2000 recession internet companies: their content is derived from users and their financial stability depends upon data collection.[37] In 2018, 81 percent of Americans used social media, up from 24 percent in 2008.[38] Globally, there are 3.7 billion internet users.[39] Just over 3 billion people used social media in 2018, up from just under 1 billion a decade prior.[40] In 2018, Facebook attained a patent to better determine users' opinions of select content with emotion recognition technology. Presumably, they will use webcams and imagery of users' facial expressions and social cues to determine their emotions. A year earlier, they attained a patent to have audio of advertisements turn on users' microphones in their phones and laptops in order to collect data on their reaction to that advertisement.[41] Facebook and other social media companies argue that they are adding these features in order to create a customized experience for users to enjoy.

Given the centrality of data collection and analysis to their profitability, social media companies operationalize their machine intelligence to create algorithms that will keep users on their platforms. Social media companies apply psychologist B. F. Skinner's concept of behavioral modification.[42] According to Skinner, rewards produce cogitative stimuli that can be exploited to modify an individual's behavior. In the digital realm, rewards are customized alerts, messages, and notifications that keep users addicted to their screens, where they provide lucrative data that can be utilized to modify users' purchase habits and preferences.[43] For example, the social media platform Snapchat successfully keeps teenagers addicted to their phone through a system that offers rewards, such as emojis, for people who have long Snapchat streaks, typically one hundred days. A streak is measured by the back-and-forth communication between two participants; the less time with communication, the shorter the streak.[44] Industry insiders have warned that this amounts to "brain-hacking" because it effectively directs people's behavior toward their screens.[45] However, what is rarely discussed is the way in which screen addiction and brain-hacking popularize the fake news content on the internet.

The economic goals that shape social media algorithms have the side effect of popularizing fake news content. Arizona State University's Kai Shu and colleagues found that "humans are naturally not very good at differentiating between real and fake news" because they tend to believe their conception of reality is the only reality and "prefer to receive information that confirms their existing views."[46] This tendency extends to the internet, where data reveal that internet users desire content that confirms rather than challenges their views. In an effort to keep users on their platform, tech companies create a bubble around each user that filters out the content that challenges users' beliefs and popularizes content that confirms their ideological position. For example, if a user believes the world is six thousand years old, companies such as Facebook will populate that user's social media feed with stories about the world being six thousand years old.[47] By repeatedly bombarding users with confirmation, filter bubbles serve to strengthen users' false beliefs, because users conflate familiarity with veracity.[48] This helps explain why studies show that fake news is 70 percent more likely to spread than truth in social media.[49] In fact, that is why bots (software that perform automated tasks such as sharing content) are a pernicious force when it comes to fake news. Although they do not create fake news, bots spread fake content further and faster than any human could possibly achieve.[50]

The political economy of the internet is responsible for the spread of fake news but is not responsible for its production. Much of that is a result of two types of institutions, internet fake news outlets and digital propaganda machines: both exploit internet technology companies' economic models for their own purposes. Fake news outlets rely on emotion-filled fake news content to build their audience, revenue, and influence. Meanwhile, digital propaganda machines consolidate power and spread their hegemony through similar internet content and data analysis. Their goals are achieved by exploiting the economic model of technology companies.

Internet Fake News Outlets and the Privileging of Fake News

Since the internet became available for in-home use, it has been plagued with fake news. Fake news producers, like other producers, can create internet websites with the veneer of a legitimate news source. In the early days of in-home internet, fake news content included hoaxes or pranks such as beach towns in the 1990s reporting on April Fool's Day that the city had banned surfing; individuals claiming to have found dead "fairies"; chain letter messages promising bad things to readers unless they sent out their own chain letters; and the invention of a kitten that could be grown in a jar.[51] However, the majority of fake news centered on celebrities such as Microsoft founder and billionaire Bill Gates buying the Catholic Church in 1994; Gates giving away all of his money in 1997; entertainer Justin Bieber being active in an elite cohort of reptiles that ruled the earth; "J. K. Rowling" being a pen name; Michelle Obama hiding that she was a man and had murdered Joan Rivers; Queen Elizabeth's cannibalism; and Melania Trump's doppelganger who followed the president around on official business.[52]

The post-Web 2.0 era afforded internet users new opportunities to produce and circulate sophisticated fake news content to a global audience. On social media websites, fake news producers can exploit the platform's inability or unwillingness to verify the veracity of users' identity and content. For example, for years Jennifer Hart's social media profile included pictures and stories that portrayed her as the matriarch of a loving and healthy family of eight. In 2018, it was revealed that the Hart family suffered from horrific abuse, including imprisonment and withholding of food from children. However, by then Hart had driven a car s off a cliff in California with her partner and their six children inside, resulting in their deaths.[53]

The internet and digital tools also enabled fake news producers to access Hollywood-like video production tools for constructing "deepfake" videos. Deepfake videos are "videos that have used artificial intelligence techniques to combine and superimpose multiple images or videos onto source material."[54] For example, in 2019 a video of Nancy Pelosi was altered to make the speaker of the House appear intoxicated during a speech.[55] Similarly, that same year a fabricated video showed Facebook CEO Mark Zuckerberg making the chilling statement, "Whoever controls the data, controls the future."[56] Fake news producers have also used deepfake videos to superimpose celebrity and noncelebrity women's faces on women in pornographic videos. Women are being notified by friends and loved ones that they are in pornographic films despite their never taking part in a pornographic production.[57] The political economy of the internet not only enabled the relatively easy production and dissemination of fake news but created structural mechanisms for popularizing and legitimizing fake news.

The Political Economy of Digital Fake News

The political economy of the internet has created a profitable market for fake news peddlers. In the digital age, companies pay top dollar to have their company's advertisement placed near or on the content with the most user engagement because algorithms privilege engaging content over other content in users' news feeds and internet searches.[58] This means that an advertisement will reach a larger audience if it is near or on engaging content. As a result, website operators, bloggers, and other content producers strive to construct and share engaging content as a way to access advertising revenue. Fake news is some of the most engaging content because it appeals to strong lower emotions that have been shown to increase user engagement, such as "fear, disgust, and surprise."[59] As a result, social media platforms privilege fake news on their platform over fact-based content.[60]

The privileging of fear-laden and hate-based fake news over journalism has seen the internet transform into a space of division and hate. In fact, a 2018 study found that the social media platform Twitter is overrun with divisive themes of "racism, misogyny, and homophobia."[61] Even though social media founders such as Facebook CEO Mark Zuckerberg claimed that their goal was not just about "connecting the world" but about "giv[ing] people the power to build community and bring[ing] the world closer together," the reality is that they have created some of the most divisive platforms in human history.[62] It's not just social media that act as fake news–fueled hate disseminators. Safiya Umoja Noble's 2018 *Algorithms of Oppression* found that racism shapes the ways in which searches are conducted on the internet, especially via Google. In addition to reinforcing stereotypes, such as facial recognition software that made Google label images of black men and women as gorillas, these searches privilege white supremacists messaging to users.[63]

The Hyperpartisan Fake News Profiteers

In terms of ideological spectrum, Right-leaning US voters are some of the biggest consumers of fake news. *Network Propaganda,* an exhaustive quantitative study by Harvard University's Yochai Benkler, Robert Faris, and Hal Roberts that traced news consumption patterns from 2015 to 2017, revealed that Right-leaning news consumers are more likely to accept falsehoods and half truths as fact because they are more likely to consume polarized content that aims to humiliate ideological opponents and misinform consumers. The study found that there is nothing comparable for Left-leaning voters, arguing that centrist, leftist, and Left-leaning voters do spread fake news but often recognize and correct errors, whereas fake news tends to spread unchallenged among Right-leaning users.[64] This makes sense given these groups' differing views on gatekeepers. Liberals tend to have more faith in gatekeepers such as government and professionals, whereas conservatives tend to be skeptical of gatekeepers; consider Ronald Reagan's "government is the problem" position in the 1980s.[65]

For decades, conservatives believed that the news media had a liberal bias that led them to censor conservative perspectives. However, much of the conservative content that was ignored by traditional media was unsubstantiated stories. For example, the John Birch Society was a well-funded ultraconservative group that lobbied for conservative causes by spreading fake news that the United Nations was "an instrument of Communist global conquest," that the goal of the civil rights movement was to inaugurate an "independent Negro-Soviet Republic," and that Dwight D. Eisenhower was "a dedicated, conscious agent of the Communist conspiracy."[66] These unsubstantiated claims and others like them were ignored by traditional news media not because of a liberal bias but rather because of a propensity to publish factual content.[67]

The internet finally provided an outlet for conservative circles to share their baseless claims and false tales. In fact, studies as late as 2018 reveal that conservative fake news is unmatched in terms of ubiquity and acceptability on the internet.[68] Matt Drudge was the first to conceptualize how reporting polarizing fake news on the internet could ameliorate conservatives' perceived information marginalization while maximizing profits for his nascent news outlet the

Drudge Report. By the mid-1990s, as more people attained in-home internet access, the Drudge Report established itself as a premier conservative news outlet. Its launch coincided with Bill Clinton's presidency, and soon Drudge became the bane of the Democratic Party. The Drudge Report published fake news content claiming that: President Bill Clinton's White House assistant Sidney Blumenthal was physically abusing his wife, that former secretary of state John Kerry had had an affair with an intern, that Bill Clinton had an illegitimate child, and that CNN reporters had heckled Republicans; it also published numerous inaccurate details about Clinton's affair with a White House intern named Monica Lewinsky.[69] Much of the Drudge Report's fake news had racist themes, such as stories claiming Senator John McCain's white aide had been attacked by a black man and that President Barack Obama was not born in the US.[70]

By the twenty-first century, Breitbart and the Drudge Report competed to draw the attention of conservative audiences with fake news. Breitbart was founded by Andrew Breitbart, who ran the company until his death in 2012, when he was succeeded by Steve Bannon, who would become an adviser to President Donald Trump. Breitbart relied on fear-inspiring racist and xenophobic narratives that had salience with whites who were reacting to the economic anxiety over the Great Recession with racial resentment over the election of the first self-identified black president and the increase in the proportion of the US population made up of racial minorities.[71] Breitbart's articles demonized Democratic Party members with fake news stories such as Pizzagate, which claimed that Hillary Clinton knew about and had covered up a Democratic Party child molestation ring.[72] The election of President Barack Obama saw Breitbart continue the long-standing American practice of spreading racist-laden fake news stories. For example, Breitbart stories claimed that Obama was born in Kenya and supported terrorist organizations.[73] Breitbart's fake news stories were not only racist but xenophobic and

Islamophobic, asserting that Democratic Party aide Huma Abedin sponsored Muslim terrorists. that Obama's nominee for US secretary of defense Chuck Hagel (R-Nebraska) had received payment for speaking at an event sponsored in part by a terrorist organization called Friends of Hamas, that a Muslim mob had inspired a civil war in Germany; and that a rash of Northern California wildfires had been started by an undocumented Latinx immigrant.[74]

Breitbart revolutionized fake news videos on the internet, disseminating manipulated content that influenced policy makers. The speed at which these false videos could be made, spread, and shared undermined the old adage "Seeing is believing." Though using new technologies, Breitbart was focused on achieving familiar goals of spreading racism and influencing public policy. For example, the Association of Community Organizations for Reform Now (ACORN), once the nation's largest community development organization, primarily serving people of color, lost its government funding after a fake news video published by Breitbart. In 2010, with the use of conservative activist-actors, Breitbart's source edited a video to make it appear that ACORN staff members were talking to and aiding a pimp and a prostitute in receiving government funding and facilitating underage prostitution. By the time the story was proven false, the government had already cut funding for ACORN.[75]

Also in 2010, Breitbart edited a video of a speech at an NAACP fund-raiser delivered by African American Shirley Sherrod, then the head of rural development for the US Department of Agriculture. The edits made her speech appear to embrace "racism" against whites who were seeking economic relief from the government.[76] Obama asked Sherrod to step down from her position after the video surfaced. Later, a full video came out proving that Breitbart's staff had doctored their video, but by then Sherrod was unemployed because, in a situation reminiscent of Eric Tucker's tweet, fake news was more pervasive than truth on the internet.

Few have profited as much from internet falsehoods as Alex Jones. Jones launched his radio show in 1996 and soon thereafter developed InfoWars, a website that offered articles, videos, and his radio show. Jones's fake news is a mix of the fear that is central to state-sponsored propaganda machines and the sensationalism that defines news media. Much of his fake news is tied to the theory that an elite group of powerful and influential politicians and business people, sometimes called the Illuminati, meet in places like Northern California's Bohemian Grove with a goal of world domination.[77] His fake news stories have claimed that the world was ending in real time on January 1, 2000 (Y2K), that the government orchestrated 9/11, that the US government uses "weather weapons" to create natural disasters in an effort to manufacture public support for a green economy, that government aid locations for natural disasters are actually concentration camps, and that school shootings are fake events, with those suffering in the images and videos being "crisis actors" hired by the federal government to legitimize plans to take away Americans' guns.[78] The reach of Jones's fake news is vast and is one of the main sources of information for President Donald Trump.[79] Commentators mistakenly dismiss his loud voice, boisterous demeanor, and wild claims as buffoonish behavior, but according to his divorce proceedings Jones is "a performance artist." He operationalizes fake news in order to line his own pockets. Jones's estimated worth is reportedly $10 million.[80]

The Alt-Right: An Internet Phenomenon

The fake news stories from InfoWars, Breitbart, and the Drudge Report are repeatedly reinforced through filter bubbles and social media algorithms, which have the dual effect of increasing profits for fake news producers while legitimizing falsehoods to users. Mike Wendling's 2018 book *Alt-Right,* based on his study of conservative and extreme Right chatroom logs, blogs, videos, websites, and interviews, concluded that the internet has shaped the way these users, which he refers to as the Alt-Right, communicate and consume news. They do not have a dominant ideology but share an opposition to feminism, Islam, and racial and ethnic minorities, as well as anxiety and antagonism about diversity in terms of race, religion, sexuality, and gender; many of them also engage with Nazi imagery and jokes. Most are young and white men, but some are middle-aged people in established professions who feel completely alienated from society, and they are scattered throughout the United States as well as other English-speaking countries including Britain, Canada, and Australia. They see themselves as fundamentally countercultural, with their own protoinstitutions such as white supremacist Richard Spencer's National Policy Institute, media outlets such as InfoWars and Breitbart, sections of the image-based bulletin board 4chan, numerous accounts on Twitter, popular Reddit forums, YouTube accounts, and websites.[81]

In the predigital age, these racist caves of information existed, but only through an extensive and carefully managed process. For example, by the 1940s, American southerners lived in an epistemological bubble of racism built from fake news stories that legitimized Jim Crow segregation and the lynching of thousands of African Americans.[82] Southerners were repeatedly consuming fake news stories that claimed black men were "buying up ice picks to attack the whites," planning to "take over the entire area during a blackout," orchestrating a "take over [of the] government after the war [World War II] through an organized Negro revolution," and working with First Lady Eleanor Roosevelt to promote racial violence.[83] The racist fake news tales of the Old South as a place of happy, well-cared-for slaves experiencing gracious plantation living were passed along and reinforced so often that consumers conflated repetition with veracity. The fake news stories that germinated in the white supremacist press of the time were cited by the white supremacist political class and passed on through oral transmission.[84] Those wishing to puncture the southern information bubble faced insurmountable odds: the foreign press had no circulation or radio broadcasts, national newspapers were scarce, and oppositional voices were threatened with censorship by groups such as the Ku Klux Klan and the Virginia State Assembly's "Board of Censor."[85] Thus white supremacist ideology and racist narratives were continuously reinforced.

The Alt-Right digital cave dwellers differ from twentieth-century southern whites in that the internet has provided a global space for them to connect, discuss, hate, and expand their influence. In fact, a Southern Poverty Law Center study found that the number of neo-Nazi groups in the US had increased from 892 in 2015 to 917 in 2017.[86] It would be difficult to find an individual who attracted more racist fake news content than America's first self-identifying black president, Barack Obama. An oft-repeated racist fake news story was that Obama was not an American. The story was bolstered by an image of Obama's 1981 digital Columbia University student identification card that listed him as a "foreign student." However, the internet photo was an obvious fake because Columbia University did not issue digital cards until 1996, long after Obama graduated.[87] The author of the falsified picture remains anonymous, but the lie continues to circulate throughout the internet.

From Fake News to Real Violence

The harm caused by fake news is not limited to spreading and legitimizing hateful ideas; it also includes the instigation of violence. For example, Islamophobic fake news has circulated on the internet since the events of September 11, 2001, and subsequent acts of violence by Muslim extremists throughout the Western world. Islamophobic fake news refers to false content that spreads fear and hate about the religion of Islam; this content has served as a justification for violence. For example, in 2018, three men in Kansas concluded from fake news that Muslims were attempting to take over the federal government in what they described as a "civilization jihad." They then colluded to massacre Somali Muslim immigrants who lived in close proximity.[88] Authorities were tipped off about the plan and stopped the men before they could act. However, the victims of twenty-eight-year-old Alexandre Bissonnette were not so lucky. In 2018, he shot and killed six individuals at a mosque after consuming Islamophobic and white supremacist fake news on the internet. Bissonnette was a major consumer of Alt-Right content from Breitbart, the Daily Wire, Fox News, InfoWars, former Ku Klux Klan grand wizard David Duke, and former White House strategist Steve Bannon. His favorite fake news provocateur was Ben Shapiro, famous for touting Islamophobic falsehoods such as "We're above 800 million Muslims radicalized, more than half the Muslims on Earth. That's not a minority. That's now a majority." Bissonnette visited Shapiro's website ninety-three times before his murder spree at the mosque.[89]

In addition to violence against Muslims, hateful fake news content has led to violence against women. Social media subcultures like that of incels ("involuntary celibates") use members-only discussion websites to rage against and dehumanize women who will not have sex with them, often advocating rape as a male right. Meninists take it a step further, posting Elliot Rodgers's manifesto about retaliation against women who refuse sexual advances, a manifesto in which he threatens murder. In May of 2014, Rodgers followed through on his threats with a rampage of stabbings and shootings in Isla Vista, California, that left six people dead and fourteen injured.[90] In 2014, in what became known as Gamergate, a group of anonymous internet users organized on websites such as 4chan, Internet Relay Chat, Twitter, and Reddit to devise and execute a doxing scheme and a series of threats of rape and murder against women suspected of making feminist video games.[91] The users' anger was sparked by a fake news story, posted online, by a game creator's former boyfriend, alleging that the game creator had received a favorable review for her video game by having sex with a reviewer.[92] In actuality the reviewer named in the story had never reviewed the game, something the former boyfriend later acknowledged. The episode would be part of a much larger violent campaign against women fomented on the internet.[93]

In the digital age, fake news plays a central role in creating the digital caves that internet users occupy. The popularity of fake news websites on the internet derives from the political economy of the internet. Internet companies privilege hate-laden, fear-driven fake news content because of its engaging properties. For this reason, fake news content reaches vast audiences, constructing digital caves where users conflate familiarity with veracity. This series of events results in the radicalization of internet users and the widespread adoption of falsehoods as facts. In addition to internet users, digital propaganda machines are some of the most influential fake news producers.

Digital State-Sponsored Propaganda Machines

Digital state-sponsored propaganda machines include all of the aspects of twentieth-century state-sponsored propaganda machines, enhanced with the propagandistic opportunities afforded by the internet. Since 2012, the internet ushered in a global information war in which nations as large as Russia and the US and as small as Turkey and Saudi Arabia rely on cyberspace to influence domestic and international behaviors and attitudes.[94] In fact the demand for fake news content is so high that it is has created new employment opportunities around the world. For example, in the tiny town of Veles, Macedonia, teenagers made over $60,000 in six months during the 2016 US presidential election producing and distributing fake news.[95] Just as companies seek data-based predictive analytic products to maximize their profits, nation-states seek them to more effectively operationalize their twenty-first-century propaganda machines. Predictive analytic products enable state-sponsored digital propaganda machines to microtarget domestic and international audiences.

Nation-states attain data in numerous ways. One is hacking. Technopedia defines hacking as the "unauthorized intrusion into a computer or a network."[96] For example, in 2014 hackers allegedly connected to the Chinese government were arrested and indicted for hacking a series of companies including: U.S. Steel, J.P. Morgan, Alcoa, Westinghouse Electrical Co., Solar World, and the United Steelworkers.[97] Nation-states can perform data breaches for numerous reasons such as theft but often do so for the purposes of cyber-espionage. the "deliberate activities taken to penetrate computer systems or networks used by an adversary in order to obtain information resident on or transiting through these systems or networks."[98]

Another way nation-states collect data is by requesting it from technology companies. Companies such as Facebook not only collect but share user data with third parties who are interested in creating applications and features for their own platforms. However, as late as 2018, Facebook had not developed a mechanism to determine if a third party had shared users' data with anyone else.[99] The threat to democracy posed by Facebook's ineptitude was exemplified by Cambridge Analytica, a British political consulting firm, hired by Donald Trump's presidential campaign and pro-Brexit groups in 2016. Unbeknownst to Facebook, an individual who had received user data, largely from personality quizzes completed by users on the platform, for the purpose of academic research forwarded it to Cambridge Analytica. During the 2016 presidential election, Cambridge Analytica used the data to target undecided voters in swing states with fake news content that exploited users' anxiety about the economy and immigration.[100]

From the Cold War to the present, technology companies have collaborated with the US federal government, largely through university research, to develop tools for surveillance and data collection. In fact, it was this collaboration that led to the creation of the internet and key features such as email.[101] In 2013, Edward Snowden, a former National Security Agency (NSA) employee-turned-whistleblower, released a series of files documenting how the US and its allies—such as Germany, France, Spain, Great Britain, Sweden, and Canada—had received access to user data from companies such as Microsoft, Yahoo!, Facebook, Google, Apple, Verizon, and Dropbox.[102] Originally, the US government claimed that the data collection was focused on overseas efforts,[103] but soon it admitted that domestic collection had been done as well.[104] In recent decades technology companies have expanded beyond the US, helping nation-states around the globe manage their data collection and analysis. For example, in 2018, Microsoft, Apple, Google, Amazon, and Facebook were working with India's government on a project called Aadhaar, which sought to collect the fingerprints, iris scans, and photos of nearly 1.3 billion Indian people.[105] Similarly, technology companies have worked with Russia and China to develop predicative analytic tools.[106] These cases illustrate a global effort by nation states to weaponize data against rival nations and their own people.

The Purpose of Digital Fake News

Digital propaganda machines employ digital fake news for a variety of functions. Improving a nation's international image is one of them.[107] For example, North Korea sought to quell international criticism about its waning rate of technological innovation with fake news stories about North Koreans' invention of a waterproof liquid.[108] Russia has built a massive infrastructure for influencing foreign elections that includes the Internet Research Agency (IRA), a factory of internet trolls who start quarrels and offend people. It has been accused of spreading fake news that influenced the Crimean people to secede from the Ukraine; influenced Greek politicians to prevent Macedonia from joining the North Atlantic Treaty Organization (NATO); and persuaded Great Britain's electorate to approve Brexit, a national referendum for Britain to leave the European Union.[109]

The efforts of Russia's digital propaganda machine to influence the outcome of the 2016 US presidential election demonstrated how the divisive force of fake news can destabilize a democracy. Russia's IRA troll factory published fake news content on Twitter, reaching 1.4 million users, and maintained 3,800 accounts on Facebook, as well as advertising space that reached 126 million users.[110] They developed bots that promoted pro-Trump messaging among Republicans while trying to create discord in the Democratic Party by stoking hatred for presidential primary frontrunner Hillary Clinton among the supporters of her primary opponent Bernie Sanders.[111]

In addition, Russians exploited real problems in American society, such as racism and xenophobia, by creating fake political groups, such as the "Blaktivists," to enflame already-existing conflicts between people of color and law enforcement. Although they were a fake group, they exploited the real racial divisions created by America's long history of white supremacy. The Blaktivists, for example, had a website claiming that "our race is under fire" and linking to news stories about antiblack police violence, giving them inflammatory headlines like "Insane! Cops Pulverized Handcuffed Man."[112] Fake groups such as these promoted fake events that were set up to provoke violent clashes in American cities. For example, in 2016, according to a report commissioned by a US Senate Select Committee, the IRA created "the Heart of Texas," a Facebook group that supported Texan secession, attracted gun owners, and spread fake news about Muslims taking over Texas. They arranged for it to advertise a

"Stop Islamification of Texas" rally in Houston, then had another fake group, the "United Muslims of America," which sought to attract liberal voices of inclusivity in Texas, advertise a "Save Islamic Knowledge" rally for the same place and time in Houston as the Heart of Texas event. The dueling rallies collided in a shouting match that required police intervention before both sides were shut down.[113]

Counterdisinformation in the United States

Although Russia's propaganda machine is active in spreading fake news, it has a formidable adversary in the US. The US is an active player in the twenty-first-century digital propaganda war. As the home of many technology companies, the US has unique opportunities to work with the industry to protect national interests, but, conversely, the vast amount of data makes the industry more vulnerable to hacks and disinformation campaigns than other nations. The US has been compromised on numerous occasions, for instance in 2012 when China collected US communications and again in 2014 when North Korea hacked Sony. In response, the US updated its propaganda machine infrastructure to carry out far-reaching cyber activity such as hacking into Iran's nuclear program and spying on domestic and foreign communications.[114]

The US's digital propaganda machine most commonly responds to digital disinformation by exposing it and its sources and by repeating desired messages.[115] In 2014, Obama's administration created the Counter-Disinformation Team under the Bureau of International Information Programs to influence internet users by these means.[116] Even earlier, US government agencies had begun to combat stories they assessed as disinformational by entering social media debates with falsified online personas.[117] In 2013, for example, the Department of Defense hired numerous people to create social media accounts using fake personas with the intent of engaging and countering bloggers who were posting what the department considered to be "inaccurate or untrue information."[118] The government also has become more focused on monitoring the media generally. In 2018, the Department of Homeland Security posted a job search for a contractor for a "media monitoring services" project.[119] The job entailed creating a searchable database that could track about 290,000 news sources, both foreign and domestic, in order to monitor "traditional news sources as well as social media, identify any and all media coverage related to the Department of Homeland Security or a particular event," and track that coverage's "sentiment" and "momentum."[120]

In addition to shaping online discourses, the US government uses digital communications to enhance fake news production and dissemination. US efforts to propagandize Cubans date back to the 1950s but have been amplified by the internet. For example, in 2018 the US created Facebook, Google, and YouTube accounts falsely accredited to Cubans living in Cuba.[121] These accounts spread even further the fake news reported by the US Office of Cuba Broadcasting (OCB) Radio and TV Martí, a propaganda arm of the US that broadcasts Spanish news in Cuba.[122] The reach of digital propaganda machines into other nations means that democracies must be concerned not only about domestic politicians engaging in fake news but about international ones as well. This serves to further complicate the relationship between fake news and democracy in the twenty-first century.

Digital Propaganda Apparatuses of Political Parties

The internet has made the digitizing of political propaganda apparatuses possible. They have all the hallmarks of predigital digital political propaganda apparatuses, but also use predictive analytic products and microtargeting to influence and direct voters' attitudes and behaviors with fake news. The press is entrusted with exposing the lies and misinformation of elected officials, but they have largely abdicated that responsibility for profit. As a result, voters are left to make electoral determinations on the basis of a mix of journalism and fake news.

Trump's digital optimization of fake news illustrates a global trend in which feeble press outlets are no match for leaders legitimizing fake news through social media. Obama's 2008 campaign relied on social media to reach voters but on a far smaller scale than Trump.[123] By the 2016 election, social media had become a much more influential mode of communication. During the election, Trump's digital media director Brad Parscale spent $100 million on Facebook's predictive analytic products to promote Trump's candidacy.[124] Parscale worked with members of Facebook to develop strategies for the most effective dissemination of fake news content.[125] Facebook sent an executive to teach Parscale how to identify and microtarget audiences on Facebook with fake news stories claiming that Trump was endorsed by Pope Francis, and that Trump had used his private jet to rescue stranded Marines.[126] Because of the opportunities that data affords, Trump's campaign had a powerful and influential window into voters' attitudes in 2016 that ultimately contributed to his victory.

Similarly, an ineffective press corps and digital tools enabled Rodrigo Duterte's political propaganda apparatus to rise to power through fake news optimization in the Philippines. The Philippines has more smartphones than people. Nearly 97 percent of Filipinos who have online capabilities have Facebook accounts. Just prior to their 2016 presidential election, some candidates, including Duterte, invited three Facebook representatives to teach them best practices for using Facebook's predictive analytic products. That meeting led Duterte to construct a political propaganda apparatus including hundreds of volunteers operating domestically and abroad. With a focus on repetition, they constructed and disseminated fake news through fake social media accounts. One webpage posted the false claim that Pope Francis had endorsed Duterte with the words, "Even the Pope Admires Duterte." Duterte's content was so dominant on Facebook (constituting 64 percent of all election discussion on the platform) that he was referred to as "undisputed king of Facebook conversations."[127]

During Trump's presidency, the Republican Party digital political propaganda apparatus demonstrated how social media can optimize fake news to create the illusion of widespread support for a leader. This illusion can be a powerful tool in discouraging dissent. Scholars have long noted the existence of a "spiral of silence," where citizens are less likely to make a statement if they fear that they are in the minority opinion or ideology.[128] As a result, leaders strive to construct a "spiral of silence" around opinions, issues, and facts that threaten their power by making themselves appear more popular than they actually are. Digital technologies have made this much easier. For example, on Trump's Inauguration Day, photos surfaced demonstrating that Obama's inauguration had a larger crowd size. On January 21, 2017, the day after his inauguration, Trump was infuriated. He called the National Park Service (NPS) director, Michael Reynolds and demanded that more flattering photos be provided. White House press secretary Sean Spicer worked with Trump and the NPS to crop the existing photos where the crowd ended in order to make the crowd look larger. That evening, Spicer claimed at a press conference that "this was the largest audience to ever witness an inauguration—period."[129] The doctored photo was released to buttress the false claim. Rather than denounce Trump's contention as false, the press treated it as a legitimate issue for hyperpartisan debate. On January 22, 2017, MSNBC's Chuck Todd pressured White House counselor Kellyanne Conway to explain the discrepancy in crowd sizes based on the inauguration photos. Conway argued that Todd was wrong about the discrepancy because the White House utilized "alternative facts."[130] The comment was mocked on Trevor Noah's *The Daily Show* and defended by conservative outlets such as Breitbart.[131] It essentially became a political question rather than a review of the evidence. A week later, nearly half of Trump voters believed his inauguration crowd was bigger than Obama's inauguration crowd.[132]

Digital political propaganda apparatuses outside the US have created a spiral of silence around their leaders through fake news stories. In North Korea, fake news serves to make leaders seem like deities. For example, fake stories have claimed that "Supreme Leader of North Korea Kim Jong Un Climbed an Active Volcano"; military operas have been written by the first supreme leader of North Korea, Kim Il Sung; calendars begin in 1910 (year 0 in North Korea), when Kim Il Sung was born; and the second supreme leader of North Korea, Kim Jong Il, holds the world record in golf after purportedly shooting a 38-under-par game that included eleven hole-in-ones and was twenty-five strokes better than the game of the actual record holder.[133] Similarly, the Chinese government's political propaganda apparatus has centralized its power by controlling national discourse through the "50 Cent Party," a collection of bloggers, social media accounts, and Wiki editors whose content is employed to cultivate a positive image of the regime.[134] It is estimated that some 300,000 members make 440 million posts every year through such accounts.[135] In the cases of North Korea and China there is no vibrant opposition press to counter the government's fake news narratives, illustrating what can happen in a country lacking a strong and free press.

During Trump's presidency, it was revealed that when a digital political propaganda apparatus optimizes fake news about an "other" for electoral purposes, it has the potential to radicalize news consumers and instigate violence. During the 2016 election there was greater polarization on social media than anywhere else.[136] Trump's political propaganda apparatus cultivated polarization by spreading fear about Muslim violence through a series of false stories about Muslim terror attacks in Atlanta, Georgia, and Bowling Green, Kentucky, and about an immigrant coup in Sweden.[137] The goal of these fake news tales was to garner support for his candidacy with promises to address the manufactured threat.[138] The content was so effective that in addition to ginning up support for his presidency and Islamophobic policies, the hate-filled rhetoric inspired crimes against Muslims. For example, two mothers in Arizona broadcasted themselves on Facebook teaching their children how to be "patriots" by vandalizing a mosque. A video posted the same day on social media, by one of the mothers, showed the mothers and children singing, "Build a wall. Ten feet, twenty feet, one hundred feet tall," which is a portion of the "Donald Trump song."[139]

The successful legitimization of fake news from Trump's political propaganda apparatus has not only revealed the press's ineptitude at exposing lies, but also radicalized individuals against the press to the point of violence. Trump's fake news narratives about the press and the Democratic Party have inspired violence among his supporters.[140] In 2018, a loyal Trump supporter named Cesar Sayoc mailed pipe bombs to Trump critics such as former president Barack Obama, former secretary of state Hillary Clinton, former vice president Joe Biden, Representative Maxine Waters, Senator Cory Booker, Senator Kamala Harris, former CIA director John Brennan, former director of National Intelligence James Clapper, and CNN.[141] The violence against political enemies spurred by Trump's fake news is eerily reminiscent of Duterte's "drug war," which optimized fake news tying "police, judges, and local community leaders, as well as 'mayors and governors,'" to drug violence in order to justify and legitimize murder and violence against them.[142] In June 2018, thirty-eight United Nations member states, including the US, through the United Nations Human Rights Council (UNHRC), called on Duterte to end this murderous campaign.[143]

Digital tools have enabled fake news to become an influential force shaping national discourses and eroding democracy. The advent of the internet brought new possibilities for manipulating the electorate that had been unimaginable just a few decades prior. Nonetheless, to focus solely on digital tools and their users is to miss the ways in which political parties and the press have contributed to the current threats facing democracy. The pursuit of profit at the expense of journalism, and electoral victory at the expense of truth, have had negative effects on democracy. These realities are illuminated by post-2016 electoral and governing practices around the world.

In an interview with the *New York Times* that traced the progression of his original post, Eric Tucker admitted he could have used better judgment before sharing his fake news story: "I think it goes without saying I would have tried to make a more objective statement." Tucker was astonished that his tweet, a message from a "private citizen who had a tiny Twitter following," had had such a massive societal impact.[144] Tucker's story demonstrates the information predicament facing twenty-first-century news consumers. Citizens have the potential to use digital tools as a basis for becoming the most informed electorate in the history of democracy. Yet as the Tucker episode illustrates, these very same tools, if used irresponsibly, can erode the foundation of democracy. Case in point, Trump was a "birther" spreading fake news before he was running for president. He relied on fake news outlets such as InfoWars to the point that he decreed any challenge to his reality to be fake news. Furthermore, rather than hold his statements accountable to facts, the media in the internet age allowed his campaign to purchase influence over the electorate with sophisticated tools and data analysis.

In the twenty-first century, the fate of democracy hinges upon citizens becoming responsible media consumers and producers. As Tucker's story illustrates, responsible media consumption and production do not result from some form of osmosis; in which mere use of technology magically endows the user with responsible media consumption habits. Instead, users need education about the veracity of content, vulnerabilities created by the internet, and how vulnerabilities can be mitigated when users control their data and consumption patterns. Without these skills and perspectives, digital users such as Tucker are susceptible to legitimizing the very falsehoods that threaten the democratic process. One bright spot for democracy in 2016 was an increased awareness about the real threat posed by fake news. This offers some hope that necessary action will be taken to alleviate the pernicious influence of fake news. In fact, throughout history, a variety of solutions for mitigating the negative influence of fake news have been suggested and implemented. The next two chapters examine and evaluate those solutions. Chapter 6 addresses each solution in turn, noting that the majority fail to mitigate the influence of fake news because they incorrectly assume that news consumers can distinguish between false content and journalism. However, there is one exception to that failure: critical media literacy education. That is why the final chapter proposes it as the most viable solution for addressing fake news.'

6 *Fighting Fake News*

Solutions and Discontent

On December 4, 2016, twenty-eight-year-old Edgar Maddison Welch loaded three guns into his Toyota Prius and drove six hours from his hometown of Salisbury, North Carolina, to Washington, D.C. Welch had spent the previous month obsessively reading blog posts and watching YouTube videos about a nonexistent pedophile ring at the Comet Ping Pong pizza restaurant in Washington, D.C., supposedly operated by members of the Democratic Party including presidential candidate Hillary Clinton. The purported scandal began appearing on the internet in late 2016, after leaked emails from members of the Democratic Party were made public. Welch, a father of two young girls, was outraged for the victims. As he walked into the Comet Ping Pong restaurant, he took a deep breath, brandished his weapon, and began rapidly pulling the trigger. Employees and patrons panicked at the sound of spraying bullets as they fled in horror. Welch was soon arrested and sentenced to four years in prison.[1]

Court documents would later reveal that Welch had secured in-home internet access shortly before his rampage.[2] Internet access gave Welch a seemingly limitless supply of information. His propensity to believe fake news, even though fact-based content was just a keystroke away, illustrates the dilemma facing the twenty-first-century American news consumers: they cannot distinguish false content from legitimate journalism.[3] In fact, as late as 2015, a Public Mind poll from Fairleigh Dickinson University found that 42 percent of all voters believed the false story that the US had found weapons of mass destruction in Iraq.[4] Similarly, an NBC News and Survey Monkey poll in 2016 found that 41 percent of self-identified Republicans incorrectly believed the fake news that former US president Barack Obama was born outside of the US.[5] Another 2016 study found that news consumers who were shown headlines for false stories and said they recalled having run across those stories were highly likely to believe them: individuals being paid to protest Trump (79 percent), FBI agents being murdered for investigating the Clintons (72 percent); FBI director James Comey posting a Trump campaign sign on his front lawn (81 percent); and Trump using his private airplane to rescue two hundred US soldiers (84 percent).[6] As these studies emerged, Aviv Ovadya, chief technologist at the Center for Social Media Responsibility and Knight Tow Fellow, famously warned that an internet "Infocalypse" was eroding the American conception of truth by weakening consumers' grip on reality.[7] Indeed, a multitude of studies since 2016 have demonstrated that the electorate is constantly inundated with false content and unable to determine fact from fiction.[8]

The perceived influence of fake news on the 2016 elections in Britain and the US fostered a renewed interest in addressing fake news consumption.[9] Since 2016, France has constructed a bill to repress false stories; Great Britain has set up a unit to tackle fake news; Malaysia has banned news fables; the Philippines has taken away news outlets' licenses; Senegal has censored fake news during their elections; and Google's China website censors information deemed by the Chinese government to be false or dangerous.[10] In the US, numerous states have sought to address fake news with changes in education policy. This has led to disagreements about the most effective pedagogical approach to media literacy.[11] Some Americans dismiss media literacy education, arguing that censorship, regulation, and techno-logical innovation are more viable solutions.

Through a historical and educational lens, this chapter analyzes each of the various proposals for addressing fake news. Many of the non-education-based proposals are ineffective because they ignore the central reason why fake news is effective: news consumers cannot distinguish fake news from journalism. In fact, most of the proposed solutions, such as crowdsourcing or exposing fake news with factual analysis, operate from the false assumption that individuals organi-cally accumulate the knowledge and skills to differentiate fake news from journalism. Furthermore, many of the non-educated-based pro-posals empower rather than weaken the influence of known fake news producers in government and private industry. In fact, when such policies have been implemented, they have exacerbated the problems associated with fake news. That is why this chapter argues that the implementation of critical media literacy education is the most effective solution for countering the pernicious influence of fake news because it empowers users, not fake news producers.

Governmental Responses

Historically, the citizenry's concerns about fake news have spurred governmental efforts to censor and regulate the flow of information. However, in recent decades, private industry has increasingly been called upon to help censor fake news content. Regardless of its source, censorship aggravates the problem of fake news. As a result, some policy makers have avoided censorship in favor of piecemeal regulation. However, regulation has historically failed to stop the pernicious influence of fake news because in practice these laws cre-ate protected space for fake news content; empower fake news pro-ducers; and incorrectly assume that the electorate can distinguish fake news from journalism. Despite these poor outcomes, citizens continue to champion censorship and regulation as effective measures to curtail the production and dissemination of fake news.

Censorship

Recently, public concern about the increasing influence of fake news has spurred a renewed interest in censorship.[12] In fact, nations such as Singapore, China, and France have been accused of using the fears about fake news as a pretext for engaging in censorship.[13] There have even been calls by US citizens for the federal government to consider censorship as a solution to fake news.[14] By the *Academic American Encyclopedia*'s definition, censorship is "suppression of information, ideas, or artistic expression by anyone, whether government officials, church authorities, private pressure groups, or speakers, writers, and artists themselves."

Historically, Americans' anxiety about fake news has resulted in government attempts to censor content. In 1645, the Massachusetts Bay Colony responded to fears about false information countering the colonial leadership by outlawing content "pernicious to the publick weal, or tending to the damage or injury of any particular person, or with the intent to deceive and abuse the people with false news and reports."[15] In the eighteenth century, as political fake news threatened his presidency, President John Adams empowered the federal government to suppress news content with the Alien and Sedition Act.[16] In 1916, in an effort to protect America's interests in World War I, the House of Representatives debated a proposed "peace censorship" bill that forbade "false news."[17] During the Cold War, the federal government pressured private groups and companies to censor select content and speakers domestically with unsubstantiated claims that they had evidence that the person or content was serving a foreign adversary.[18]

In the twenty-first century, the US government has increasingly depended upon censorship by proxy to address fake news. *Censorship by proxy* refers to the censorship of information performed by a third party, but at the behest of government.[19] America's war on terror saw technology companies transform into the government's censorship proxies.[20] Their unparalleled control over communication made them valuable and attractive proxies for government agencies struggling with political and legal obstacles to censorship.[21] For their part, the electorate has lauded technology companies such as Facebook, Apple, YouTube, and Spotify for censoring fake news outlets such as InfoWars and ideologies grounded in falsehoods such as white separatism and white supremacy.[22] By 2018, public support for censorship by technology companies was so high that Twitter was chided for not participating in the industry-wide suppression.[23] Although proponents saw the technology industry's action as a crucial step toward the goal of mitigating the influence of fake news, historically censorship has not achieved this goal.

Scholars agree that censorship tends to strengthen rather than weaken the influence of fake news. Historically, censorship has failed to eradicate targeted content because it results in a rise in demand for that content, thereby incentivizing the producers to "learn methods of censorship evasion" and identify or create nontraditional but effective avenues for content dissemination.[24] For example, thousands of people avoided Soviet censorship during the Cold War through the practice of *samizdat*, which refers to the creation of a distribution network for reproduced pieces of censored content.[25] The ineffectiveness of censorship is further compounded by the Streisand effect, which is "defined as the inadvertent popularity of any material as a result of its suppression."[26] By attracting new audiences to the very content that censorship laws aims to conceal, censorship achieves the exact opposite of its stated purpose.

In addition to compounding the problems of fake news, censorship enables repressive measures by fake news producers. Scholars have found that rather than open up spaces where truth can circulate, censorship campaigns create a chilling effect among the electorate that fosters the antidemocratic climate in which repressive regimes manifest.[27] In fact, studies show that public awareness of censorship results in broader censorship because nontargeted communities' fears of persecution result in acts of self-censorship.[28] In addition to self-policing, censorship campaigns often silence other unintended targets such as journalists. For example, the recent wave of technology company–led censorship failed to make a distinction between those promoting and those reporting on hate speech.[29] As a result, legitimate journalists have had their stories become inaccessible to news consumers. Historically, the US electorate has preferred haphazard legal mechanisms rather than censorship when it comes to mitigating the influence of fake news.

Regulation

Traditionally, government regulation, like censorship, has failed to combat fake news because it operates from the false assumption that news consumers can differentiate between fake news and journalism. For example, in an effort to provide a diversity of views in news media, the Communication Act of 1934 empowered the federal government to limit the number of media outlets a company could own in a particular market.[30] However, as a consequence, the act created more opportunities for all content creators, including fake news producers, to own and operate a media outlet. For example, the *National Review* published news stories falsely absolving Pinochet from committing acts of terrorism and murder in the US.[31] Despite these false stories and others from conservative commentator William Buckley, it was able to operate under the guise of diversifying media content. Similarly, in the 1940s the federal government instituted the Federal Communications Commission (FCC)'s Fairness Doctrine, which required media outlets to offer contrasting views on issues of public importance, and the US Office of War Information's (OWI) Rumor Project, which sought to have legitimate journalists discredit false rumors.[32] These policies did little to address the influence of fake news because they operated from the false premise that news consumers who came into contact with falsehoods in news media would reject them if presented with factual analysis countering those falsehoods.[33] However, news consumers have repeatedly demonstrated the opposite. For example, the OWI's Rumor Project was closed a few years after it opened because research showed that it actually helped spread fake news.[34]

Between 1937 and 1942, the federal government created and operated the nation's first media literacy program, the Institute for Propaganda Analysis (IPA). The IPA sought to teach citizens how to critically analyze propaganda by offering study guides and classroom exercises.[35] But by 1942, a month after the US entered World War II, the federal government abolished the IPA over fears that its analysis could be "easily misunderstood during a war emergency, and more important, the analyses could be misused for undesirable purposes by persons opposing the government's effort."[36] Given that the US government's state-sponsored propaganda machine was disseminating fake news at the time, this statement hints that citizens who were capable of analyzing propaganda posed a threat to the government's efforts to spread propaganda.

Governmental regulatory mechanisms falsely assume that a heavy media diet of fake news can be offset by some journalism. Similarly, government censorship campaigns strip citizens of their intellectual autonomy by normalizing a situation in which bureaucrats determine which information is true. By the twenty-first century, the electorate's faith in government solutions to these problems waned.[37] The Fairness Doctrine and the Communication Act were eliminated in 1987 and 1996 respectively.[38] Over time, an emphasis on governmental solutions was eclipsed by techno-utopian ideology, which promised that human ingenuity and the entrepreneurial spirit of capitalism could solve problems that had evaded policy makers, including fake news.

Technology Industry Responses

Techno-Utopianism

In the twenty-first century, techno-utopianism became a dominant ideology among the American electorate.[39] Techno-utopianism is a deterministic ideology that assumes advances in science and technology will unequivocally transform the human experience in a positive way.[40] They view government regulation and taxation as hindrances to industries' ability to improve the human condition. Despite their bravado, techno-utopian solutions, like governmental solutions, fail to mitigate the influence of fake news because they do not equip citizens with the knowledge and skills to determine false content from journalism. In fact, techno-utopian ideology is predicated on the notion that technology, not the human mind, should direct citizens' decision-making processes.[41] In this respect, techno-utopian ideology disregards human cognitive ability as a major factor in human progress. Instead, it empowers technology companies to act as information authoritarians that manage and direct human behavior and attitudes. The technology industry's slick advertising and political maneuvering have privileged techno-utopianism as a guiding ideology to solve America's fake news problem.

The promise of techno-utopianism is belied by a set of false assumptions. First, techno-utopians falsely claim that government intervention in the market prevents industry innovation, but government is actually responsible for many of the industry's greatest achievements. For example, the main features of Steve Jobs's iPhone resulted from government funding and research: internet, GPS, touchscreen display, and the recent Siri voice-activated personal assistant. Similarly, Tesla's battery technologies and solar panels as well as Google's search engine algorithm came from government-funded research.[42] Second, techno-utopian ideology argues that technology has made humans' lives easier and less labor intensive. However, scholars contend that America's digital society has led to increased wealth inequality, poverty, and work hours.[43] Third, techno-utopians argue that new technologies empower users with choice, but customized internet experiences, such as filter bubbles that provide users with a predetermined set of options, actually replace the freedom of choice with the illusion of choice.[44] In fact, *The Age of Surveillance Capitalism*, by Harvard Business School professor Shoshana Zuboff, illustrates that the techno-utopian goal is to erase human autonomy by directing every human action through the stealthy entrenchment of technology in every aspect of human life.[45] Fourth, techno-utopians claim that algorithms provide the most fair and accurate readings of data because they lack the biases that shape human decision-making. However, scholars have found that algorithms not only mirror the prejudices of their creators but optimize those prejudices into public policy that compounds inequality.[46]

Last, techno-utopians claim to value human knowledge, but in practice they disregard it for profit. For example, rather than explore the expanses of human knowledge offered in higher education, Elizabeth Holmes of Theranos and Mark Zuckerberg of Facebook dropped out of college. Holmes, without any doctoral-level biological knowledge, promised that an entire lab, staff, and waiting process for blood analysis would be replaced with a box she called Edison. By the time Theranos Inc. determined that their proposed invention was a physical impossibility, they had already secured and lost billions of dollars in funding.[47] Similarly, Zuckerberg, with no prior civics knowledge to speak of, promised that his Facebook platform could deliver democracy to the world.[48] Instead, it caused division and instability in countless democratic nations while empowering antidemocratic regimes such as those of Rodrigo Roa Duterte in the Philippines and Donald Trump in the US.[49] In 2019, Facebook tacitly admitted their role in undermining democracy by censoring certain voices and perspectives while scaling the platform's interactions to smaller, more private online communities.[50] The stories of Holmes and Zuckerberg demonstrate a disregard for human knowledge and innovation. Rather than utilize existing scholarship to inform the process of achieving their stated goals, they believed technological solutions would randomly emerge.

Techno-Utopian Policies for Combating Fake News

Policy proposals aimed at combating fake news through regulation of the technology-industry have been stymied by industry lobbying. Many technology companies profit from the engagement derived from fake news content.[51] As a result, the technology industry largely views the debate around fake news as a public relations issue, not an issue of democracy. They have stifled attempts to regulate their industry by funding political campaigns; sharing domestic and international data with the intelligence community; performing opposition research on their critics; and offering employment to elected officials and their loved ones, especially in the Democratic Party.[52] These efforts have succeeded in achieving legislative inaction favorable to the industry, such as the federal government's refusal to fine Facebook in 2011 for illegally sharing users' data; to intervene in Facebook's platform during the 2016 election despite proof of election meddling; and to carry out the proposed reforms suggested by US senator Mark Warner's (D-VA) 2018 investigation into social media companies' mismanagement of data.[53] Facebook has become so sophisticated at thwarting government regulation that an eighteen-month British Parliament investigation to Facebook concluded in

2019 that the social media giants are "digital gangsters."[54] With the federal government abdicating its responsibility to address fake news, the technology industry has increasingly led US efforts.

Most of the techno-utopian solutions claim that technological innovation and crowdsourcing will mitigate the influence of fake news. *Crowdsourcing* refers to "the process of taking into account the collective input of a group of individuals rather than of a single expert (or small number of experts) to answer a question."[55] For example, YouTube added the crowdsourced content from Wikipedia pages to their videos as a factual source; CNN's 2017 *Full Circle* program works with Facebook to report on audience-requested stories; and Facebook replaced its "trending" feature with a feature that ranks news organizations according to trust based on crowdsourced data.[56] However, crowdsourcing is an ineffective tool for addressing false content because the belief of the majority is irrelevant if the majority cannot delineate journalism from fake news. As a result, some industry insiders have proposed "customizing the crowd."

Techno-utopian solutions that customize the crowd, or crowdsource using a particular group that may be considered more knowledgeable, mitigate some of the issues with traditional crowdsourcing but as a consequence empower known fake news producers. For example, Steve Brill's NewsGuard relies on a community of thousands of independent journalists and power brokers to rate the validity of news stories and press outlets with a colored emblem on a user's browser: green for true and red for false.[57] Where traditional crowdsourcing enables nonexperts to influence news consumers, NewsGuard empowers the ideology of the political and economic elite to dominate news consumption patterns. NewsGuard's custom crowd is composed of a limited number of corporate-owned press outlets; members of the political class; and intelligence community insiders.[58] Historians have pointed out that a homogeneity of ideas in the political class and news media led to the false reporting that shaped

Americans' conceptions of the Vietnam War.[59] In fact, some researchers argue that NewsGuard's class bias is revealed by their categorization of news sites that challenge corporate news media discourses with a red label, while Fox News, a news outlet known for distributing fake news content, has a green light, meaning that it "maintains basic standards of credibility and transparency."[60] In essence, Brill has created a think tank that seeks to influence news consumption patterns rather than mitigate the influence of fake news.

Proponents of media literacy education rightly argue that only an effective education can mitigate the influence of fake news by giving citizens the skills to recognize false content. However, techno-utopians have worked arduously to undermine these efforts by shaping media literacy education into a pedagogy that celebrates rather than critically examines media.

Acritical Media Literacy: A Techno-Utopian Approach to Fake News

Despite its devaluing of human knowledge, techno-utopianism has been a strong influence on American media literacy education programs. In the US, media literacy is defined as "the ability to access, analyze, evaluate, create, and act using all forms of communication."[61] The growing threat of fake news and the dismal state of news literacy in the US accentuate the need for a new, critical approach to news literacy. News literacy is a component of media literacy that is defined as "the critical thinking skills necessary to evaluate news publications for their credibility and reliability."[62] Few Americans are offered a media literacy education, let alone a news literacy education. In fact, only about 50 to 60 percent of US high school students are ever taught to critique the trustworthiness of internet sources. That number is 7 to 15 percent for college students.[63] Techno-utopians have long used their political and economic influence to shape the US's limited media education programs into an acritical corporate marketing mechanism.

In addition to lobbying elected officials and partnering with government agencies, the technology industry attempts to spread its techno-utopian ideology through media literacy education. Historically, industries have sought to use media education as an advertising mechanism for their product or brand. Media scholar Zoë Druick contends that since World War II corporations such as Ford have used their funding as a mechanism to shape America's limited media literacy programs into ideological tools that transform the classroom into a space of corporate colonization.[64] In fact, Nickelodeon, Facebook, Microsoft, Apple, and Sony have developed and distributed educational materials to school districts that normalize rather than analyze their companies and content.[65] Their content reinforces students', parents', and educators' habit of conflating students' familiarity and use of corporate platforms with their being media literate. In fact, Professor Sam Wineburg, a contributor to a 2019 national study of students' online civic reasoning by the Stanford History Education Group, argues that "Many people assume that because young people are fluent in social media they are equally perceptive about what they find there. Our work shows the opposite to be true."[66]

In the age of surveillance capitalism, the technology corporations' interest in education is rooted in their desire for access to lucrative data, not quality education. Dr. Ben Williamson, Chancellor's Fellow at the Centre for Research in Digital Education and the University of Edinburgh Futures Institute, explains that in recent decades there has been a "datafication" of education. With the support of companies such as IBM, Google, Uber, PayPal, Chegg and Edmodo, state and local governments, who are enamored by the techno-utopian vision for education, are collecting and analyzing students' data, which includes grades, attendance, graduation rates, and submitted assignments, in order to inform better pedagogical practices.[67] Public schools are particularly valuable because they provide limitless data from a diverse population with almost no concern for cost. Where the private sector will generally limit spending on data analysis once it threatens to reduce profits, forty years of neoliberal reform have afforded public institutions a limitless opportunity to spend taxpayer dollars under the auspices of serving the public's demand for accountability.[68] This essentially guarantees a steady flow of user data to these companies regardless of the quality of education. Indeed, scholars have concluded that the datafication going on in law enforcement, the military, and higher education illustrates that the techno-utopian vision of improving institutions through data analysis is at best an exaggeration and at worse a ruse that exploits the citizenry at the expense of taxpayers. Not only does the datafication process fail to measure the desired outcome, leaving the institution with worthless data, it also introduces and reinforces prejudices.[69] Indeed, often the algorithms, which are falsely portrayed as objective, reflect the racist and sexist attitudes of their creators.[70] These tropes and biases are adopted by the users that encounter them. Essentially, techno-utopians' datafication of education has been shown to be ineffective, futile, and problematic.

The successful implementation of an industry curriculum is dependent upon educators to act as willing participants. Educators play a crucial role in determining what content enters a classroom. They are increasingly persuaded to use industry marketing content, disguised as effective curricula, in their classroom, from organizations such as National Association for Media Literacy Education (NAMLE), NAMLE is one of the biggest sources of media literacy content in the US. Their content derives from a collaboration of scholars such as NAMLE cofounder Renee Hobbs and corporations such as Nickelodeon, Google, Facebook, and Twitter.[71] This is no secret. In fact, Hobbs lauds the technology industry as "a significant player in advancing the media literacy competencies."[72] Furthermore, in 2015,

NAMLE hosted Brooke Oberwetter, a manager of external affairs at Facebook, at its annual conference, where she informed "parents, teachers, and young people about the tools, settings, and resources available on Facebook [to] help keep people safe." Oberwetter's contention rings especially insincere given that Facebook has actively targeted online game-playing children and their parents in a scheme to collect thousands of dollars.[73] However, techno-utopian scholars defend their acceptance of corporate money. Verónica Donoso, Valerie Verdoodt, Maarten Van Mechelen, and Lina Jasmontaite wrote in the *Journal of Children* that "without industry collaboration, the work of media scholars presents a missed opportunity to ensure that children are better protected and empowered."[74] In fact, NAMLE's wealth and resources are unmatched by other media literacy organizations, making their approach the most dominant in the US.

The acritical approach to media literacy prevents practitioners from addressing, introducing, or analyzing the power dynamics that are crucial for understanding how fake news is produced and disseminated. Citizens need to question how the ideology and vested interests of media producers shape their content. With regard to fake news, this requires knowledge of the fake news producers and their interests. However, many of those same fake news producers are shaping media literacy education. As a result, they do not discuss or encourage students to analyze how the ideological or economic motives of the content producer may shape the accuracy of their content. Students are better served by a critical approach to fake news—one that not only takes account of the vested interests of fake news producers but teaches students how to withstand the pernicious influence of fake news.

Developing Critical News Literacy Education

Critical scholars advocate for a critical framework to be applied to media education. A critical framework derives from the Frankfurt school, which argues that dominant ideologies result from power inequities that are strengthened and fortified through media and communication.[75] Members of the Frankfurt school contend that liberation from the dominant ideologies is possible through a critical examination of the power dynamics that drive the media.[76] Critical scholars are not interested in attacking techno-utopianism. Rather, they strive to critically examine and understand the influence of all dominant ideologies in media. That is why, in addition to appreciating media, critical scholars interrogate "the ways media tend to position viewers, users, and audiences to read and negotiate meanings about race, class, gender, and the multiple identity markers that privilege dominant groups."[77] Whereas acritical media literacy educators teach students to accept the techno-utopian view of media, a critical analysis of media content explores the vested ideologies and interests in media and their influence on users.[78]

A critical news literacy pedagogy applies a critical framework to news literacy education with the goal of mitigating the influence of fake news. The most accepted theoretical design of a critical media literacy pedagogy derives from Douglas Kellner and Jeff Share of University of California, Los Angeles, who argue that effective critical media literacy is demonstrated when students can critically dissect media forms; discriminate and evaluate media content; investigate media effects and uses; construct alternative media; and use media intelligently.[79] When applied to news literacy, Kellner and Share's critical framework reveals the components of effective critical news literacy education.

Effective critical news literacy pedagogy promotes the intelligent use of media.[80] Intelligent media use is defined by acts of liberation from the dominant ideologies that are communicated and fortified through media.[81] Liberation "refers to the process of resisting oppressive forces. As a state, liberation is a condition in which oppressive forces no longer exert their dominion over a person or a group."[82] Liberation is dependent upon analyzing the process by which media is used to strengthen dominant ideologies. To become more aware of the ways that media can act as tool of liberation or exploitation, students need to analyze if their media use is an act of liberation or exploitation: *Are they serving the demands of the media producer or acting in their self-interest?* An awareness of the crucial role technology plays in furthering cognitive subjugation through fake news acts as a foundation for students to explore their media consumption habits by documenting who produces the media they consume; what platforms they use; how much time they spend consuming media; and how the information they receive compares to the information they produce.

Effective critical news literacy pedagogy is an exploration of the ways in which technology simultaneously acts as a tool of ideological hegemony and a tool of liberation. Each new piece of new technology historically presents consumers with what media scholar Neil Postman referred to as a Faustian bargain, opportunities for exploitation and liberation.[83] Earlier examples discussed in this text, such as the printing press, photography, radio, television, and film, have all enabled fake news producers to exploit users. However, the internet in particular has taken fake news consumption to a new level where power is manifested through the practices of brain-hacking, microtargeting, data collection, filter bubbles, and algorithms.[84] Part of being news literate is assessing the relationship between these practices and the pillars of democratic freedom such as privacy, free expression, and political organizing.

Yet media can also be used as a tool of cognitive liberation. Cognitive liberation refers to a "three-stage shift in consciousness: first, individuals no longer perceive the system as legitimate or just; second, those who once saw the system as inevitable begin to demand change; and third, those who normally considered themselves powerless come to believe that they can alter their lot in life."[85] Critical news literacy classrooms first spotlight the ways in which media exposes societal injustices but then explore the way media, such as podcasts and hip-hop, have been used as a tool to demand change.[86] Students are expected to assess the effectiveness of these efforts in liberating oppressed communities. This has the dual function of assessing their knowledge of course concepts while providing a framework for assessing how they use media. Given that a critical news literacy curriculum teaches students how to distinguish fake news from journalism, critical news literacy offers the best solution for mitigating the influence of fake news.

Welch's shooting rampage, dubbed Pizzagate, quickly became a media poster child for discussions about guns and conspiracy theories in the US. However, little discussion emerged about Welch's inability to distinguish fake news from journalism. Perhaps it was because, in the vast landscape of internet users, Welch was not an outlier. In fact, in 2016, 46 percent of Trump voters believed that leaked Democratic Party emails specifically confirmed "human trafficking," "Pizzagate," and "pedophilia." However, neither those terms nor the purported scandal was ever mentioned in the emails.[87] Despite the Pizzagate example, and numerous studies, the proposed solutions to fake news focus on eradicating false content rather than giving the electorate the skills to discern falsehood and choose journalism. Corporations and governments have offered to act as information authoritarians, determining what is true and what is false for consumers. However, these actions have done nothing more than eliminate users' autonomy, while empowering the fake news producers in government and private industry.

Despite their best intentions, acritical media literacy scholars' embrace of techno-utopian ideology has relegated them to nothing more than a public relations arm of the fake news producers in the technology industry. In contrast, critical media literacy scholars have proposed a pedagogy to mitigate the influence of fake news without empowering its producers. However, until this text, the construction of a critical news literacy praxis was hampered by the limited research on fake news. As a result, the concluding chapter is a fake news detection kit that explains how to achieve the learning outcomes of an effective critical news literacy pedagogy.

7 *The Fake News Detection Kit*
The Ten-Point Process to Save Our Democracy

If a nation expects to be ignorant & free, in a state of civilisation, it expects what never was & never will be. The functionaries of every government have propensities to command at will the liberty & property of their constituents. There is no safe deposit for these but with the people themselves; nor can they be safe with them without information. Where the press is free and every man able to read, all is safe.

— THOMAS JEFFERSON TO CHARLES YANCEY, January 6, 1816

Scholars have long echoed Jefferson's claim that democratic freedom is girded by a free and vibrant press.[1] However, since Jefferson's time, it has become increasingly clear that democracy is equally dependent upon a news-literate citizenry.[2] Seth Ashley, Adam Maksl, and Stephanie Craft explain that "news media literacy takes the broad goals of media literacy—the ability to access, analyze, evaluate, and create media—and applies them to news content specifically with a focus on the contexts of news production."[3] Contrary to Jefferson's claims, access to journalism does not guarantee that a citizenry will be informed or free. However, citizens' access to seemingly endless information on the internet has not mitigated the influence of fake news. That is why, in addition to a free and vibrant press, democracy depends on the electorate having the skills to recognize and interpret journalism, while detecting and guarding against fake news. Otherwise, we run the risk of fake news having a dominant influence on the electorate, or even worse, we abdicate our democratic responsibility and entrust self-serving authorities, such as President Donald Trump or Facebook, with determining what is fake news and journalism for the electorate.

Until this study, efforts at constructing effective critical news literacy pedagogy were hindered by the incomplete scholarship on fake news. Essentially, solutions were designed for a problem that was not fully understood. This ten-part proposal, which is based on critical news literacy scholarship and the findings of this text, seeks to hone your fake news detection skills. The detection skills are not intended to be practiced in any particular order. Collectively, these skills, organized in a series of questions, will help you better determine the validity of news content.

1. Do I Want to Be Informed or a Fake News Disseminator?

Allison Butler, copresident of the national critical media literacy organization Action Coalition for Media Literacy Education (ACME), argues that, as citizens in a democracy, we must recast ourselves as media citizens rather than media consumers.[4] Indeed, our democracy is best served when we use news as means of becoming more informed rather than as commodities to be shared or liked on social media. In 2016, Maksym Gabielkov, a professor of computer science at the University of Helsinki, and his colleagues found that nearly two-thirds of the internet links shared on social media had never been clicked.[5] The findings are strong evidence that the majority of content shared online is posted and reposted without being read, let alone investigated. This presents two critical problems. First, people are basing their decision to share an item on the headline rather than on the content's veracity. Depending on a headline for accuracy is foolish given that scholars have found that from newspapers to the internet, headlines are often misleading or simply unsupported by the evidence in the article.[6] The second problem posed by not reading articles before sharing them is that the user has not vetted the content. By helping to spread unverified content, social media users effectively become accomplices to fake news producers.

Andy Lee Roth, the associate director of the anticensorship news literacy organization Project Censored, argues that users can become more informed and less susceptible to headlines if they avoid news inflation.[7] News inflation is news consumers' habit of privileging the amount of content they encounter over the amount of quality information they encounter or retain. There is a massive amount of news available on the internet, but sharing more content than you investigate does not make you more informed. It is better to scrutinize a few high-quality stories than to share an endless stream of unverified content.

2. Should I React or Investigate?

As noted throughout this text, fake news is designed to elicit a specific emotional response and subsequent action. Think back to the demonization of Germans by Lord Kitchener's World War I state-sponsored propaganda machine. It used fear to motivate troop enlistment. When you are consuming news content, rather than react, consider listening to Allison Butler, who reminds us to "slow down."[8] When we react without thinking, for example by sharing content after reading only the headline, we behave in accordance with the wishes of fake news producers. When we slow down, we can investigate the content and its underlying evidence. Before you share or like, investigate!

3. Why Was My Attention Drawn to This Content?

When you encounter content, consider practicing self-reflection. Analyze how your personal biases make you susceptible to false content. Each person has a unique set of factors that attract them to a particular piece of content. Analyze what role, if any, your preferences or behavior play in shaping your news habits. Consider what changes you can make to recognize and resist fake news in the future, including turning off the data sharing permissions on your digital devices. The more you limit fake news producers' access to your data, the less vulnerable you become to their content. This is a crucial step in circumventing the influence of fake news in the future.

4. Who Is the Publisher of This Content?

Inquiries into the validity of content often begin by identifying the publisher. A content publisher has enormous power to determine what users will or will not see. As a result, it is crucial to identify the publisher and any potential conflicts of interest. The publisher's identity is not always easy to find, but with a little digging it is usually attainable. A broadcast program will typically include the publisher's identity in its introductory or concluding credits. A website should have its publisher listed on an About Us or Contact Us webpage. Once you are aware of a publisher's identity, it is then crucial to consider their intent in producing media. As a reminder:

a. *The press* spreads fake news in order to build its audience and revenue.
b. *State-sponsored propaganda machines* seek to centralize the government's power with fake news.

c. *Satirical fake news* seeks to entertain and influence audiences through partisan narratives and appeals to emotion.

d. *Nation-states* aim to serve their foreign and domestic policy interests with fake news.

e. *Political party propaganda apparatuses* optimize fake news to win elections and policy debates.

f. *Self-interested actors* engage in the construction and dissemination of fake news for a host of reasons, including entertainment and self-aggrandizement.

Once you have identified the publisher, consider how their interests may have shaped the frame, slant, or bias of the content. If you are unfamiliar with the publisher, research them. Some resources online can be helpful, such as Media Matters, Fairness and Accuracy in Reporting (FAIR), Snopes, PolitiFact, and FactCheck. Not only do they fact-check news outlets, but they keep a substantial archive of publishers' content. Consider whether the publisher has a history of publishing false content. If they do, you should be suspicious of the content's accuracy.

5. Who Is The Author of This Content?

As Judith Miller's *New York Times* reporting (discussed in chapter 3) reveals, sometimes it is the author, not the publisher, who is responsible for the dissemination of fake news. Thus it is beneficial to investigate the author. First, look into the author's background to see if they are qualified to discuss the topic at hand. The author should have a biography on the publisher's website that can help you determine their qualifications. You should also consider the author's affiliations. If this person is affiliated with known fake news producers, you need to consider how that relationship might affect the reliability of their content.

In the world of journalism, nothing is more valuable than credibility. As a result, consider whether the author has a history of publishing false, misleading, or unsubstantiated content. You can use the same fact-checking resources used to investigate the publisher: Media Matters, FAIR, Snopes, PolitiFact, and FactCheck. Either through an archival page or a search on these websites, you can find all of the fact-checking that has been done on the author in question.

6. Do I Understand the Content?

In addition to researching the author and publisher, you want to evaluate the evidence in the news story. However, that requires familiarity with the content in question. A misunderstanding or an incomplete read leaves you ill-prepared to evaluate the story's veracity. A great way to ensure that you understand the article is to ask the 5Ws (and an H). The 5Ws are a ubiquitous tool, often used in journalism, to gather information. When you are asked about the content, you should be able to give a factual answer to each of the following:

- Who?
- What?
- Where?
- When?
- Why?
- How?

After you answer the 5Ws (and the H), consider reviewing the content to ensure that you have a clear understanding about the news story and underlying evidence. If any of the questions have not been answered or addressed, you should be suspicious of the content's accuracy.

7. Does the Evidence Hold Up under Scrutiny?

When you encounter fake news, analyze the evidence used by the author. Although it takes more time, Michael Caulfield, the director of blended and networked learning at Washington State University, Vancouver (WSU), recommends that when you are reading a news article, you find out if other people have checked the source, go upstream to the story's source, read what other net sources say on the topic, then "circle back" to reread the original story you're trying to fact-check and apply to it whatever new information you have gleaned. "If you get lost, hit dead ends, or find yourself going down an increasingly confusing rabbit hole, back up and start over knowing what you know now. You're likely to take a more informed path with different search terms and better decisions."[9]

To determine a news story's veracity, you will need to evaluate the evidence provided. Some news stories might initially appear compelling or convincing because of the use of linguistic tricks or visual and audio manipulation. For example, think back to the ACORN video, which provided compelling evidence of a government-assisted human-trafficking scam. Upon further examination, it was revealed that only manipulated evidence existed to support the video's claims. Similarly, when you complete a piece of news content, you want to evaluate how well the evidence supports the author's claims.

One way to evaluate the evidence is to identify any fallacious claims. Douglas Walton, a Distinguished Research Fellow at the University of Windsor, defines fallacies as "commonly used sophisms or errors in reasoning."[10] Think back to the ad hominem attacks that Bill O'Reilly and Keith Olbermann lobbed at each other during their news broadcasts. These were not news, they were fallacious arguments. You will hone your ability to spot fake news if you habitually search for fallacies in news content.[11] There are numerous fallacies, but the ones that are most pertinent to the study of fake news include

- Rival causes/post hoc
- Inferred justification/motivated reasoning
- Ad hominem
- Straw person
- Equivocation
- Obfuscation
- Non sequitur
- False dilemma
- Red herring
- Appeal to questionable authority
- Ad populum (bandwagon fallacy)
- Begging the question (circular reasoning)
- Value conflict/value assumption
- Slippery slope
- Explain by naming
- Glittering generality
- Hasty generalization
- Oversimplification
- Appeal to perfect solution (utopian fallacy)
- Wishful thinking[12]

In addition to assessing the author's logic, analyzing your logic can aid in spotting fake news. Ask yourself: *How do I know this is true?* Truth is generally found in news content when there are verified sources. The Center for News Literacy provides five questions to determine if an author's sources are trustworthy:

- Is this an independent source?
- Are there multiple sources?
- Can the source's information be verified?
- Is this an authoritative and/or informed source?
- Is this a named source?

If the answer is "no" to any of these questions, this should raise suspicion about the story's validity. Think back to your guiding question: If you cannot identify or trust the sources, how can you trust the content?

8. What Is Missing from This Content?

When it comes to detecting fake news, the absence of information is just as revealing as the information that is present. The political party propaganda apparatuses detailed in chapter 3 often used select factual information to present a false interpretation of events. For example, the Republican Party propaganda apparatus exploited the actual arrest of a drug dealer in front of the White House by neglecting to mention that the government had selected the arrest location. Although news stories such as these include verifiable facts, they are fake news because they are missing crucial facts. Thus you want to investigate what is missing from a piece of news content.

One way you can determine what is missing is by cross-checking the content with other news stories on the same topic. Given the different biases and interests that frame content, you want to compare corporate versus independent news outlets as well as Right-leaning versus Left-leaning affiliated outlets. One great resource is All Sides (https://www.allsides.com/unbiased-balanced-news), which on a daily basis introduces the same article from multiple news outlets with competing political ideologies. Another is Project Censored (www.ProjectCensored.org), which posts stories that are published by the independently funded press but are ignored by the corporate-funded press. In addition to political and economic influence, you should account for the ways in which select identities can frame a story. Critical media literacy scholars Jeff Share, Tessa Jolls, and Elizabeth Thoman, writing for the Center for Media Literacy, remind us of the importance of identity and ask us to consider the question "What values, lifestyles, and points of view are represented in, or omitted from, this message?"[13] In practice, this means identifying the racial, ethnic, gendered, regional, sexual, and class identities that shape a piece of news content before examining how competing identity groups have reported on the same topic.

Another way you can determine what is missing from a piece of content is by reaching out to an expert. This could be an elected official or someone employed in the industry or academic discipline in question. You can start by looking at the webpage for a relevant department at a local public university. Their contact information should be available for you to use. Reach out to them and see if they have any commentary or resources to offer that may help you better evaluate your news content.

9. Who Might Benefit from or Be Harmed by This Message?

When determining the legitimacy of news content, the reaction that people have to a particular piece of content can be as revealing as anything else. Think back to the numerous examples of how fake news by the press produced public support for war; political party propaganda apparatuses cultivated hyperpartisan division; and state-sponsored propaganda machines bolstered authoritarian regimes. In each case, the content was meticulously designed to engender a specific response from the news consumer that served the interests of the producer.

Identifying the desired purpose of a particular piece of content can help you determine if it is fake news. If the intended purpose is to cultivate the known outcomes of fake news, that should raise your suspicion about the news story's trustworthiness. As a reminder, the outcomes of fake news consumption are

- Moral panic
- Moral outrage
- Radicalization of consumers

- Marginalization of the press
- Social division
- Manipulation of democracy
- The implementation of an authoritarian regime

These behaviors and attitudes do not alone prove that the content is fake news. However, before you believe or share the content, you should investigate if one or more of these outcomes was the producer's intended purpose.

To determine the purpose of a piece of content, you want to ask yourself: Why was this made? If it is a website, sometimes the domain name, such as .com, .org, .gov, or .edu, can reveal the website's purpose. Generally speaking, websites that end in .com are for commercial purposes; .org are for nonprofit purposes; .gov are for governmental purposes; and .edu are for educational purposes. However, there is no mechanism to enforce these boundaries, so dig deeper. The Newseum, a Washington, D.C., news history and media literacy organization, offers some crucial evaluation criteria for identifying the purpose behind a piece of content:

- Context: What's the big picture?
- Audience: Who is the intended audience?
- Execution: How is the information presented?[14]

Because our identity plays a key role in how we interpret content, we must consider the influence that individuals' race, gender, sexuality, region, age, or ability may have on their interpretation of content. Indeed, as University of Colorado, Denver's communication professor Brenda Allen notes, 'Differences matter.' Our identity and lived experience are intertwined, shaping how we interpret and negotiate messages.[15] To be able to identify all types of fake news, we must consider how differences in identity are expressed in differing interpretations of news and fake news content. Theoretical frameworks help provide, especially to those with privilege, the perspectives of others. For example, ask, *How might I interpret this content through a feminist lens as compared to a critical race framework?* The usage of theoretical frameworks can build our awareness of who, how, and why a particular story is marginalizing a particular group. If the story targets one or more identity groups with known recurring themes in fake news—nationalism, fear, hate, and celebrity gossip—it is a strong sign that it is fake news. For example, fake news about slave uprisings in the eighteenth and nineteenth centuries targeted whites with themes of fear and hate against African American slaves.

10. Does the Content Qualify as Journalism?

As discussed in chapter 1, journalism is a well-defined field. When a piece of content does not adhere to journalistic standards, its legitimacy is worthy of investigation. It is important to remind yourself that just because someone is employed as a journalist or working at a known news media outlet does not mean that he or she is practicing sound journalism. In fact, think back to the examples of employed journalists and reporters who engaged in the production and dissemination of fake news, such as Stephen Glass, Jayson Blair, Bill O'Reilly, Brian Williams, and Judith Miller. They illustrate why it is crucial to investigate everyone, including employed journalists, when you assess the validity of news content.

A news story is legitimate journalism if it is adheres to the functions of the press; is newsworthy; and follows the journalistic code of ethics. First, determine if the news story serves one of these five critical democratic functions discussed in chapter 1:

- Marketplace of ideas
- Agenda setter

- Watchdog
- Information disseminator
- Public mobilization

If it does not serve one of these functions, you should be skeptical of its legitimacy. Either way, additional investigative work is needed to determine the news story's validity.

Next, you want to determine if the content is newsworthy as defined by the press. The press generally follows five criteria to decide if something is newsworthy:

- Is it new?
- Is it unusual?
- Is it interesting?
- Is it significant?
- Is it about people?[16]

If the answer is no to any of these, that raises serious questions about why the content was created. In response, you will want to investigate the purpose of the content.

Finally, you want to determine if the author has acted as a journalist. Media scholar Alan Knight and his colleagues define a journalist as "anyone applying professional practices within recognized codes of ethics."[17] To determine if a piece of content is real news or actual journalism, you need to determine if it adheres to the ethical practice of journalism. According to the Ethical Journalism Network, the ethical practice of journalism is rooted in five principles:

- Truth and Accuracy: Although journalists cannot guarantee truth, they can and must present facts as part of their reporting. In addition, they need to be transparent about whether those facts have been corroborated.

- Independence: Journalists should never act on behalf of someone else's interest.
- Fairness and Impartiality: Journalists must strive for objectivity and provide as many differing viewpoints as possible.
- Humanity: Journalists ought to avoid causing harm and be aware of the impact of their stories on other people's lives.
- Accountability: Journalists must hold themselves and their colleagues accountable. This includes illuminating errors, taking responsibility, and offering corrections.[18]

If the author has not exhibited journalistic ethics, you should not use them as a news source. Instead seek out other journalists who are reporting on the same topic but adhering to journalistic ethics.

Jefferson warned future generations about the fragility of democracy by referring to American democracy as an "experiment."[19] Jefferson was aware that all of the previous democracies had failed. As this book has illustrated, fake news has played a crucial role in weakening democracies and empowering authoritarian regimes. The power of autocrats manifests in environments saturated with fake news. In the twenty-first century, Americans, like much of the global community, must heed Jefferson's warning as they are bombarded with fake news from journalists, governments, satirical entertainers, political parties, self-interested actors, bots, and algorithms. These producers disseminate content through numerous media with unimaginable capabilities for directing human behavior. The implications for democracy are catastrophic.

Despite the real threat facing democracy, fake news has not been adequately addressed by American institutions. Each new communication technology has enabled an increasing number of fake news producers to develop more sophisticated means of manipulating the electorate. Throughout that same time, lawmakers, private industry, the press, and educators have made valiant efforts to eradicate or mitigate the influence of fake news. However, these efforts have failed to address the central factor legitimizing fake news: consumers' inability to distinguish fake news from journalism. This dilemma persists because of insufficient scholarship about fake news.

This text has provided a wide-ranging study of fake news that serves as the foundation for a promising proposal about how critical news literacy educators can mitigate the pernicious influence of fake news. As this text goes to press, the discourses around the Covid-19 virus demonstrate the urgency with which America must consider critical news literacy curriculum. The pandemic has been complicated by fake news that denies the virus's existence, promotes false cures, and provides baseless assertions about its origins. Much like the impact of a virus on the body, fake news emaciates and incapacitates the electorate from engaging in meaningful democratic action. By integrating critical news literacy into our curriculum we equip future generations with the tools to preserve our democracy. It is worth reminding our students and ourselves of the words of the former prime minister of the United Kingdom, Winston Churchill, who noted that democracy is "the worst form of government except for all those other forms that have been tried from time to time."[20]

Notes

Introduction

1. Amber Jamieson, "'You Are Fake News': Trump Attacks CNN and Buzz-Feed at Press Conference," *Guardian,* January 11, 2017, https://www.theguardian.com/us-news/2017/jan/11/trump-attacks-cnn-buzzfeed-at-press-conference.

2. Brian Stelter, "Trump Averages a 'Fake' Insult Every Day. Really. We Counted," CNN, January 17, 2018, https://money.cnn.com/2018/01/17/media/president-trump-fakenews-count/index.html.

3. Dino-Ray Ramos, "Ed Helms' 'The Fake News' Special Gets Premiere Date on Comedy Central," *Deadline,* November 14, 2017, https://deadline.com/2017/11/ed-helms-comedy-central-the-fake-news-with-ted-nelms-1202207636/; "The Fake News Show," *British Comedy Guide,* n.d., accessed December 19, 2019, https://www.comedy.co.uk/tv/the_fake_news_show/; "*Murphy Brown* (1988–2018), Season 11, Episode 1," IMDB, aired September 27, 2018, https://www.imdb.com/title/tt8074972/.

4. Allcott and Gentzkow, "Social Media"; Broniatowski et al., "Weaponized Health Communication."

5. On the dangers of fake news peddled by TV news personalities, see Bakir and McStay, "Fake News"; Benkler, Faris, and Roberts, *Network Propaganda;* Ovadya, "What's Worse," 43–45. On the dangers of fake news from online news outlets, see Wendling, *Alt-Right.*

6. On proposed government regulations, see Goldberg, "Responding to Fake New." On proposed legal action against individuals, see Nathan Schneider, "Antitrust for the Many, Not the Few," *Nation,* November 20, 2018, https://www

.thenation.com/article/facebook-monopoly-antitrust-facebook/, and against nations, see McIntyre, *Post-truth.*

7. Goldberg, "Responding to Fake News"; R. Hobbs, "Teach the Conspiracies"; Williams, "Fighting 'Fake News.'"

8. Cheung, "Media Education"; R. Hobbs and Frost, "Measuring the Acquisition."

9. "Media Literacy Legislative Roundup: 21 Bills, 11 States, 5 New Laws," Media Literacy Now, January 2, 2018, https://medialiteracynow.org/media-literacy-legislative-roundup-21-bills-11-states-5-new-laws/; "15 Bills in 12 States," Media Literacy Now, https://medialiteracynow.org/your-state-legislation/.

10. Aufderheide, *Media Literacy,* 6; Mihailidis, "Civic Media Literacies."

11. Mihailidis and Viotty, "Spreadable Spectacle."

12. Bulger and Davison, "Promises, Challenges and Futures."

13. Funk, Kellner, and Share, "Critical Media Literacy," 1.

14. Kellner and Share, "Critical Media Literacy"; Goldberg, "Responding to Fake News."

15. Nolan Higdon and Ben Boyington, "Has Media Literacy Been Hijacked?," Project Censored, March 19, 2019, https://www.projectcensored.org/has-media-literacy-been-hijacked/.

16. J. Fleming, "Media Literacy, News Literacy."

17. R. Hobbs, Seyferth-Zapf, and Grafe, "Using Virtual Exchange."

18. Tandoc, Lim, and Ling, "Defining 'Fake News,'" 2.

19. Goldberg, "Responding to Fake News," 418.

20. Barclay, *Fake News, Propaganda;* Young, *Bunk.*

21. Hsia, *Trent* 1475.

22. Araújo, "Lisbon Earthquake of 1755."

23. Kate Irby, "You Think You Can Recognize Fake News? So Does Most of the Country," *Sacramento Bee,* December 15, 2016, https://www.sacbee.com/latest-news/article121063928.html.

24. Claire Fallon, "Where Does the Term 'Fake News' Come From?," *Huffington Post,* March 24, 2017, https://www.huffingtonpost.com/entry/where-does-the-term-fake-news-come-from_us_58d53c89e4b03692bea518ad; "The Daily Rabid," *San Francisco Call,* October 15, 1899, https://cdnc.ucr.edu/cgi-bin/cdnc?a=d&d=SFC18991015.2.59&srpos=13&e=-------en--20--1--txt-txIN--------1.

25. David Lieberman, "Fake News," *TV Guide,* February 1992.

26. Amarasingam, *Stewart/Colbert Effect;* Baym, "Daily Show."

27. Farsetta and Price, "Fake TV News"; R. Hobbs, Seyferth-Zapf, and Grafe, "Using Virtual Exchange."

28. Mike Wendling, "The (Almost) Complete History of 'Fake News,'" BBC Trending, January 22, 2018, https://www.bbc.com/news/blogs-trending-42724320.

29. Higdon and Huff, *United States of Distraction.*

30. Staff, "Indicators of News Media Trust," Knight Foundation, report, September 11, 2018, https://www.knightfoundation.org/reports/indicators-of-news-media-trust.

31. Barclay, *Fake News, Propaganda*; Bartlett, *Truth Matters*; Levitin, *Weaponized Lies*; McIntyre, *Post-truth.*

32. Glenn Kessler, Salvador Rizzo, and Meg Kelly, "President Trump Has Made 4,229 False or Misleading Claims in 558 Days," *Washington Post,* August 1, 2018, https://www.washingtonpost.com/news/fact-checker/wp/2018/08/01 /president-trump-has-made-4229-false-or-misleading-claims-in-558-days /?utm_term=.d8e57745b22d.

33. Jack Holmes, "To Supporters, Trump Isn't Just Right—He Controls the Truth," *Esquire,* July 31, 2018, https://www.esquire.com/news-politics/a22600827 /donald-trump-supporters-believe-the-media/.

34. Stanford History Education Group, "Evaluating Information: The Cornerstone of Civic Online Reasoning," Stanford University, November 22, 2016, https://stacks.stanford.edu/file/druid:fv751yt5934/SHEG%20Evaluating%20 Information%20Online.pdf.

35. McGrew et al., "Can Students Evaluate Online Sources?," 165.

36. Guess, Nagler, and Tucker, "Less Than You Think."

37. Breakstone et al., "Students' Civic Online Reasoning," 3.

38. Lazer et al., "Science of Fake News," 1094.

39. M. Stephens, *History of News.*

40. Allcott and Gentzkow, "Social Media," 213; Broniatowski et al., "Weaponized Health Communication."

41. Guo and Vargo, "'Fake News,'"; Chris Rozvar, "Damaging Brooklyn ACORN Sting Video Ruled 'Heavily Edited,' No Charges to Be Filed," *New Yorker,* March 2, 2010; Young, *Bunk.*

42. Lazer et al., "Science of Fake News."

43. Bolsover and Howard, "Computational Propaganda," 8.

44. R. Hobbs, "Teaching and Learning," 31.

45. Bernhard, *U.S. Television News*; Wu, *Attention Merchants.*

46. Brett Samuels, "Carl Bernstein: I Wonder if We Would Have Been Fired Today for Mistake in Watergate Story," *Hill,* December 10, 2017, https://thehill .com/homenews/media/364164-carl-bernstein-i-wonder-if-we-would-have-been-fired-today-for-mistake-in; Wu, *Attention Merchants.*

47. Barclay, *Fake News, Propaganda*; Bartlett, *Truth Matters*; Levitin, *Weaponized Lies*; Stephens-Davidowitz, *Everybody Lies*; Vaidhyanathan, *Anti-social Media*.

48. McIntyre, *Post-truth*; Fuchs, *Digital Demagogue*.

49. Blumer, *Symbolic Interactionism*.

50. McLuhan, *Understanding Media*; Postman, *Teaching*; Strate, "Media Ecology."

51. N. Stephens, "Toward a More Substantive Media Ecology," 19.

52. McLuhan, Fiore, and Agel, *Medium Is the Massage*; McLuhan, *Gutenberg Galaxy*.

53. Heyer, *Communications and History*; G. Patterson, *History and Communications*; Stamps, *Unthinking Modernity*.

54. Kelly, Foucault, and Habermas, *Critique and Power*; Horkheimer, *Critical Theory*; Piccone, *Essential Frankfurt School Reader*.

55. Piccone, *Essential Frankfurt School Reader*; Hall et al., *Culture, Media, Language*.

56. M. Stephens, *History of News*.

57. Saldaña, *Coding Manual*.

58. Saldaña, *Coding Manual*.

59. Rich Buchler and Staff, "Six Corporations Own 90% of News Media—Truth!," *Truth or Fiction*, https://www.truthorfiction.com/six-corporations-own-90-percent-of-news-media/; Ashley Lutz, "These 6 Corporations Control 90% of the Media In America," *Business Insider*, June 14, 2012, www.businessinsider.com/these-6-corporations-control-90-of-the-media-in-america-2012-6.

1. The Fourth Estate

1. Copeland, *Idea of a Free Press*.

2. Lepore, *These Truths*.

3. Kinsbruner, *Independence in Spanish America*.

4. Tocqueville, *Democracy in America*, 389.

5. Eisenstein, *Printing Press*.

6. M. Stephens, *History of News*.

7. Laura Crombie, "A Brief History of How People Communicated in the Middle Ages," *History Extra*, October 24, 2014, https://www.historyextra.com/period/medieval/a-brief-history-of-how-people-communicated-in-the-middle-ages/.

8. M. Stephens, *History of News*.

9. M. Stephens, *History of News*.

10. M. Stephens, *History of News*.

11. M. Stephens, *History of News*.

12. C. W. Anderson, Downie, and Schudson, *News Media*.

13. Straubhaar, LaRose, and Davenport, *Media Now*.

14. C. W. Anderson, Downie, and Schudson, *News Media*.

15. Straubhaar, LaRose, and Davenport, *Media Now*.

16. Tocqueville, *Democracy in America*, chap. 6.

17. Thomas Jefferson to Edward Carrington, January 16, 1787, extract, Thomas Jefferson's Monticello, tjrs.monticello.org/letter/1289.

18. Gentzkow, Glaeser, and Goldin, "Rise of the Fourth Estate."

19. Volokh, "Freedom for the Press."

20. Editorial Board, "British Press Freedom under Threat," *New York Times,* November 14, 2013.

21. Laursen, "David Hume"; "The Constitution of the Italian Republic," Presidenza della Repubblica, archived from the original (PDF), www.quirinale.it /qrnw/costituzione/pdf/costituzione_inglese.pdf, on November 27, 2016.

22. Staff, "2018 World Press Freedom Index," Reporters without Borders, 2018, https://rsf.org/en/ranking.

23. Richard Perez-Pena, "American Newspapers Have Relied on Government Subsidies since Washington's Day, but That Support Has Dropped Sharply in the Last Four Decades," *New York Times,* January 27, 2010, https://www.nytimes .com/2010/01/28/business/media/28subsidy.html; Laura McGann "Separation of News and State? How Government Subsidies Buoyed Media," Nieman Lab, January 28, 2010, www.niemanlab.org/2010/01/separation-of-news-and-state-how-government-subsidies-buoyed-media/.

24. Perez-Pena, "American Newspapers."

25. Johnson, *Your Second Priority,* i.

26. These five functions are discussed in Overholser and Hall Jamieson, *Press*.

27. Lee Hamilton, "Why Good Journalism Is Crucial to Our Democracy," *Detroit News,* August 17, 2016, https://www.detroitnews.com/story/opinion/2016 /08/17/journalism-democracy/88933512/.

28. Hamilton, "Why Good Journalism."

29. Jensen, *Censored* 1996.

30. Peter Henshall and David Ingram, *The News Manual,* Online Edition, 2012, chapter 1, "What Is News?," https://www.thenewsmanual.net/Manuals Volume 1/volume1_01.html.

31. Snell quoted in Roy Greenslade, "Reporting Is Different from Journalism, and It's the Latter We Need to Protect," *Guardian,* December 10, 2009, https://

www.theguardian.com/media/greenslade/2009/dec/10/newspapers-pressand-publishing.

32. D'Angelo and Kuypers, *Doing News Framing Analysis*.

33. Nielsen, "The Total Audience Report: Q1 2016," July 27, 2016, www.nielsen.com/us/en/insights/reports/2016/the-total-audience-report-q1-2016.html.

34. Leah Christian, Amy Mitchell, and Tom Rosentiel, "Mobile Devices and News Consumption: Some Good Signs for Journalism," Pew Research Center, March 18, 2012, www.journalism.org/2012/03/18/mobile-devices-and-news-consumption-some-good-signs-for-journalism/1-23-percent-of-u-s-adults-get-news-on-at-least-two-digital-devices-300x155/.

35. American Press Institute, "The Personal News Cycle: How Americans Choose to Get Their News," American Press Institute, March 17, 2014, https://www.americanpressinstitute.org/publications/reports/survey-research/personal-news-cycle/.

36. All these statistics are from Michael Barthel et al., "Pathways to News," Pew Research Center, July 7, 2016, www.journalism.org/2016/07/07/pathways-to-news/.

37. Kalev Leetaru, "'Fake News' and How the Washington Post Rewrote Its Story on Russian Hacking of the Power Grid," *Forbes,* January 1, 2017, https://www.forbes.com/sites/kalevleetaru/2017/01/01/fake-news-and-how-the-washington-post-rewrote-its-story-on-russian-hacking-of-the-power-grid/#573fdf57ad51.

38. Adornato, *Mobile and Social Media Journalism*.

39. Bebić and Volarević, "Viral Journalism."

40. Ayman M. Mohyeldin, "No One Is Safe: How Saudi Arabia Makes Dissidents Disappear," *Vanity Fair,* July 29, 2019, https://www.vanityfair.com/news/2019/07/how-saudi-arabia-makes-dissidents-disappear.

41. Elana Beiser, "Record Number of Journalists Jailed as Turkey, China, Egypt Pay Scant Price for Repression," Committee to Protect Journalists, December 13, 2017, https://cpj.org/reports/2017/12/journalists-prison-jail-record-number-turkey-china-egypt.php.

42. Staff, "RSF Index 2018: Hatred of Journalism Threatens Democracies," Reporters without Borders, https://rsf.org/en/rsf-index-2018-hatred-journalism-threatens-democracies.

2. The Faux Estate

1. G. Knight, *Joseph Bates,* 71.

2. Dick, *William Miller.*

3. Miller, *William Miller's Apology.*

4. Billington, "Millerite Adventists"; Bliss, *Memoirs of William Miller,* 141–44.

5. Bliss, *Memoirs of William Miller,* 141–44.

6. Steuter and Wills, *At War with Metaphor,* 40.

7. Ubelaker, "North American Indian Population."

8. Coward, *Newspaper Indian,* 149–52.

9. "Columbus Reports on His First Voyage, 1493: A Spotlight on a Primary Source by Christopher Columbus," Gilder Lehrman Institute of History, https://www.gilderlehrman.org/content/columbus-reports-his-first-voyage-1493.

10. Zinn, *People's History,* chap. 1.

11. Carrasco, "Give Me Some Skin."

12. Zinn, *People's History,* chap. 1.

13. Zinn, *People's History,* chap. 1.

14. Cave, *Pequot War.*

15. Zinn, *People's History,* chap. 1.

16. Bradford, "Of Plymouth Plantation," 84.

17. Cave, *Pequot War,* 86.

18. Silver, *Our Savage Neighbors.*

19. Cohen, *Folk Devils,* 9.

20. Schinkel, "Contexts of Anxiety."

21. Russell, *Witchcraft.*

22. Kat Eschner, "How New Printing Technology Gave Witches Their Familiar Silhouette," *Smithsonian,* October 30, 2017, https://www.smithsonianmag.com/smart-news/how-new-printing-technology-gave-witches-their-familiar-silhouette-180965331/.

23. Holmes, "Opinion"; Ronan, "'Young Goodman Brown.'"

24. Stacy Schiff, "The Witches of Salem: Diabolical Doings in a Puritan Village," *New Yorker,* September 7, 2015, https://www.newyorker.com/magazine/2015/09/07/the-witches-of-salem.

25. Mather, *Wonders.*

26. Calef, More Wonders, 152; Holmes, "Opinion."

27. Calef, *More Wonders,* 26, 27, 28.

28. Lepore, *These Truths.*

29. Zhou et al., "Fake News."

30. Huddy, Bankert, and Davies, "Expressive versus Instrumental Partisanship."

31. Hogeland, *Whiskey Rebellion.*

32. Krom and Krom, "Whiskey Tax of 1791."

33. Spencer, "Democratic-Republican Societies."

34. Rorabaugh, *Alcoholic Republic.*

35. Betsy Golden Kellem, "The Resistance Files: The (18th-Century) War on the Mainstream Media," *Historista,* March 6, 2017, www.megankatenelson.com /the-resistance-files-the-18th-century-war-on-the-mainstream-media/.

36. Ray, "'Not One Cent for Tribute.'"

37. Callender, *Prospect before Us,* vol. 2.

38. Kellem, "Resistance Files."

39. Kellem, "Resistance Files."

40. C. Smith, "Alien and Sedition Crisis."

41. M. Stephens, *History of News.*

42. Wu, *Attention Merchants.*

43. Rosenheim, *Cryptographic Imagination.*

44. Vida, "'Great Moon Hoax.'"

45. Wu, *Attention Merchants.*

46. Wu, *Attention Merchants.*

47. Petra S. McGillen, "Techniques of 19th-Century Fake News Reporter Teach Us Why We Fall for It Today," *Conversation,* April 5, 2017, https:// theconversation.com/techniques-of-19th-century-fake-news-reporter-teach-us-why-we-fall-for-it-today-75583.

48. Dain, *Hideous Monster.*

49. Elliott, "Nat Turner Insurrection."

50. Dain, *Hideous Monster.*

51. Hedges, *War Is a Force.*

52. Winders, *Mr. Polk's Army;* Henderson, *Glorious Defeat.*

53. Reilly, *War with Mexico!;* Reilly, "Newspapers: U.S. Press."

54. Reilly, *War with Mexico!*

55. Evan Andrews, "Things You May Not Know about the Mexican-American War," History.com, April 22, 2016, https://www.history.com/news/10-things-you-may-not-know-about-the-mexican-american-war.

56. D. Davis, *Slave Power Conspiracy;* Foner, *Give Me Liberty!*

57. Nevins, *Ordeal of the Union,* vol. 1; D. Davis, *Slave Power Conspiracy.*

58. D. Davis, *Slave Power Conspiracy.*

59. D. Davis, *Slave Power Conspiracy;* Lowry, *Photographer and the President.*

60. Ratner and Teeter, *Fanatics and Fire-Eaters.*

61. Mott, *American Journalism.*

62. Kinzer, *True Flag.*

63. Vaughn, *Encyclopedia of American Journalism.*

64. Foner, *Give Me Liberty!*; Kinzer, *True Flag*; Vaughn, *Encyclopedia of American Journalism*.

65. Anne Leland, *American War and Military Operations Casualties: Lists and Statistics* (Washington, DC: Congressional Research Service, 2010); Herring, *From Colony to Superpower*; Keenan, *Encyclopedia*.

66. Kazanjian and Enss, *Trials of Annie Oakley*.

67. Tandoc and Jenkins, "Out of Bounds?"; Petersen, "Towards an Industrial History."

68. Justin Anderson, "WaPo Picks a Side in Maryland Race—the Side That's Offering Billions to Amazon," FAIR, October 11, 2018, https://fair.org/home/wapo-picks-a-side-in-maryland-race-the-side-thats-offering-billions-to-amazon/.

69. Goodwin, *Bully Pulpit*.

70. David Folkenflik, "Tribune, Tronc and Beyond: A Slur, a Secret Payout and a Looming Sale," NPR, December 12, 2018, https://www.npr.org/2018/12/12/675961765/tribune-tronc-and-beyond-a-slur-a-secret-payout-and-a-looming-sale?sc=tw.

71. Harris, "Xenophobia."

72. Foner, *Give Me Liberty!*

73. Kindleberger, Manias, Panics and Crashes.

74. Villanueva, "Gilded Freedom," 70.

75. Villanueva, "Gilded Freedom," 72.

76. Lyman, "'Yellow Peril' Mystique."

77. Laurie, "'Chinese Must Go.'"

78. Aysa-Lastra and Cachón, *Immigrant Vulnerability and Resilience*.

79. Wu, *Attention Merchants*.

80. Olson and Cloud, *Murrow Boys*; Wu, *Attention Merchants*.

81. Porch, "'No Bad Stories.'"

82. Kennett, *For the Duration*.

83. Porch, "'No Bad Stories.'"

84. "'Private Snafu' Fights Fake News in 1944," History.com, n.d., accessed December 29, 2019, https://www.history.com/topics/world-war-ii/world-war-ii-history/videos/private-snafu-fights-fake-news-in-1944.

85. Ambrose, *Citizen Soldiers*, 342.

86. Sheldon, *Father Coughlin*; Schrag, *Not Fit*.

87. Schrag, *Not Fit*.

88. Friendly, *Good Guys*.

89. Higdon and Huff, *United States of Distraction*.

90. Staff, "All Pants on Fire! Statements Involving Rush Limbaugh," PolitiFact, 2019, www.politifact.com/personalities/rush-limbaugh/statements /byruling/pants-fire/.

91. Berry and Sobieraj, *Outrage Industry.*

92. Wu, *Attention Merchants.*

93. Hallin, *Uncensored War.*

94. Wu, *Attention Merchants.*

95. Staff, "1957: BBC Fools the Nation," On This Day: April 1, BBC, news.bbc. co.uk/onthisday/hi/dates/stories/april/1/newsid_2819000/2819261.stm.

96. Fried, *Russians Are Coming!*

97. Wire, "50 Years Ago, Mosinee Staged a Mock Communist Takeover," *Journal Times,* May 2, 2000, https://journaltimes.com/news/state-and-regional/ years-ago-mosinee-staged-a-mock-communist-takeover/article_3d94ab53-b652-5aac-a554-d12ae08c93f1.html; Fried, *Russians Are Coming!*

98. Berlinger and Zacharias, "Resources for Teaching."

99. Hammond, *Reporting Vietnam.*

100. "Military Pressures against North Vietnam, February 1964-January 1965," in Gravel, Chomsky, and Zinn, *Pentagon Papers,* vol. 3, chap. 2, 106–268.

101. Jeff Cohen and Norman Solomon, "30-Year Anniversary: Tonkin Gulf Lie Launched Vietnam War," FAIR, July 27, 1994, https://fair.org/media-beat-column/30-year-anniversary-tonkin-gulf-lie-launched-vietnam-war/.

102. "Gulf of Tonkin's Phantom Attack: Faulty Intelligence Played Role in Decision to Engage Viet Cong," NPR, August 2, 2004, https://www.npr.org/templates /story/story.php?storyId=3810724; Cohen and Solomon, "30-Year Anniversary"; "Gulf of Tonkin," National Security Administration, May 30, 2006, https://www .nsa.gov/news-features/declassified-documents/gulf-of-tonkin/.

103. Hallin, "Media, the War," 2–24; Hammond, *Reporting Vietnam.*

104. Herring, *Secret Diplomacy.*

105. Gabriel Voiles, "On Cronkite as (Belatedly) 'Courageous Truth-Teller,'" FAIR, July 20, 2009, https://fair.org/uncategorized/on-cronkite-as-belatedly-courageous-truth-teller/; Jeff Cohen, "The Myth of the Media's Role in Vietnam," FAIR, May 6, 2001, https://fair.org/article/the-myth-of-the-medias-role-in-vietnam/.

106. Foer, *World without Mind.*

107. "Vietnam War U.S. Military Fatal Casualty Statistics," National Archives, https://www.archives.gov/research/military/vietnam-war/casualty-statistics; Hirschman, and Loi, "Vietnamese Casualties."

108. Lee B. Becker, Mengtian Chen, and James M. Cox Jr., "Public Trust in Journalism and Media: Analysis of Data from 1970 to 2015," Kettering Foundation, 2016, *https://www.kettering.org/catalog/product/public-trust-journalism.*; Rudenstine, *Day the Presses Stopped.*

109. Higdon and Huff, *United States of Distraction.*

110. Higdon and Huff, *United States of Distraction.*

111. Jennifer Saba, "Specifics on Newspapers from 'State of News Media' Report," *Editor and Publisher,* March 16, 2009, www.editorandpublisher.com /PrintArticle/Specifics-on-Newspapers-from-State-of-News-Media-Report; Elizabeth Grieco, "Newsroom Employment Dropped Nearly a Quarter in Less Than 10 Years, with Greatest Decline at Newspapers," Pew Research, FactTank, July 30, 2018, https://www.pewresearch.org/fact-tank/2018/07/30/newsroom-employment-dropped-nearly-a-quarter-in-less-than-10-years-with-greatest-decline-at-newspapers/.

112. Adrian Uribarri, "Ethics Case Studies: The Times and Jayson Blair," Society of Professional Journalists, n.d., accessed December 29, 2019, https://www .spj.org/ecs13.asp.

113. Carolyn Wilder, "Times Reporter Who Resigned Leaves Long Trail of Deception," *New York Times,* May 11, 2003, https://www.nytimes.com/2003/05/11/us /correcting-the-record-times-reporter-who-resigned-leaves-long-trail-of-deception.html.

114. Hanna Rosin, "Hello, My Name Is Stephen Glass, and I'm Sorry," *New Republic,* November 10, 2014, https://newrepublic.com/article/120145/stephen-glass-new-republic-scandal-still-haunts-his-law-career.

115. Rachel Brody, "Brian Williams' Years-Long Lie: The NBC Nightly News Anchor Apologized for Saying He'd Faced Enemy Fire in 2003 While Reporting in Iraq," *U.S. News,* February 5, 2015, https://www.usnews.com/opinion /articles/2015/02/05/brian-williams-admits-to-lying-about-facing-rpg-fire-in-iraq-pundits-react; Peter Bergen, "Did Brian Williams Embed with SEAL Team 6?," CNN, February 13, 2015, https://www.cnn.com/2015/02/13/opinion/bergen-brian-williams-seal-team-six/index.html; Tom Kludt, "Brian Williams' Reporting on Katrina: What We Know," CNN Money, February 7, 2015, http://money. cnn.com/2015/02/07/media/brian-williams-hurricane-katrina/index.html.

116. Tom Kludt, "Bill O'Reilly Faces New Questions: His JFK Story," CNN Money, February 25, 2015, http://money.cnn.com/2015/02/25/media/bill-oreilly-jfk-george-de-mohrenschildt/index.html; Husna Haq, "Bill O'Reilly Claims False, Admits Fox News Channel: Why That Won't Hurt Him at Fox," *Christian*

Science Monitor, March 2, 2015, https://www.csmonitor.com/USA/Politics
/Decoder/2015/0302/Bill-O-Reilly-claims-false-admits-Fox-News-Why-that-
won-t-hurt-him-at-Fox.

117. Foner, *Give Me Liberty!*

3. Satirical News and Political Party Propaganda Apparatuses

1. "By the Way, All Those People in the Back Are Fake News," CSPAN, November 5, 2018, https://www.c-span.org/video/?c4759166/all-people-back-fake-news.

2. Brian Stelter, "Trump Averages a 'Fake' Insult Every Day. Really. We Counted.," CNN, January 17, 2018, https://money.cnn.com/2018/01/17/media/president-trump-fake-news-count/index.html.

3. Lutz, "Fourteen Years of Doublespeak," 40.

4. David Bauder, "Fox's Hannity Speaks Onstage at Trump Campaign Rally," Associated Press, November 6, 2018, https://www.apnews.com/20f240baf0674 2c79de711d7e8580eb9.

5. Bauder, "Fox's Hannity."

6. Higdon and Huff, *United States of Distraction.*

7. Horne and Adali, "This Just In."

8. Jeffrey Gottfried, Katerina Eva Matsa, and Michael Barthel, "As Jon Stewart Steps Down, 5 Facts about *The Daily Show*," Pew Research Center, FactTank, August 6, 2015, www.pewresearch.org/fact-tank/2015/08/06/5-facts-daily-show/.

9. Staff, "Journalism, Satire or Just Laughs? 'The Daily Show with Jon Stewart,' Examined," Pew Research Center, Journalism and Media, May 8, 2008, www.journalism.org/2008/05/08/journalism-satire-or-just-laughs-the-daily-show-with-jon-stewart-examined/#fn4.

10. Horne and Adali, "This Just In," 388.

11. Lynn Smith, "On the Other Side of the Desk, Stewart Puts the Jokes Aside," *Los Angeles Times,* October 18, 2004, https://www.latimes.com/archives/la-xpm-2004-oct-18-et-stewart18-story.html.

12. Tim Stanley, "Jon Stewart, a Comic Genius Who Became Just as Partisan as His Targets," *Telegraph,* August 7, 2015, https://www.telegraph.co.uk/culture/tvandradio/11788512/Jon-Stewart-a-comic-genius-who-became-just-as-partisan-as-his-targets.html.

13. Higdon and Huff, *United States of Distraction.*

14. *Red Eye* transcript, May 19, 2012, Fox News Channel, saved on Internet Archive, https://archive.org/details/FOXNEWS_20120519_070000_Red_Eye.

15. "Larry King Live: Are Fatty Foods Good for You?," CNN, October 19, 2007, transcripts.cnn.com/TRANSCRIPTS/0710/19/lkl.01.html.

16. "Joy Behar Gets a TV Show All Her Own," CNN, June 11, 2009, https://people.com/tv/joy-behar-gets-a-tv-show-all-her-own/.

17. Michael Fumento, "The Little Black Book of Billionaire Secrets: Toyota Hybrid Horror Hoax," *Forbes,* March 12, 2010, https://www.forbes.com/2010/03/12/toyota-autos-hoax-media-opinions-contributors-michael-fumento.html#5f482b86164b.

18. Amarasingam, *Stewart/Colbert Effect.*

19. Levendusky, "Why," 50.

20. Levendusky, "Why"; Amarasingam, *Stewart/Colbert Effect.*

21. Taibbi, *Hate Inc.*

22. Staff, "Journalism, Satire or Just Laughs?"

23. Caitlin Flanagan, "How Late-Night Comedy Fueled the Rise of Trump," *Atlantic,* May 2017, https://www.theatlantic.com/magazine/archive/2017/05/how-late-night-comedy-alienated-conservatives-made-liberals-smug-and-fueled-the-rise-of-trump/521472/.

24. Jack Mirkinson, "MSNBC Almost Entirely Dominated by Opinion," *Huffington Post,* March 18, 2013, https://www.huffingtonpost.com/2013/03/18/msnbc-opinion-cable-news_n_2900160.html.

25. *Red Eye* transcript, May 19, 2012.

26. Dan Fletcher, "Prickly Personalities: Bill O'Reilly vs. Keith Olbermann," *Time,* March 12, 2009, content.time.com/time/specials/packages/article/0,28804,1884499_1884515_1884471,00.html.

27. Levendusky, "Why"; Stroud, "Polarization"; N. Davis and Dunaway, "Party Polarization."

28. Levendusky, "Why"; Staff, "Indicators of News Media Trust."

29. Elizabeth Grieco, "Newsroom Employment Dropped Nearly a Quarter in Less Than 10 Years, with Greatest Decline at Newspapers." Pew Research Center, FactTank, July 30, 2018, https://www.pewresearch.org/fact-tank/2018/07/30/newsroom-employment-dropped-nearly-a-quarter-in-less-than-10-years-with-greatest-decline-at-newspapers/. Jennifer Saba, "Specifics on Newspapers from 'State of News Media' Report," *Editor and Publisher,* March 16, 2009, www.editorandpublisher.com/PrintArticle/Specifics-on-Newspapers-from-State-of-News-Media-Report, traces the loss of newspaper positions specifically for 2001 through 2008. On the increase in digital-news positions, see Grieco, "Newsroom Employment," and Paul Bedard, "Online Media Jobs Up 209%, Helps Offset Print's 53% Decline," *Washington Examiner,* July 24, 2018, https://www

.washingtonexaminer.com/washington-secrets/online-media-jobs-up-209-helps-offset-prints-53-decline.

30. Lepore, *These Truths*.

31. Antonino D'Ambrosio, "Lee Atwater's Legacy," *Nation*, October 20, 2008, https://www.thenation.com/article/lee-atwaters-legacy/.

32. Tom Turnipseed, "What Lee Atwater Learned and the Lesson for His Protégés," *Washington Post*, April 16, 1991, A19.

33. Robin Toner, "Washington at Work; The New Spokesman for the Republicans: A Tough Player in a Rough Arena," *New York Times*, July 31, 1990, https://www.nytimes.com/1990/07/31/us/washington-work-new-spokesman-for-republicans-tough-player-rough-arena.html; Evan Thomas, "The Slickest Shop in Town," *Time*, March 3, 1986, content.time.com/time/magazine/article/0,9171,960803,00.html.

34. Stefan Forbes, dir., *Boogie Man: The Lee Atwater Story*, documentary, Interpositive Media, 2008.

35. Franklin Foer, "The Quiet American Paul Manafort Made a Career Out of Stealthily Reinventing the World's Nastiest Tyrants as Noble Defenders of Freedom," *Slate*, April 28, 2016, www.slate.com/articles/news_and_politics/politics/2016/04/paul_manafort_isn_t_a_gop_retread_he_s_made_a_career_of_reinventing_tyrants.html.

36. Roger Simon, "How a Murderer and Rapist Became the Bush Campaign's Most Valuable Player," *Baltimore Sun*, November 11, 1990, http://articles.baltimoresun.com/1990-11-11/features/1990315149_1_willie-horton-fournier-michael-dukakis.

37. Germond and Witcover, *Whose Broad Stripes*.

38. Simon, "How a Murderer."

39. Dan Rodricks, "Trying to Find the Real Willie Horton," *Baltimore Sun*, August 12, 1993, http://articles.baltimoresun.com/1993-08-12/news/1993224224_1_willie-horton-willie-horton-jeffrey-elliot.

40. Erin Blakemore, "How the Willie Horton Ad Played on Racism and Fear," History.com, November 2, 2018, https://www.history.com/news/george-bush-willie-horton-racist-ad.

41. Reinarman and Levine, "Crack Attack."

42. James C. Moore, "Don't Expect the Truth from Karl Rove," *Los Angeles Times*, March 23, 2007, https://www.latimes.com/la-oe-moore23mar23-story.html.

43. Richard Gooding, "The Trashing of John McCain," *Vanity Fair*, September 24, 2008. https://www.vanityfair.com/news/2004/11/mccain200411; Ann Banks, "Dirty Tricks, South Carolina and John McCain," *Nation*, January 28, 2008, https://www.thenation.com/article/dirty-tricks-south-carolina-and-john-mccain/.

44. Minnite, *Myth of Voter Fraud;* Al Kamen, "Miami 'Riot' Squad: Where Are They Now?," *Washington Post,* January 24, 2005, www.washingtonpost.com/wp-dyn/articles/A31074-2005Jan23.html.

45. McConnell, "Two-and-a-Half Cheers."

46. Patrick Matrisciana, dir., *The Clinton Chronicles: An Investigation into the Alleged Criminal Activities of Bill Clinton,* 1994; Carrie Johnson, "Clinton Scandals: A Guide from Whitewater to the Clinton Foundation," NPR, June 21, 2016, https://www.npr.org/2016/06/12/481718785/clinton-scandals-a-guide-from-whitewater-to-the-clinton-foundation.

47. "Changing Attitudes on Gay Marriage," Pew Research Center, June 26, 2017, www.pewforum.org/fact-sheet/changing-attitudes-on-gay-marriage/; Victoria A. Brownworth, "Hillary Clinton Is a Lesbian," *Curve* magazine, May 26, 2012, www.curvemag.com/News/Hillary-Clinton-Is-A-Lesbian-1230/; Wendy Stokes, "A Brief History of Hillary Clinton Lesbian Rumors," *Frisky,* September 4, 2018, https://thefrisky.com/a-brief-history-of-hillary-clinton-lesbian-rumors/; Jaime Fuller, "Matt Drudge and Hillary Clinton: A History," *Washington Post,* February 12, 2014, https://www.washingtonpost.com/news/the-fix/wp/2014/02/12/matt-drudge-and-hillary-clinton-a-history/?utm_term=.d3e5c48b4239; Joel Keller, "Jenny McCarthy Implies Hillary Clinton Is a Lesbian during 'The View,'" *Wrap,* July 22, 2014, https://www.thewrap.com/jenny-mccarthy-implies-that-hillary-clinton-has-girlfriends-on-the-view/.

48. Hunter Schwarz, "Did you Hear the One about the Muslim, Socialist, Kenyan President? The Joke Obama Can't Stop Telling," *Washington Post,* April 26, 2015, https://www.washingtonpost.com/news/the-fix/wp/2015/04/26/obama-jokes-about-being-a-socialist-kenya-born-muslim-at-every-whcd/?noredirect=on&utm_term=.f71d93ef793b; Esposito, "White Fear."

49. Halperin and Heilemann, *Double Down.*

50. Kellner, *Persian Gulf TV War.*

51. Goodwin, *Bully Pulpit.*

52. Goodwin, *Bully Pulpit.*

53. Goodwin, *Bully Pulpit.*

54. Youssef Ibrahim, "Iraq Threatens Emirates and Kuwait on Oil Glut," *New York Times,* July 18, 1990, https://www.nytimes.com/1990/07/18/business/iraq-threatens-emirates-and-kuwait-on-oil-glut.html; Kellner, *Persian Gulf TV War.*

55. Tom Regan, "When Contemplating War, Beware of Babies in Incubators," *Christian Science Monitor,* September 6, 2002, https://www.csmonitor.com/2002/0906/p25s02-cogn.html.

56. Phillips, *Giants.*

57. Sherman, *Loudest Voice.*

58. Steve Rendall, "Fox's Slanted Sources," FAIR, July 1, 2001, https://fair.org /extra/foxs-slanted-sources/; Tim Dickinson, "Political Hitman Lee Atwater on 'Soul Brother' Roger Ailes," *Rolling Stone,* June 1, 2011, https://www.rollingstone .com/politics/politics-news/political-hitman-lee-atwater-on-soul-brother-roger-ailes-235688/; William Shawcross "Rupert Murdoch," *Time,* November 3, 1999; Gaby Hinsliff, "The PM, the Mogul and the Secret Agenda," *Observer,* July 23, 2006.

59. US Government Accounting Office, "GAO Decision—Matter of: Department of Health and Human Services, Centers for Medicare & Medicaid Services—Video News Releases," December 7, 2006, File: B-302710, US House of Representatives. May 19, 2004; US Government Accounting Office, "GAO Decision B-304228, "Department of Education—No Child Left Behind Act Video News Release and Media Analysis," September 30, 2005; Jon Schwartz, "Donald Trump Makes the New York Times Great Again!," *Intercept,* November 23, 2016, https://theintercept.com/2016/11/23/donald-trump-makes-the-new-york-times-great-again/; Ken Silverstein, "The CIA's Mop-Up Man: L.A. Times Reporter Cleared Stories with Agency before Publication," *Intercept,* September. 4, 2014, https://theintercept.com/2014/09/04/former-l-times-reporter-cleared-stories-cia-publication/; David Margolick and Richard Gooding, "Wrong Man, Wrong Place," *Vanity Fair,* April 29, 2008, https://www.vanityfair.com/style/2005 /06/gannongate200506; David Barstow and Robin Stein, "The Message Machine: How the Government Makes News; Under Bush, a New Age of Prepackaged News," New York Times. March 13, 2005, http://select.nytimes.com/gst /abstract.html?res=F50914FC3E580C708DDDAA0894DD404482.

60. Steve Young, "Bill O'Reilly Mocks Homeless Veterans, Who John Edwards Fights For, as Nonexistent," *Huffington Post,* January 16, 2008, https://www .huffingtonpost.com/steve-young/bill-oreilly-mocks-homele_b_81798.html.

61. Mitchell T. Bard, "Propaganda, Persuasion, or Journalism? Fox News' Prime-Time Coverage of Health-Care Reform in 2009 and 2014," *Electronic News* 11, no. 2 (2017): 100–118; Staff, "Echoing Palin, Kilmeade Said Health Care Bill Mandates Elderly Go 'in Front of Death Panel,'" *Media Matters,* August 10, 2009, https://www.mediamatters.org/video/2009/08/10/echoing-palin-kilmeade-said-health-care-bill-ma/153089; D. Skinner, "'Keep Your Government Hands Off.'"

62. James L. Krahenbuhl, "Truth, Fiction and Lou Dobbs," *New York Times,* May 30, 2007, https://www.nytimes.com/2007/05/30/business/30leonhardt. html; John Kruzel, "No Evidence 'Many' Illegal Immigrants Voted in Midterm Elections, as Lou Dobbs Said," PolitiFact, November 16, 2018, https://www .politifact.com/punditfact/statements/2018/nov/16/lou-dobbs/no-evidence-

many-illegal-immigrants-voted-midterm-/; Jon Greenberg, "Ann Coulter Wrongly Claims That U.S. 'Has Already Taken in One-Fourth of Mexico's Entire Population,'" PolitiFact, June 2, 2015, https://www.politifact.com/punditfact /statements/2015/jun/02/ann-coulter/no-us-has-not-taken-14-mexicos-popula-tion/; Adam B. Lerner, "Ann Coulter: Immigrants Are Worse Than ISIL," *Politico*, May 26, 2015, https://www.politico.com/story/2015/05/ann-coulter-immigrants-are-worse-than-isil-118297; Coulter, *Adios, America!*; Wiley, "Brief History."

63. Cardaras, *Fear, Power, and Politics.*

64. Cardaras, *Fear, Power, and Politics*; Andrew Kirell, "If Bill Maher Made the Same Controversial 9/11 Comments Today, Would He Have Lost His Show?" *Medialite*, October 9, 2012, http://www.mediaite.com/tv/if-bill-maher-made-the-same-controversial-911-comments-today-would-he-have-lost-his-show/; Press, *Toxic Talk*; Dennis J. Bernstein, "Silencing Donahue and Anti-war Voices," *Consortium News*, January 15, 2012, https://consortiumnews.com/2012/01/15 /silencing-donahue-and-anti-war-voices/.

65. Judith Miller, "Illicit Arms Kept till Eve of War, an Iraqi Scientist Is Said to Assert," *New York Times*, July 31, 2016, https://www.nytimes.com/2003/04/21 /world/aftereffects-prohibited-weapons-illicit-arms-kept-till-eve-war-iraqi-scientist.html: Editors, "The Times and Iraq: A Sample of the Coverage," *New York Times*, https://archive.nytimes.com/www.nytimes.com/ref/international /middleeast/20040526CRITIQUE.html?_r=1; Russ Baker, 'Scoops' and Truth at the Times: What Happens When Pentagon Objectives and Journalists' Needs Co-incide," *Nation*, June 5, 2003, https://www.thenation.com/article/scoops-and-truth-times/; Ed Pilkington, Helen Pidd, and Martin Chulov, "Colin Powell Demands Answers over Curveball's WMD Lies," *Guardian*, February 16, 2011, https://www.theguardian.com/world/2011/feb/16/colin-powell-cia-curveball.

66. Staff, "'Scooter' Libby Indicted in CIA Leak Case, Resigns," ABC News, October 28, 2005, https://abcnews.go.com/Politics/CIALeak/story?id=1259169.

67. Norman Solomon, "The Military-Industrial-Media Complex: Why War Is Covered from the Warriors' Perspective," FAIR, August 2005, https://fair.org /extra/the-military-industrial-media-complex/.

68. Frank Newport, "Seventy-Two Percent of Americans Support War against Iraq; Bush Approval Up 13 Points to 71%," Gallup, March 24, 2003, https://news. gallup.com/poll/8038/seventytwo-percent-americans-support-war-against-iraq. aspx; Kerry Sheridan, "Iraq Death Toll Reaches 500,000 since Start of U.S.-Led Invasion," *Huffington Post*, October 15, 2013, https://www.huffingtonpost .com/2013/10/15/iraq-death-toll_n_4102855.html; Staff, "Iraq Conflict Has Killed a Million Iraqis: Survey," Reuters, January 30, 2008, https://www.reuters

.com/article/us-iraq-deaths-survey/iraq-conflict-has-killed-a-million-iraqis-survey-idUSL3048857920080130.

69. Rob Tornoe, "Here's What Fake Russian Facebook Posts during the Election Looked Like," *Philadelphia Inquirer,* October 6, 2017, www.philly.com/philly/news/politics/presidential/facebook-russia-fake-posts-trump-election-clinton-20171006.html.

70. "20 Forgotten Bush Scandals," *Daily Beast,* January 6, 2009, https://www.thedailybeast.com/20-forgotten-bush-scandals; Mark Mazzetti and Borzou Daragahi, "U.S. Military Covertly Pays to Run Stories in Iraqi Press," *Los Angeles Times,* November 30, 2005, https://www.latimes.com/archives/la-xpm-2005-nov-30-fg-infowar30-story.html.

71. Hamm, *New Blue Media;* Brian Stelter, "Air America to Cease Broadcasting Immediately," *New York Times,* January 21, 2010, https://mediadecoder.blogs.nytimes.com/2010/01/21/air-america-to-cease-broadcasting-immediately/.

72. Howard Kurtz, "MSNBC, Leaning Left And Getting Flak from Both Sides," *Washington Post,* May 28, 2008, https://www.washingtonpost.com/wp-dyn/content/article/2008/05/27/AR2008052703047_pf.html.

73. Pew Research Center, "The Color of News | Project for Excellence in Journalism (PEJ)," Journalism and Media, October 29, 2008, www.journalism.org/2008/10/29/the-color-of-news/; Ben Norton, "MSNBC Ignores Catastrophic US-Backed War in Yemen; Finds Russia 5000% More Newsworthy," FAIR, January 8, 2018, https://fair.org/home/msnbc-yemen-russia-coverage-2017; Eoin Higgins, "Russia or Corporate Tax Cuts: Which Would Comcast Rather MSNBC Cover?," FAIR, December 13, 2017, https://fair.org/home/russia-or-corporate-tax-cuts-which-would-comcast-rather-msnbc-cover/; Jason Schwartz, "MSNBC's Surging Ratings Fuel Democratic Optimism," MSNBC, April 11, 2018, https://www.politico.com/story/2018/04/11/msnbc-democrats-ratings-cnn-fox-513388; Jacques Steinberg, "Cable Channel Nods to Ratings and Leans Left," *New York Times,* November 6, 2007, https://www.nytimes.com/2007/11/06/business/media/06msnb.html?mtrref=www.google.com&gwh=CCD517C50A9C944B6349F47CD3889B20&gwt=pay&assetType=REGIWALL.

74. Henry J. Gomez, "Rachel Maddow Says That Ohio Budget Includes Requirement for Transvaginal Ultrasound," PolitiFact, July 9, 2013, https://www.politifact.com/ohio/statements/2013/jul/09/rachel-maddow/rachel-maddow-says-ohio-budget-includes-requiremen/.

75. "Did Sanders Supporters Throw Chairs at Nevada Democratic Convention?," Snopes, https://www.snopes.com/fact-check/did-sanders-supporters-throw-chairs-at-nevada-democratic-convention/; "Former Democratic Chief:

Clinton 'Took Control' of Party," BBC, November 3, 2017, https://www.bbc.com /news/world-us-canada-41850797; Ezra Klein, "Was the Democratic Primary Rigged?," *Vox*, November 14, 2017, https://www.vox.com/policy-and-politics /2017/11/14/16640082/donna-brazile-warren-bernie-sanders-democratic-primary-rigged; Hadas Gold, "CNN's Jeff Zucker Defends Paying Political Surrogates at Company Town Hall," *Politico*, November 2, 2016, https://www .politico.com/blogs/on-media/2016/11/cnns-zucker-continues-to-defend-paying-political-surrogates-230639; Dara Linddara, "Bernie Bros, Explained," *Vox*, February 5, 2016, https://www.vox.com/2016/2/4/10918710/berniebro-bernie-bro.

76. William Saletan, "Stop Talking about "Republican Talking Points," *Slate*, August 1, 2019, https://slate.com/news-and-politics/2019/08/democratic-debate-warren-sanders-republican-talking-points-stop.html.

77. Higdon and Huff, *United States of Distraction*; Taibbi, *Hate Inc.*

78. William Cummings, "Fox News Denounces 'Unfortunate' Sean Hannity Appearance at Donald Trump Rally," *USA Today*, November 6, 2018, https:// www.usatoday.com/story/news/politics/elections/2018/11/06/election-day-2018-sean-hannity-appearance-trump-rally-denounced/1904090002/.

79. Mike Snider, "Fox News' Sean Hannity Absent from Election Coverage after Appearing at Rally with Trump," *USA Today*, November 7, 2018, https:// www.usatoday.com/story/money/nation-now/2018/11/07/sean-hannity-fox-news-absent-election-night-coverage/1917432002/.

80. Media Matters Staff, "Sean Hannity Suggests Florida Recount Is an Illegal Democratic Plot to Steal the Election," Media Matters, November 8, 2018, https://www.mediamatters.org/video/2018/11/08/sean-hannity-suggests-florida-recount-illegal-democratic-plot-steal-election/222037.

4. The Roots of State-Sponsored Propaganda

1. "Speech: Donald Trump in Cleveland, OH," October 22, 2016, https:// factba.se/transcript/donald-trump-speech-cleveland-oh-october-22-2016.

2. Kaitlin Kimont, "What Does 'Lügenpresse' Mean? The Troubling Phrase Has Been Recently Revived," Romper, October 24, 2016, https://www.romper .com/p/what-does-lugenpresse-mean-the-troubling-phrase-has-been-recently-revived-21169.

3. Sasha Abram, "As Trump Consolidates His Power, the History of 1930s Germany Repeats Itself," *Sacramento Bee*, March 18, 2018, https://www.sacbee .com/opinion/california-forum/article205750864.html.

4. Kimont, "What Does 'Lügenpresse' Mean?"

5. Guilday, "Sacred Congregation," 478–94.

6. Benkler, Faris, and Roberts, *Network Propaganda*, 29.

7. Lippmann, *Public Opinion*, 248.

8. Roskos-Ewoldsen, Roskos-Ewoldsen, and Dillman Carpentier, "Media Priming," 97–120.

9. Wu, *Attention Merchants*, 38.

10. Wu, *Attention Merchants*.

11. Terraine, *Mons*.

12. Batson et al., "Anger at Unfairness," 1272.

13. Simmonds, *Britain and World War One*.

14. Wu, *Attention Merchants*, 38.

15. Geissler, *God and Sea Power*; Tucker, *Woodrow Wilson*; P. Roberts, "Paul D. Cravath."

16. Brune, *Chronological History*, 365; Wu, *Attention Merchants*; Creel, *How We Advertised America*; Newton-Matza, *Espionage and Sedition Acts*.

17. Wu, *Attention Merchants*; T. Fleming, *Illusion of Victory*.

18. T. Fleming, *Illusion of Victory*.

19. Wu, *Attention Merchants*; Bailey, *Essays Diplomatic and Undiplomatic*.

20. Paddock, *Call to Arms*; Bailey, *Essays Diplomatic and Undiplomatic*; "Lusitania Was Unarmed," *New York Times*, May 10, 1915.

21. *Tucson Daily Citizen*, December 13, 1918, https://newspaperarchive.com /tucson-citizen-dec-13-1918-p-1/.

22. Trommler, "Lusitania Effect."

23. Trommler, "Lusitania Effect."

24. Quinn, *Conning of America*; *Lexington Progress* (Lexington, TN), October 11, 1918, Chronicling America: Historic American Newspapers, Library of Congress, http://chroniclingamerica.loc.gov/lccn/sn89058168/1918-10-11/ed-1 /seq-2/; Staff, "The Corpse Factory and the Birth of Fake News," BBC, February 17, 2017, https://www.bbc.com/news/entertainment-arts-38995205.

25. Zembylas, "Politics of Shame."

26. Wu, *Attention Merchants*; T. Fleming, *Illusion of Victory*.

27. R. Roberts, "Vice of Pride."

28. Thaler, "Was He or Wasn't He?"

29. Foner, *Give Me Liberty!*

30. Ponder, *Managing the Press*.

31. Christopher B. Daly, "How Woodrow Wilson's Propaganda Machine Changed American Journalism," *Smithsonian*, April 28, 2017, https://www

.smithsonianmag.com/history/how-woodrow-wilsons-propaganda-machine-changed-american-journalism-180963082/.

32. Vaughn, *Holding Fast*, 397.

33. Daly, "How Woodrow Wilson's Propaganda Machine."

34. Hagedorn, *Savage Peace*, 29.

35. *Clearwater Republican* (Orofino, ID), July 6, 1917, Chronicling America: Historic American Newspapers, Library of Congress, http://chroniclingamerica.loc.gov/lccn/sn86091128/1917-07-06/ed-1/seq-4/.

36. *New-York Tribune*, February 28, 1915, Chronicling America: Historic American Newspapers, Library of Congress, http://chroniclingamerica.loc.gov/lccn/sn83030214/1915-02-28/ed-1/seq-8/.

37. *Clinch Valley News* (Jeffersonville, VA), May 18, 1917, Chronicling America: Historic American Newspapers, Library of Congress, http://chroniclingamerica.loc.gov/lccn/sn85034357/1917-05-18/ed-1/seq-2/.

38. Wever and Van Bergen, "Death"; Patterson, *Search for Negotiated Peace.*

39. Wu, *Attention Merchants*, 50.

40. Hitler, *Mein Kampf*, 181.

41. "Research Starters: Worldwide Deaths in World War II," National World War II Museum, https://www.nationalww2museum.org/students-teachers/student-resources/research-starters/research-starters-worldwide-deaths-world-war; "World War 2 Statistics," Second World War History, https://www.secondworldwarhistory.com/world-war-2-statistics.php.

42. Reuth, *Goebbels.*

43. Thacker, *Joseph Goebbels.*

44. Wu, *Attention Merchants.*

45. "The Press in the Third Reich," United States Holocaust Memorial Museum, https://www.ushmm.org/wlc/en/article.php?ModuleId=10007655; Berkhoff, *Harvest of Despair.*

46. Anthony Smith, "How Hitler's Attacks on the German Press Helped One of History's Greatest Despots Rise to Power," *Mic,* January 11, 2018, https://mic.com/articles/187354/how-hitlers-attacks-on-the-german-press-helped-one-of-historys-greatest-despots-rise-to-power#.xCbz2VVox.

47. Wolin, *Democracy Incorporated.*

48. Paxton, *Anatomy of Fascism.*

49. "Nazi Persecution of the Disabled: Murder of the 'Unfit,'" United States Holocaust Memorial Museum, https://www.ushmm.org/information/exhibitions/online-exhibitions/special-focus/nazi-persecution-of-the-disabled; Burleigh, *Third Reich.*

50. Hartman, "Psychoanalytic View."

51. Paxton, *Anatomy of Fascism*.

52. Timothy Snyder, "Hitler vs. Stalin: Who Was Worse?," *New York Review of Books*, January 27, 2011, https://www.nybooks.com/daily/2011/01/27/hitler-vs-stalin-who-was-worse/.

53. Maddock et al., "Characterizing Online Rumoring Behavior."

54. Overy, 1939; Lightbody, *Second World War*.

55. Paxton, *Anatomy of Fascism*.

56. Lightbody, *Second World War*.

57. Bellamy, *Absolute War*.

58. "Das ist Heldentum!," *Illustrierter Beobachter*, January 21, 1943, 2–3, research.calvin.edu/german-propaganda-archive/illbeo01.htm; Joseph Goebbels, "Missed Opportunities," in *Die Zeit ohne Beispiel* (Munich: Zentralverlag der NSDAP, 1941), research.calvin.edu/german-propaganda-archive/goeb17.htm; Aufklärungs- und Redner-Informationsmaterial der Reichspropagandaleitung der NSDAP, *Lieferung* 20, 21, 23, 24 (August, September, October, November, December 1935), 1–25 (Juden Allgemeines), research.calvin.edu/german-propaganda-archive/rim3.htm.

59. Joseph Goebbels, "Die Weltkrise," *Das Reich*, December 17, 1944, research.calvin.edu/german-propaganda-archive/goeb57.htm; "Das ist Heldentum!"; Goebbels, "Missed Opportunities"; Aufklärungs- und Redner-Informationsmaterial der Reichspropagandaleitung der NSDAP, *Lieferung* 20, 21, 23, 24.

60. Goebbels, "Weltkrise."

61. Doherty, *Nazi Wireless Propaganda*.

62. Marc Wort, "The Fake British Radio Show That Helped Defeat the Nazis," *Smithsonian*, February 28, 2017, https://www.smithsonianmag.com/history/fake-british-radio-show-helped-defeat-nazis-180962320/.

63. Lucas, *Axis Sally*.

64. Alan Taylor, "American Nazis in the 1930s: The German American Bund," *Atlantic*, June 5, 2017, https://www.theatlantic.com/photo/2017/06/american-nazis-in-the-1930sthe-german-american-bund/529185/.

65. Gordon F. Sander, "When Nazis Filled Madison Square Garden in 1939," *Politico*, August 23, 2017, https://www.politico.com/magazine/story/2017/08/23/nazi-german-american-bund-rally-madison-square-garden-215522.

66. John Broich, "The Press Has Fallen for Fascists Before," *Guardian*, December 12, 2016, https://www.theguardian.com/commentisfree/2016/dec/12/media-coverage-facists-leaders-mussolini-hitler.

67. Hunt, Martin, and Rosenwein, *Making of the West.*

68. Rhodes, *Propaganda.*

69. Diggins, *Mussolini and Fascism.*

70. Broich, "Press Has Fallen."

71. Jordan, *America's Mussolini.*

72. McClain, *Japan;* Jansen, *Making of Modern Japan.*

73. Howe, *Hunt for Tokyo Rose.*

74. Masaharu, "'Negro Propaganda Operations.'"

75. Dizard, *Inventing Public Diplomacy;* Phillip W. Stewart, "A Reel Story of World War II: the United News Collection of Newsreels Documents the Battlefield and the Home Front," *Prologue Magazine* 47, no. 3 (Fall 2015), https://www.archives.gov/publications/prologue/2015/fall/united-newsreels.html.

76. Sweeney, *Secrets of Victory.*

77. "Japanese Relocation during World War II," National Archives, https://www.archives.gov/education/lessons/japanese-relocation.

78. Geoffrey Ross, "Newspapers of the New Deal Concentration Camps," *University of Illinois Urbana-Champaign,* March 8, 2017, https://www.library.illinois.edu/hpnl/blog/internment-camp-newspapers/.

79. Koppes and Black, "Blacks, Loyalty."

80. Applebaum, *Iron Curtain.*

81. Applebaum, *Iron Curtain.*

82. P. O'Neil, *Post-communism and the Media;* Major and Mitter, "East Is East."

83. Crampton, *Eastern Europe.*

84. Michael Specter, "Russia's Purveyor of 'Truth,' Pravda, Dies after 84 Years," *New York Times,* July 31, 1996, accessed October 19, 2015, https://www.nytimes.com/1996/07/31/world/russia-s-purveyor-of-truth-pravda-dies-after-84-years.html.

85. Applebaum, *Iron Curtain.*

86. United States Information Agency, "Crude, Anti-American Disinformation: 'Geheim' and 'Top Secret' Magazines: Purveyors of Crude, Defamatory Disinformation," United States Government Report (Washington, DC, 1992), http://intellit.muskingum.edu/russia_folder/pcw_era/sect_09b.htm.

87. Ivanova et al., *Labor Camp Socialism.*

88. Service, *History of Modern Russia,* 186.

89. Earley, *Comrade J,* 167–77; Goulden, "Disinformation (dezinformatsiya)"; Waller, *Strategic Influence,* 159–61.

90. Ross, Essien, and Torres, "Conspiracy Beliefs."

91. Suri, *Henry Kissinger.*

92. Bernhard, *US Television News;* Dizard, *Inventing Public Diplomacy.*

93. Bernhard, *US Television News.*

94. Bernhard, *US Television News;* Dizard, *Inventing Public Diplomacy;* Carl Bernstein, "The CIA and the Media: How America's Most Powerful News Media Worked Hand in Glove with the Central Intelligence Agency and Why the Church Committee Covered It Up," *Rolling Stone,* October 20, 1977, www.carlbernstein.com/magazine_cia_and_media.php.

95. Myrna Oliver, "Joseph Alsop, Columnist, Dead at 78: Powerful Political Writer Known for His Interpretation of News," *Los Angeles Times,* August 29, 1989, articles.latimes.com/1989-08-29/news/mn-1197_1_joseph-alsop;   Bernstein, "CIA and the Media."

96. Bernstein, "CIA and the Media"; Hadley, *Rising Clamor.*

97. Bernstein, "CIA and the Media."

98. Foer, *World without Mind;* Jeffrey St. Clair and Alexander Cockburn, "The CIA and the Press: When the Washington Post Ran the CIA's Propaganda Network," *CounterPunch,* November 30, 2016, https://www.counterpunch.org/2016/11/30/the-cia-and-the-press-when-the-washington-post-ran-the-cias-propaganda-network/.

99. A. Brinkley, *Publisher;* D. Brinkley, *Cronkite.*

100. Kinzer, *Brothers;* Bernstein, "CIA and the Media."

101. Ian Shapira, "Long-Ago Wiretap Inspires a Battle with the CIA for More Information," *Washington Post,* March 2, 2013, https://www.washingtonpost.com/local/long-ago-wiretap-inspires-a-battle-with-the-cia-for-more-information/2013/03/02/8ebaa924-77b0-11e2-aa12-e6cf1d31106b_story.html.

102. Kinzer, *Brothers;* Kinzer, *Overthrow.*

103. James Risen, "Secrets of History: The C.I.A. in Iran—a Special Report; How a Plot Convulsed Iran in '53 (and in '79)," *New York Times,* April 16, 2000, https://www.nytimes.com/2000/04/16/world/secrets-history-cia-iran-special-report-plot-convulsed-iran-53-79.html.

104. Joseph and Grandin, *Century of Revolution;* Kornbluh, *Pinochet File;* Schlesinger, Kinzer, and Coatsworth, *Bitter Fruit;* Kinzer, *All the Shah's Men.*

105. Risen, "Secrets of History."

106. Talbot, *Devil's Chessboard.*

107. Kornbluh, *Pinochet File.*

108. T. Davis, "Operation Northwoods."

109. Kornbluh, *Pinochet File;* Talbot, *Devil's Chessboard;* Kinzer, *Brothers;* Schlesinger, Kinzer, and Coatsworth, *Bitter Fruit;* Kinzer, *All the Shah's Men.*

110. Dorman and Farhang, *U.S. Press and Iran.*

111. Talbot, *Devil's Chessboard.*

112. Gleijeses, *Shattered Hope.*

113. Cowie, *Stayin' Alive;* Schulman, *Seventies;* Stein, *Pivotal Decade.*

114. Bernstein, "CIA and the Media."

115. Talbot, *Devil's Chessboard.*

116. John Hudson, "U.S. Repeals Propaganda Ban, Spreads Government-Made News to Americans," *Foreign Policy,* July 14, 2013, https://foreignpolicy.com/2013/07/14/U-S-REPEALS-PROPAGANDA-BAN-SPREADS-GOVERN-MENT-MADE-NEWS-TO-AMERICANS/.

117. Staff, "How 9/11 Changed How Americans View the World," National Public Radio, September 10, 2012, https://www.npr.org/2012/09/10/160886676/how-9-11-changed-how-america-sees-the-world.

118. Michael Weiss and Hassan Hassan, "Everything We Knew about This ISIS Mastermind Was Wrong," *Daily Beast,* April 15, 2016, https://www.thedailybeast.com/everything-we-knew-about-this-isis-mastermind-was-wrong.

119. Frank Newport, "Seventy-Two Percent of Americans Support War against Iraq; Bush Approval Up 13 points to 71%," Gallup, March 24, 2003, https://news.gallup.com/poll/8038/seventytwo-percent-americans-support-war-against-iraq.aspx; Kerry Sheridan, "Iraq Death Toll Reaches 500,000 since Start of U.S.-Led Invasion," *Huffington Post,* October 15, 2013, https://www.huffingtonpost.com/2013/10/15/iraq-death-toll_n_4102855.html; Staff, "Iraq Conflict Has Killed a Million Iraqis: Survey," Reuters, January 30, 2008, https://www.reuters.com/article/us-iraq-deaths-survey/iraq-conflict-has-killed-a-million-iraqis-survey-idUSL3048857920080130.

120. David Zucchino, "Army Stage-Managed Fall of Hussein Statue," *Los Angeles Times,* July 3, 2004, https://web.archive.org/web/20041209035238/http://www.commondreams.org/headlines04/0703-02.htm.

121. John Kampfner, "The Truth about Jessica," *Guardian,* May 15, 2003, https://www.theguardian.com/world/2003/may/15/iraq.usa2.

122. Anna Mulrine, Shoshana Johnson, and Patrick Miller, "Former POW Jessica Lynch Recalls Her Captivity in Iraq," *U.S. News,* March 18, 2008, https://www.usnews.com/news/iraq/articles/2008/03/18/jessica-lynch-recalls-her-captivity-in-iraq.

123. Josh White, "Army Withheld Details about Tillman's Death," *Washington Post*, May 4, 2005, www.washingtonpost.com/wp-dyn/content/article/2005/05/03/AR2005050301502.html.

124. "Soldier: Army Ordered Me Not to Tell Truth about Tillman," CNN, April 25, 2007, www.cnn.com/2007/POLITICS/04/24/tillman.hearing/.

125. Frank James, "Pat Tillman Deserved Silver Medal: McChrystal," NPR, June 2, 2009, https://www.npr.org/sections/thetwo-way/2009/06/pat_tillman_deserved_silver_me.html.

126. David Barstow, "Message Machine: Behind Analysts, the Pentagon's Hidden Hand," April 20, 2008, *New York Times*, https://www.nytimes.com/2008/04/20/us/20generals.html?.

127. Avi Zenilman and Michael Calderone, "'Deafening' Silence on Analyst Story," *Politico*, May 8, 2008, https://www.politico.com/story/2008/05/deafening-silence-on-analyst-story-010204.

128. US House of Representatives Bill 5736, May 10, 2012, https://www.gpo.gov/fdsys/pkg/BILLS-112hr5736ih/pdf/BILLS-112hr5736ih.pdf.

129. Michael Hastings, "Congressmen Seek to Lift Propaganda Ban," Buzzfeed News, May 18, 2012, https://www.buzzfeednews.com/article/mhastings/congressmen-seek-to-lift-propaganda-ban.

130. Andrew Marantz, "Scholar of Conspiracy Theories Became the Subject of a Right-Wing Conspiracy Theory," *New Yorker*, December 27, 2017, https://www.newyorker.com/culture/persons-of-interest/how-a-liberal-scholar-of-conspiracy-theories-became-the-subject-of-a-right-wing-conspiracy-theory.

131. Ken Silverstein, "The CIA's Mop-Up Man: L.A. Times Reporter Cleared Stories with Agency before Publication," *Intercept*, September 4, 2014, https://theintercept.com/2014/09/04/former-l-times-reporter-cleared-stories-cia-publication/.

132. *Glenn Greenwald, "The Inspector General's Report on* 2016 FBI Spying Reveals a Scandal of Historic Magnitude: Not Only for the FBI but Also the U.S. Media," December 12, 2019, !!*Intercept*, https://theintercept.com/2019/12/12/the-inspector-generals-report-on-2016-fb-i-spying-reveals-a-scandal-of-historic-magnitude-not-only-for-the-fbi-but-also-the-u-s-media/?comments=1; John Solomon, "FBI's Steele Story Falls Apart: False Intel and Media Contacts Were Flagged before FISA," *Hill*, May 9, 2019, https://thehill.com/opinion/whitehouse/442944-fbis-steele-story-falls-apart-false-intel-and-media-contacts-were-flagged.

133. Julia MacFarlane, "Angela Merkel and Emmanuel Macron Show Liberal Unity on Armistice Day as Alt-Right Movements Rise across Europe," ABC News,

November 11, 2018, https://abcnews.go.com/International/angela-merkel-emmanuel-macron-show-liberal-unity-armistice/story?id=59122446.

5. Fake News and the Internet Economy

1. Sapna Maheshwari, "How Fake News Goes Viral: A Case Study," *New York Times,* November 20, 2016, https://www.nytimes.com/2016/11/20/business/media/how-fake-news-spreads.html.

2. Maheshwari, "How Fake News Goes Viral."

3. Maheshwari, "How Fake News Goes Viral."

4. Maheshwari, "How Fake News Goes Viral."

5. Maheshwari, "How Fake News Goes Viral."

6. Maheshwari, "How Fake News Goes Viral."

7. Oliver Burkeman, "Forty Years of the Internet," *Guardian,* October 23, 2009, https://www.theguardian.com/technology/2009/oct/23/internet-40-history-arpanet.

8. Dumas, *Diving into the Bitstream,* 18.

9. "The New Clash between Free Speech and Privacy," NPR, March 21, 2018, https://www.npr.org/sections/alltechconsidered/2018/03/21/591622450/section-230-a-key-legal-shield-for-facebook-google-is-about-to-change.

10. "Bill Gates," interview, *Charlie Rose,* November 25, 1996, PBS, https://charlierose.com/videos/12426.

11. Tanya Basu, "New Google Parent Company Drops 'Don't Be Evil' Motto," *Time,* October 4, 2015, time.com/4060575/alphabet-google-dont-be-evil/.

12. Zuboff, *Age of Surveillance Capitalism.*

13. Xing Zhang, Zhenglei Yi, Zhi Yan, Geyong Min, Wenbo Wang, Ahmed Elmokashfi, Sabita Maharjan, and Yan Zhang, "Social Computing for Mobile Big Data," *Computer* magazine, September 2016, 86–90.

14. Zuboff, *Age of Surveillance Capitalism.*

15. Buenstorf and Fornahl, "B2C—Bubble to Cluster."

16. Catherine Tymkiw, "Bleak Friday on Wall Street," CNN, April 14, 2000, https://money.cnn.com/2000/04/14/markets/markets_newyork/.

17. Richard Richtmyer, "Pets.com at Its Tail End," CNN, November 7, 2000, https://money.cnn.com/2000/11/07/technology/pets/.

18. Zuboff, *Age of Surveillance Capitalism.*

19. Levine, *Surveillance Valley.*

20. Potolsky, *National Security Sublime.*

21. Zuboff, *Age of Surveillance Capitalism.*

22. Zuboff, *Age of Surveillance Capitalism*, ix.

23. Zuboff, *Age of Surveillance Capitalism*.

24. Wu, *Attention Merchants*.

25. Zuboff, *Age of Surveillance Capitalism*.

26. Aaron Mak, "The Industry: How Facebook Made Those Eerie 'People You May Know' Suggestions," *Slate*, December 19, 2018, https://slate.com/technology/2018/12/facebook-friend-suggestions-creepy-people-you-may-know-feature.html?_twitter_impression=true.

27. All of the above statistics are in Bernard Marr, "How Much Data Do We Create Every Day? The Mind-Blowing Stats Everyone Should Read," *Forbes*, May 21, 2018, https://www.forbes.com/sites/bernardmarr/2018/05/21/how-much-data-do-we-create-every-day-the-mind-blowing-stats-everyone-should-read/#635d904a60ba.

28. Zuboff, *Age of Surveillance Capitalism*.

29. Zuboff, *Age of Surveillance Capitalism*.

30. Kruschinski and Haller, "Restrictions."

31. "Social Network Advertising Revenues in the United States from 2015 to 2018 (in Billion U.S. Dollars)," Statista, n.d., accessed January 9, 2020, https://www.statista.com/statistics/271259/advertising-revenue-of-social-networks-in-the-us/.

32. Bianca Bosker, "The Binge Breaker: Tristan Harris Believes Silicon Valley Is Addicting Us to Our Phones. He's Determined to Make It Stop," *Atlantic*, November 2016, https://www.theatlantic.com/magazine/archive/2016/11/the-binge-breaker/501122/; Eoin O'Carroll, "Are the Trackers Really Voluntary?," *Christian Science Monitor*, March 15, 2018, https://www.csmonitor.com/Technology/2018/0315/Can-your-boss-make-you-wear-a-Fitbit; Megan Molteni, "The Creepy Genetics behind the Golden State Killer Case," *Wired*, April 27, 2018, https://www.wired.com/story/detectives-cracked-the-golden-state-killer-case-using-genetics/; Tina Hesman Saey, "Crime Solvers Embraced Genetic Genealogy: The Golden State Killer Case Was Just the Beginning," *Science News*, December 17, 2018, https://www.sciencenews.org/article/genetic-genealogy-forensics-top-science-stories-2018-yir.

33. Zuboff, *Age of Surveillance Capitalism*.

34. Zuboff, *Age of Surveillance Capitalism*.

35. Benkler, Faris, and Roberts, *Network Propaganda*.

36. Duggan and Brenner, *Demographics of Social Media Users*; Monica Riese, "The Definitive History of Social Media," *Daily Dot*, September 12, 2016, https://www.dailydot.com/debug/history-of-social-media/.

37. Fuchs et al., *Internet and Surveillance*.

38. Staff, "Percentage of U.S. Population Who Currently Use Any Social Media from 2008 to 2017," Statista, n.d., accessed January 9, 2020, https://www.statista.com/statistics/273476/percentage-of-us-population-with-a-social-network-profile/.

39. Bernard Marr, "How Much Data Do We Create Every Day? The Mind-Blowing Stats Everyone Should Read," *Forbes*, May 21, 2018, https://www.forbes.com/sites/bernardmarr/2018/05/21/how-much-data-do-we-create-every-day-the-mind-blowing-stats-everyone-should-read/#635d904a60ba.

40. Staff, "Number of Social Network Users Worldwide from 2010 to 2021 (in Billions)," Statista, n.d., accessed January 9, 2020, https://www.statista.com/statistics/278414/number-of-worldwide-social-network-users/.

41. Mark Kernan, "The Dystopian Future of Facebook," *CounterPunch*, November 8, 2018, https://www.counterpunch.org/2018/11/08/the-dystopian-future-of-facebook/.

42. Julie Bort, "An Early Investor in Facebook and Google Has Slammed Them for 'Aggressive Brain Hacking,'" *Business Insider*, August 8, 2017, www.businessinsider.com/famous-facebook-and-google-investor-condemns-brain-hacking-2017-8; B. Skinner, *Behavior of Organisms*.

43. Wu, *Attention Merchants*.

44. Taylor Lorenz, "Teens Explain The World of Snapchat's Addictive Streaks, Where Friendships Live or Die," April 14, 2017, https://www.businessinsider.com/teens-explain-Snapchat-streaks-why-theyre-so-addictive-and-important-to-friendships-2017-4.

45. Bort, "Early Investor in Facebook"; B. Skinner, *Behavior of Organisms*.

46. Shu and Liu, *Detecting Fake News*, 2.

47. Pariser, *Filter Bubble*.

48. Fazio et al., "Knowledge Does Not Protect"; David Z. Hambrick and Madeline Marquardt, "Cognitive Ability and Vulnerability to Fake News: Researchers Identify a Major Risk Factor for Pernicious Effects of Misinformation," *Scientific American*, February 6, 2018, https://www.scientificamerican.com/article/cognitive-ability-and-vulnerability-to-fake-news/.

49. Robinson Meyer, "The Grim Conclusions of the Largest-Ever Study of Fake News: Falsehoods Almost Always Beat Out the Truth on Twitter, Penetrating Further, Faster, and Deeper into the Social Network Than Accurate Information," *Atlantic*, March 8, 2018, https://www.theatlantic.com/technology/archive/2018/03/largest-study-ever-fake-news-mit-twitter/555104/.

50. Stephanie Thurrott, "How to Spot Fake News in Your Social Media Feed; Are You Sharing Fake News without Knowing It?," NBC, March 13, 2018,

https://www.nbcnews.com/better/news/can-you-spot-fake-news-your-feed-ncna854036.

51. Staff, "Famous Internet Hoaxes," *Telegraph*, June 13, 2011, https://www.telegraph.co.uk/technology/internet/8571780/Famous-internet-hoaxes.html.

52. Staff, "Famous Internet Hoaxes"; Zoë Bernard, "The Queen of England Is a Cannibal and Finland Doesn't Exist—These Are the 12 Craziest Conspiracy Theories on the Internet," *Business Insider*, November 19, 2017, www.businessinsider.com/craziest-internet-conspiracy-theories-2017-11.

53. Madeline Holcombe and Augie Martin, "Jennifer Hart Drove Her Six Children to Their Deaths as Her Wife Looked Up How Much They Would Suffer, a Jury Says," CNN, April 6, 2019, https://www.cnn.com/2019/04/06/us/hart-family-crash-inquest-searches/index.html.

54. Charlotte Walsh, "What Is a Deepfake? This Video Technology Is Spooking Some Politicians," *USA Today*, March 15, 2019, https://www.usatoday.com/story/news/politics/2019/03/15/what-deepfake-video-technology-spooking-some-politicians/3109263002/.

55. Joan Donovan and Britt Paris, "Beware the Cheapfakes," *Slate*, June 12, 2019, https://slate.com/technology/2019/06/drunk-pelosi-deepfakes-cheap-fakes-artificial-intelligence-disinformation.html.

56. Bernhard Warner, "Deepfake Video of Mark Zuckerberg Goes Viral on Eve of House A.I. Hearing," *Fortune*, June 12, 2019, fortune.com/2019/06/12/deepfake-mark-zuckerberg/.

57. Jesselyn Cook, "Here's What It's Like to See Yourself in a Deepfake Porn Video," *Huffington Post*, June 23, 2019, https://www.huffpost.com/entry/deepfake-porn-heres-what-its-like-to-see-yourself_n_5d0d0faee4b0a3941861fced.

58. Voorveld et al., "Engagement with Social Media"; Vaidhyanathan, *Anti-social Media*.

59. Rhett Jones, "Gigantic Study of Fake News Online Finds the Enemy Is Humanity," Gizmodo, March 8, 2018, https://gizmodo.com/gigantic-study-of-fake-news-online-finds-the-enemy-is-h-1823594468; Vaidhyanathan, *Anti-social Media*.

60. Vosoughi, Roy, and Aral, "Spread of True and False News."

61. Auditi Guha, "Study Confirms What Women Have Long Said: Twitter Is Abusive," *Rewire News*, December 18, 2018, https://rewire.news/article/2018/12/18/study-confirms-what-women-have-long-said-twitter-is-abusive/; "Troll Patrol Findings," Amnesty International, December 12, 2018, https://decoders.amnesty.org/projects/troll-patrol/findings.

62. Sarah Frier and Max Chafkin, "Zuckerberg's New Mission for Facebook: Bringing the World Closer," Bloomberg, June 22, 2017, https://www.bloomberg.com/news/articles/2017-06-22/zuckerberg-s-new-mission-for-facebook-bringing-the-world-closer.

63. Noble, *Algorithms of Oppression*.

64. Benkler, Faris, and Roberts, *Network Propaganda*.

65. Ronald Reagan, "First Inaugural Address," Presidency Project, https://www.presidency.ucsb.edu/ws?pid=43130.

66. John Savage, "The John Birch Society Is Back," *Politico*, July 16, 2017, https://www.politico.com/magazine/story/2017/07/16/the-john-birch-society-is-alive-and-well-in-the-lone-star-state-215377.

67. Kleinknecht, *Man Who Sold the World*.

68. Benkler, Faris, and Roberts, *Network Propaganda*.

69. "Newsweek Kills Story on White House Intern," Drudge Report, January 17, 1998, http://www.drudgereportarchives.com/data/2002/01/17/20020117_175502_ml.htm; Brian Stelter, "Birthers Fanned Flames of Conspiracy for Years," *New York Times*, April 27, 2011, https://www.nytimes.com/2011/04/28/business/media/28birth.html.

70. Brian Montopoli, "Obama Birth Certificate Release Won't Kill 'Birther' Movement," CBS News, April 27, 2011, https://www.cbsnews.com/news/obama-birth-certificate-release-wont-kill-birther-movement/; Jeffrey Feldman, "Drudge Puts Dangerous Spin on Mugging, Implies Violence Targeting McCain Volunteers," *Huffington Post*, November 23, 2008, https://www.huffingtonpost.com/jeffrey-feldman/drudge-puts-dangerous-spi_b_137342.html; Benjy Sarlin, "With Drudge Report's Help, Birthers Latch onto Phony Forgery Theory," *Talking Points Memo*, April 29, 2011, https://talkingpointsmemo.com/dc/with-drudge-report-s-help-birthers-latch-onto-phony-forgery-theory.

71. Carol Anderson, *White Rage*; Zaitchick, *Gilded Rage*.

72. Tim Mak, "'Pizzagate' Gunman Liked Alex Jones," *Daily Beast*, December 4, 2016, https://www.thedailybeast.com/pizzagate-gunman-liked-alex-jones.

73. Joseph Goldstein, "Alt-Right Gathering Exults in Trump Election with Nazi-Era Salute," *New York Times*, November 21, 2016, https://www.nytimes.com/2016/11/21/us/alt-right-salutes-donald-trump.html; Peter Baker and Maggie Haberman, "A Conspiracy Theory's Journey from Talk Radio to Trump's Twitter," *New York Times*, March 5, 2017, https://www.nytimes.com/2017/03/05/us/politics/trump-twitter-talk-radio-conspiracy-theory.html; Lori Robertson, "Trump's ISIS Conspiracy Theory," FactCheck.org, Annenberg Public Policy

Center of the University of Pennsylvania, June 16, 2016, https://www.factcheck.org/2016/06/trumps-isis-conspiracy-theory/.

74. David Weigel, "'Friends of Hamas': The Scary-Sounding Pro-Hagel Group That Doesn't Actually Exist," *Slate*, February 14, 2013, http://www.slate.com/blogs/weigel/2013/02/14/_friends_of_hamas_the_scary_sounding_pro_hagel_group_that_doesn_t_actually.html; Agence France-Presse in Berlin, "German Police Quash Breitbart Story of Mob Setting Fire to Dortmund Church," *Guardian*, January 7, 2017, https://www.theguardian.com/world/2017/jan/07/german-police-quash-breitbart-story-of-mob-setting-fire-to-dortmund-church; Brianna Sacks and Talal Ansari, "Breitbart Made Up False Story That Immigrant Started Deadly Sonoma Wildfires, Sheriff's Office Says," BuzzFeed, https://www.buzzfeed.com/briannasacks/no-an-undocumented-immigrant-did-not-start-the-deadly?utm_term=.lpbyb6Oej#.rgmV5wyD2; Daniel Victor and Liam Stack, "Stephen Bannon and Breitbart News, in Their Words," *New York Times*, November 14, 2016, https://www.nytimes.com/2016/11/15/us/politics/stephen-bannon-breitbart-words.html?mtrref=undefined&gwh=67891184CB5B8760A126F2542A30FB1A&gwt=pay.

75. Chris Rozvar, "Damaging Brooklyn ACORN Sting Video Ruled 'Heavily Edited,' No Charges to Be Filed," *New Yorker*, March 2, 2010.

76. Sheryl Gay Stolberg, Shaila Dewan, and Brian Stelter, "With Apology, Fired Official Is Offered a New Job," *New York Times*, July 21, 2010, https://www.nytimes.com/2010/07/22/us/politics/22sherrod.html?mtrref=www.google.com&gwh=4DA9F04EBF1A0D80231087560B19E0A8&gwt=pay.

77. Nolan Higdon, "Disinfo Wars: Alex Jones' War on Your Mind," Project Censored, September 26, 2013, projectcensored.org/disinfo-wars-alex-jones-war-mind/.

78. Higdon, "Disinfo Wars"; Laura Bradley, "Watch the Opposition Shout Down Alex Jones—Or Was It a Crisis Actor?," *Vanity Fair*, April 13, 2018, https://www.vanityfair.com/hollywood/2018/04/the-opposition-alex-jones-defamation-crisis-actor; Eric Killelea, "Alex Jones' Mis-Infowars: 7 Bat-Sh*t Conspiracy Theories," *Rolling Stone*, February 21, 2017, https://www.rollingstone.com/culture/culture-lists/alex-jones-mis-infowars-7-bat-sht-conspiracy-theories-195468/the-government-is-controlling-the-weather-118190/.

79. Tim Murphy, "How Donald Trump Became Conspiracy Theorist in Chief: He's Made the Paranoid Style of American Politics Go Mainstream," *Mother Jones*, November/December 2016, https://www.motherjones.com/politics/2016/10/trump-infowars-alex-jones-clinton-conspiracy-theories/.

80. Corky Siemaszko, "InfoWars' Alex Jones Is a 'Performance Artist,' His Lawyer Says in Divorce Hearing," NBC, April 17, 2017, https://www.nbcnews

.com/news/us-news/not-fake-news-infowars-alex-jones-performance-artist-n747491.

81. Wendling, *Alt-Right.*

82. "Lynching, Whites and Negroes, 1882–1968," Monroe Work Collection, Tuskegee University Archives and Repository, 192.203.127.197/archive/bitstream /handle/123456789/511/Lyching 1882 1968.pdf.

83. Odum, *Race and Rumors.*

84. Jean, "'Warranted' Lynchings."

85. Stephen Smith, "Radio: The Internet of the 1930s," American Radio Works, November 10, 2014, www.americanradioworks.org/segments/radio-the-internet-of-the-1930s; D. Smith, *Managing White Supremacy.*

86. Mark Potok, "The Year in Hate and Extremism," February 17, 2017, Southern Poverty Law Center, https://www.splcenter.org/fighting-hate/intelligence-report/2017/year-hate-and-extremism.

87. David Mikkelson, "Did Barack Obama Attend Columbia University as a Foreign Student?," Snopes, February 9, 2012, https://www.snopes.com/fact-check/obama-student-id/.

88. "How Were They Radicalized? A Jury in Kansas This Week Is Deliberating Whether Three Militia Members Should Spend the Rest of Their Lives in Prison," *Huffington Post,* April 17, 2018, https://www.huffingtonpost.com/entry/domestic-terrorism-trial-kansas-trump-militia_us_5ad4e700e4b0edca2cbcb603?t1t.

89. Toula Drimonis, "Did American Right-Wing Trolls Radicalize the Quebec Mosque Shooter?" *Huffington Post,* April 20, 2018, https://www .huffingtonpost.com/entry/opinion-drimonis-montreal-mosque-trolls-shapiro_ us_5ad95a7ee4b029ebe0228dc1; Christopher Mathias and Ryan J. Reilly, "These Pro-Trump Extremists Had a Plan To Kill Muslims," *Huffington Post,* April 17, 2018, https://www.huffpost.com/entry/domestic-terrorism-trial-kansas-trump-militia_n_5ad4e700e4b0edca2cbcb603.

90. Wendling, *Alt-Right.*

91. Jane, *Misogyny Online.*

92. Chandra Steele, "Everything You Never Wanted to Know about Gamer-Gate," *PC Magazine,* October 21, 2014, https://www.pcmag.com/article2 /0,2817,2470723,00.asp.

93. Jane, *Misogyny Online.*

94. Wright, *Terror Years;* Liz Essley Whyte, "Turkey's Propaganda War Targets America's State Capitals," Center for Public Integrity, February 2, 2018, https:// www.pri.org/stories/2018-02-02/turkeys-propaganda-war-targets-americas-state-capitals; Segal, *Hacked World Order.*

95. Alexander Smith and Vladimir Banic, "Fake News: How a Partying Macedonian Teen Earns Thousands Publishing Lies," NBC, December 8, 2016, https://www.nbcnews.com/news/world/fake-news-how-partying-macedonian-teen-earns-thousands-publishing-lies-n692451.

96. "Hacking," Technopedia, https://www.techopedia.com/definition/26361/hacking.

97. Zak Doffman, "'National Security Threat' As Chinese Hackers Are 'Allowed' to Target U.S. Businesses," *Forbes*, April 13, 2019, https://www.forbes.com/sites/zakdoffman/2019/04/13/u-s-businesses-allowing-chinese-government-hackers-to-steal-american-secrets/#6b1a55eba4d4.

98. Lin, "Cyber Conflict," 77.

99. Zuboff, *Age of Surveillance Capitalism*.

100. Ward, "Social Networks."

101. Levine, *Surveillance Valley*.

102. Tim Leslie and Mark Corcoran, "Explained: Australia's Involvement with the NSA, the U.S. Spy Agency at Heart of Global Scandal," ABC, November 2013, https://www.abc.net.au/news/2013-11-08/australian-nsa-involvement-explained/5079786; Julian Borger, "GCHQ and European Spy Agencies Worked Together on Mass Surveillance," *Guardian*, November 1, 2013, https://www.theguardian.com/uk-news/2013/nov/01/gchq-europe-spy-agencies-mass-surveillance-snowden; Glenn Greenwald and Ewen MacAskill, "Boundless Informant: The NSA's Secret Tool to Track Global Surveillance Data," *Guardian*, June 11, 2013, https://www.theguardian.com/world/2013/jun/08/nsa-boundless-informant-global-datamining; Glenn Greenwald, "NSA Collecting Phone Records of Millions of Verizon Customers Daily," *Guardian*, June 3, 2013, https://www.theguardian.com/world/2013/jun/06/nsa-phone-records-verizon-court-order.

103. Charlie Savage, Edward Wyatt, and Peter Baker, "U.S. Says It Gathers Online Data Abroad," *New York Times*, June 6, 2013, https://www.nytimes.com/2013/06/07/us/nsa-verizon-calls.html.

104. Caren Bohan, "Lawmakers Urge Review of Domestic Spying, Patriot Act," *Chicago Tribune*, June 9, 2013, https://www.chicagotribune.com/news/politics/ct-xpm-2013-06-09-sns-rt-us-usa-security-lawmakersbre9580ab-20130609-story.html.

105. Paul Blumenthal and Gopal Sathe, "India's Biometric Database Is Creating a Perfect Surveillance State—and U.S. Tech Companies Are on Board," *Huffington Post*, August 25, 2018, https://www.huffingtonpost.com/entry/india-aadhuar-tech-companies_us_5b7ebc53e4b0729515109fd0.

106. "The Facebook Dilemma, Part 1," *Frontline,* PBS, season 37, episode 8; Staff, "Facebook Confirms Data-Sharing Agreements with Chinese Firms," BBC, June 6, 2018, https://www.bbc.com/news/business-44379593; Evan Perez, Donie O'Sullivan, Drew Griffin, and Curt Devine, "Russian Company Could Have Accessed Facebook Data on Millions of Americans, Source Says," CNN, July 12, 2018, https://money.cnn.com/2018/07/12/technology/facebook-mailru-russia/index.html.

107. James Titcomb, "Facebook and Twitter Delete Hundreds of Fake Accounts Linked to Iran and Russia," *Telegraph,* August 22, 2018, https://www.telegraph.co.uk/technology/2018/08/22/facebook-twitter-delete-hundreds-fake-accounts-linked-iran-russia/; Nick Schifrin, "Inside Russia's Propaganda Machine," PBS, July 11, 2017, https://www.pbs.org/newshour/show/inside-russias-propaganda-machine; Michael Pizzi, "Putin Dissolves RIA Novosti News Agency," Al Jazeera America, December 9, 2013, http://america.aljazeera.com/articles/2013/12/9/putin-dissolves-rianovostinewsagency.html; Peter Finn, "Russia Pumps Tens of Millions Into Burnishing Image Abroad," *Washington Post,* March 6, 2008, www.washingtonpost.com/wp-dyn/content/article/2008/03/05/AR2008030503539_pf.html.

108. "Craziest North Korean News Coverage," *ShortList,* January 30, 2014, https://www.shortlist.com/news/craziest-north-korean-news-coverage/42821.

109. Allen and Moore, "Victory without Casualties"; Lange-Ionatamishvili and Svetoka, "Strategic Communications"; Simon Tisdall, "Result of Macedonia's Referendum Is Another Victory for Russia," *Guardian,* October 1, 2018, https://www.theguardian.com/world/2018/oct/01/result-of-macedonia-referendum-is-another-victory-for-russia; Matthew Field and Mike Wright, "Russian Trolls Sent Thousands of Pro-Leave Messages on Day of Brexit Referendum, Twitter Data Reveal," *Telegraph,* October 17, 2018, https://www.telegraph.co.uk/technology/2018/10/17/russian-iranian-twitter-trolls-sent-10-million-tweets-fake-news/; Andrew Grice, "Fake News Handed Brexiteers the Referendum—and Now They Have No Idea What They're Doing," *Independent,* January 18, 2017, https://www.independent.co.uk/voices/michael-gove-boris-johnson-brexit-eurosceptic-press-theresa-may-a7533806.html.

110. Matt Apuzo and Sharon LeFaniere, "13 Russians Indicted as Mueller Reveals Effort to Aid Trump Camp," *New York Times,* February 16, 2016, https://www.nytimes.com/2018/02/16/us/politics/russians-indicted-mueller-election-interference.html; Nick Statt, "Twitter Says It Exposed Nearly 700,000 People to Russian Propaganda during U.S. Election," *Verge,* January 19, 2018, https://www.theverge.com/2018/1/19/16911086/twitter-russia-propaganda-us-presidential-election-

bot-accounts-findings; Ben Popken, "Twitter Deleted 200,000 Russian Troll Tweets. Read Them Here," NBC, February 14, 2018, https://www.nbcnews.com /tech/social-media/now-available-more-200-000-deleted-russian-troll-tweets-n844731; Jen Kirby, "What to Know about the Russian Troll Factory Listed in Mueller's Indictment," *Vox*, February 16, 2018, https://www.vox.com/2018/2/16/17020974 /mueller-indictment-internet-research-agency.

111. Gabriel Debenedetti, "Sanders Silent on Claim That Russians Backed Him in 2016," *Politico,* February 16, 2018, https://www.politico.com/story /2018/02/16/bernie-sanders-russia-2016-election-interference-415691.

112. Sam Levin, "Did Russia Fake Black Activism on Facebook to Sow Division in the US?," *Guardian,* September 30, 2017, https://www.theguardian.com /technology/2017/sep/30/blacktivist-facebook-account-russia-us-election.

113. Renee DiResta, Kris Shaffer, Becky Ruppel, David Sullivan, Robert Matney, Ryan Fox, Jonathan Albright, and Ben Johnson, "The Tactics and Tropes of the Internet Research Agency," New Knowledge, December 18, 2018, https://disinformationreport.blob.core.windows.net/disinformation-report/NewKnowledge-Disinformation-Report-Whitepaper-121718.pdf.

114. Segal, *Hacked World Order.*

115. Project Censored, "US Military Manipulates the Social Media," September 30, 2011, projectcensored.org/2-us-military-manipulates-the-social-media/.

116. John R. Schindler, "Obama Fails to Fight Putin's Propaganda Machine," *Observer,* November 5, 2015, https://observer.com/2015/11/obama-fails-to-fight-putins-propaganda-machine/.

117. Nick Fielding and Ian Cobain, "Revealed: US Spy Operation That Manipulates Social Media," *Guardian,* March 17, 2011, www.guardian.co.uk/technology /2011/mar/17/us-spy-operation-social-networks.

118. Project Censored, "Social Media Websites Censoring Alternative News," April 1, 2013, projectcensored.org/social-media-websites-censoring-alternative-news/.

119. Carla Herreria, "Homeland Security to Compile a Database of Journalists, Bloggers and Influencers: Many in the Media Industry Did *Not* Like the Implications," *Huffington Post,* April 6, 2018, https://www.huffingtonpost.com/entry /homeland-security-searchable-database_us_5ac7f41de4b07a3485e4bb1d?a6j.

120. Alex Kasprak, "Is Homeland Security Working to Compile a Database of Journalists and Bloggers?," Snopes, April 6, 2018, https://www.snopes.com /fact-check/dhs-compile-database-journalists-bloggers/.

121. Segal, *Hacked World Order;* Jerry Iannelli, "U.S. Government Has Plans to Spread Hidden Facebook Propaganda in Cuba," *Miami New Times,* August 21,

2018, https://www.miaminewtimes.com/news/us-planned-cuban-facebook-propaganda-on-radio-tv-marti-10625033.

122. Iannelli, "U.S. Government Has Plans"; Staff, "US 'Paid Anti-Cuba Journalists,'" BBC News, September 8, 2006, news.bbc.co.uk/2/hi/americas/5329394.stm.

123. "The Facebook Dilemma, Part 2," *Frontline*, PBS, season 37, episode 9.

124. Shaw, "Assessing the Impact."

125. "Facebook Dilemma, Part 2"; Hendricks and Schill, "Social Media Election."

126. "Facebook Dilemma, Part 2"; Allcott and Gentzkow, "Social Media."

127. Lauren Etter, "What Happens When the Government Uses Facebook as a Weapon?," Bloomberg, December 7, 2017, https://www.bloomberg.com/news/features/2017-12-07/how-rodrigo-duterte-turned-facebook-into-a-weapon-with-a-little-help-from-facebook.

128. Kim, "Spiral of Silence"; Noelle-Neumann, "Spiral of Silence."

129. Jon Swaine, "Trump Inauguration Crowd Photos Were Edited after He Intervened," *Guardian*, September 6, 2018, https://www.theguardian.com/world/2018/sep/06/donald-trump-inauguration-crowd-size-photos-edited.

130. Chuck Todd, "Conway: Press Secretary Gave 'Alternative Facts,'" *Meet the Press*, NBC News, January 22, 2017, http://www.nbcnews.com/meet-the-press/video/conway-press-secretary-gave-alternative-facts-860142147643; Brian Stelter, "White House Press Secretary Attacks Media for Accurately Reporting Inauguration Crowds," CNN, January 21, 2017, http://money.cnn.com/2017/01/21/media/sean-spicer-press-secretary-statement/; Jonathan Lemire, "Trump Draws Far Smaller Inaugural Crowd Than Obama," *U.S. News and World Report*, January 20, 2017, https://www.usnews.com/news/politics/articles/2017-01-20/trump-draws-far-smaller-inaugural-crowd-than-obama.

131. Jethro Nededog, "Trevor Noah: Here's How You Know Trump Adviser Kellyanne Conway Is Lying," *Business Insider*, January 24, 2017, https://www.businessinsider.com/trevor-noah-kellyanne-conway-lying-alternative-facts-2017-1; Benkler, Faris, and Roberts, *Network Propaganda*, 45; Adelle Nazarian, "Donald Trump: Press Lying about Inauguration Crowd Size," Breitbart, January 21, 2017, https://www.breitbart.com/live/womens-march-washington-live-updates/donald-trump-press-lying-inauguration-crowd-size/.

132. Alan Levinovitz, "Trump Supporters Refuse to Believe Their Own Eyes: They Still Think Trump's Inauguration Crowds Were Bigger, Despite the Evidence. Here's Why," *Slate*, January 27, 2017, https://slate.com/technology/2017/01/trump-supporters-think-trump-crowds-are-bigger-even-when-looking-at-photos.html.

133. "Craziest North Korean News Coverage"; Myers, *Cleanest Race*.

134. David Bandurski, "China's Guerrilla War for the Web," *Far Eastern Economic Review*, July 7, 2008, http://chinamediaproject.org/2008/07/07/feer-chinas-guerrilla-war-for-the-web/.

135. King, Pan, and Roberts, "How the Chinese Government Fabricates"; Sean Gallagher, "Red Astroturf: Chinese Government Makes Millions of Fake Social Media Posts," Ars Technica, https://arstechnica.com/information-technology/2016/06/red-astroturf-chinese-government-makes-millions-of-fake-social-media-posts/; Bandurski, "China's Guerrilla War"; Michael Bristow, "China's Internet 'Spin Doctors,'" BBC News, December 16, 2008, http://news.bbc.co.uk/2/hi/asia-pacific/7783640.stm.

136. Benkler, Faris, and Roberts, *Network Propaganda*, 45.

137. Anna Ringstrom and Jeff Mason, "Sweden Mocks Trump's 'Alternative Facts' on Fictional Refugee Incident," *National Memo*, February 19, 2017, https://www.nationalmemo.com/sweden-mocks-trump-incident/; Justin Carissimo, "Sean Spicer Cites Fake Atlanta Terror Attack Story," *Independent*, February 9, 2017, www.independent.co.uk/news/world/americas/sean-spicer-creates-fake-atlanta-terror-attack-story-a7570561.html; Samantha Schmidt and Lindsey Bever, "Kellyanne Conway Cites 'Bowling Green Massacre' That Never Happened to Defend Travel Ban," *Washington Post*, February 3, 2017, https://www.washingtonpost.com/news/morning-mix/wp/2017/02/03/kellyanne-conway-cites-bowling-green-massacre-that-never-happened-to-defend-travel-ban/?utm_term=.b269b8573955; Jack Holmes, "To Supporters, Trump Isn't Just Right—He Controls the Truth," *Esquire*, July 31, 2018, https://www.esquire.com/news-politics/a22600827/donald-trump-supporters-believe-the-media/.

138. Marie Solis, "Six Anti-Muslim Comments That Could Haunt Trump in Travel Ban Supreme Court Case," *Newsweek*, April 24 2018, www.newsweek.com/tk-trumps-anti-muslim-comments-could-come-back-haunt-him-travel-ban-supreme-898086.

139. Rowaida Abdelaziz, "Horrifying Videos Show Racist Moms Teaching Kids to Be 'Patriots,'" *Huffington Post*, March 14, 2018, https://www.huffingtonpost.com/entry/facebook-videos-mosque-vandalism-women-children_us_5aa9a121e4b0600b82ffe195.

140. Colin Horgan, "The Acosta Video Debate Is the Future of Fake News: Video Manipulation Technology Is Making It Harder Than Ever to Believe What You See," Medium, November 8, 2018, https://medium.com/s/story/the-acosta-video-debate-is-the-future-of-fake-news-bd8202902deb.

141. Vanessa Romo and Joel Rose, "Judge Orders Pipe Bomb Suspect Cesar Sayoc Held without Bail," National Public Radio, November 6, 2018, https://www.npr.org/2018/11/06/664796199/judge-orders-pipe-bomb-suspect-cesar-sayoc-held-without-bail; Emily Sullivan, "Mail Bomb Suspect Reportedly Had List of More Than 100 Potential Targets," National Public Radio, October 30, 2018, https://www.npr.org/2018/10/30/662000228/mail-bomb-suspect-reportedly-had-list-of-more-than-100-potential-targets.

142. Rishi Iyengar, "Philippine President Rodrigo Duterte Targets over 1,000 More Officials in His Drug War," *Time*, September 16, 2016, www.time.com/4496535/philippines-duterte-drug-war-list-officials/; Kate Lamb, "Thousands Dead: The Philippine President, the Death Squad Allegations and a Brutal Drugs War," *Guardian*, April 2, 2017, https://www.theguardian.com/world/2017/apr/02/philippines-president-duterte-drugs-war-death-squads; Joseph Hincks, "Duterte Is Assassinating Opponents under the Cover of the Drug War," *Time*, July 5, 2018, www.time.com/5330071/philippines-mayors-political-assassination-duterte/.

143. Vito Barcelo and Maricel V. Cruz, "38 Nations Seek End to 'Killings,'" *Manila Standard*, June 24, 2018, manilastandard.net/news/top-stories/268837/38-nations-seek-end-to-killings-.html.

144. Sapna Maheshwari, "How Fake News Goes Viral: A Case Study," *New York Times*, November 20, 2016, https://www.nytimes.com/2016/11/20/business/media/how-fake-news-spreads.html.

6. Fighting Fake News

1. Spencer Hsu, "'Pizzagate' Gunman Sentenced to Four Years in Prison, as Prosecutors Urged Judge to Deter Vigilante Justice," *Washington Post*, June 22, 2017, https://www.washingtonpost.com/local/public-safety/pizzagate-gunman-sentenced-to-four-years-in-prison-as-prosecutors-urged-judge-to-deter-vigilante-justice/2017/06/22/a10db598-550b-11e7-ba90-f5875b7d1876_story.html?utm_term=.71d5f857ffbf.

2. Adam Goldman, "The Comet Ping Pong Gunman Answers Our Reporter's Questions," *New York Times*, December 7, 2016, https://www.nytimes.com/2016/12/07/us/edgar-welch-comet-pizza-fake-news.html.

3. Stanford History Education Group, "Evaluating Information: The Cornerstone of Civic Online Reasoning," Stanford University, November 22, 2016, https://stacks.stanford.edu/file/druid:fv751yt5934/SHEG%20Evaluating%20

Information%20Online.pdf; McGrew et al., "Can Students Evaluate"; Guess, Nagler, and Tucker, "Less Than You Think."

4. Kendall Breitman, "Poll: Half of Republicans Still Believe WMDs Found in Iraq," *Politico,* January 7, 2015, https://www.politico.com/story/2015/01/poll-republicans-wmds-iraq-114016.

5. Josh Clinton and Carrie Roush, "Poll: Persistent Partisan Divide over 'Birther' Question," NBC News, August 10, 2016, https://www.nbcnews.com/politics/2016-election/poll-persistent-partisan-divide-over-birther-question-n627446.

6. Craig Silverman and Jeremy Singer-Vine, "Most Americans Who See Fake News Believe It, New Survey Says," Buzzfeed News, December 6, 2016, https://www.buzzfeednews.com/article/craigsilverman/fake-news-survey.

7. Charlie Warzel, "He Predicted the 2016 Fake News Crisis. Now He's Worried about an Information Apocalypse," BuzzFeed News, February 11, 2018, https://www.buzzfeednews.com/article/charliewarzel/the-terrifying-future-of-fake-news#.orP4p2XG.

8. Breakstone et al., "Students' Civic Online Reasoning"; Guess, Nagler, and Tucker, "Less Than You Think"; McGrew et al., "Can Students Evaluate."

9. Williams, "Fighting Fake News."

10. Jack Poulson, "I Quit Google over Its Censored Chinese Search Engine. The Company Needs to Clarify Its Position on Human Rights," *Intercept,* December 1, 2018, https://theintercept.com/2018/12/01/google-china-censorship-human-rights/.

11. "Media Literacy Legislative Roundup: 21 Bills, 11 States, 5 New Laws," Media Literacy Now, https://medialiteracynow.org/media-literacy-legislative-roundup-21-bills-11-states-5-new-laws/; "15 Bills in 12 States," Media Literacy Now, https://medialiteracynow.org/your-state-legislation/.

12. Mark Rothacher, "Letter: Let's Outlaw Fake News and Punish Everyone Who Spreads It," *Salt Lake City Tribune,* June 15, 2018, https://www.sltrib.com/opinion/letters/2018/06/14/letter-lets-outlaw-fake-news-and-punish-every-one-who-spreads-it/; Lydia O'Connor, "Twitter CEO Gives Interview to Conspiracy Theorist about Refusing to Ban Conspiracy Theorists," *Huffington Post,* August 8, 2018, https://www.huffingtonpost.com/entry/jack-dorsey-sean-hannity-twitter_us_5b6b4c9ce4b0530743c6a138.

13. Poulson, "I Quit Google"; Karishma Vaswani, "Concern over Singapore's Anti-Fake News Law," BBC, April 4, 2019; J.D. Tuccille, "Internet Censorship Is Only for the Little People," *Reason,* April 11, 2019, https://reason.com/2019/04/11/internet-censorship-in-france/ https://www.bbc.com/news/business-47782470.

14. Rothacher, "Letter"; O'Connor, "Twitter CEO Gives Interview."

15. "The Law against Lying and False News in Colonial Massachusetts," *Massachusetts Law Updates* (blog), May 7, 2018, Massachusetts Trial Court Law Libraries, https://blog.mass.gov/masslawlib/legal-history/the-law-against-lying-and-false-news-in-colonial-massachusetts/.

16. Foner, *Give Me Liberty!*

17. "Peace Censorship Bill," *Daily Home News,* July 10, 1916, www.digifind-it.com/matawan/DATA/homenews/1916/1916-07-10.pdf.

18. Kreimer, "Censorship by Proxy," 11.

19. Kreimer, "Censorship by Proxy."

20. Kreimer, "Censorship by Proxy"; Potolsky, *National Security Sublime.*

21. Kreimer, "Censorship by Proxy."

22. Aja Romano, "Apple Banned Alex Jones's Infowars. Then the Dominoes Started to Fall," *Vox,* August 6, 2018, https://www.vox.com/policy-and-politics/2018/8/6/17655516/infowars-ban-apple-youtube-facebook-spotify; Joseph Cox and Jason Koebler, "Facebook Bans White Nationalism and White Separatism," *Vice,* March 27, 2019, https://www.vice.com/en_us/article/nexpbx/facebook-bans-white-nationalism-and-white-separatism; Times Editorial Board, "Facebook Has the Right to Ban Extreme Voices, but It Needs to Tread Lightly," *Los Angeles Times,* May 7, 2019, https://www.latimes.com/opinion/editorials/la-ed-facebook-ban-20190507-story.html.

23. O'Connor, "Twitter CEO Gives Interview."

24. W. Hobbs and Roberts, "How Sudden Censorship Can Increase," 1; Nabi, "Censorship Is Futile."

25. Kind-Kovács and Labov, *Samizdat, Tamizdat, and Beyond.*

26. Nabi, "Censorship Is Futile."

27. De Baets, "Taxonomy of Concepts."

28. Townend, "Freedom of Expression"; Kaminski and Witnov, "Conforming Effect," 465.

29. Matt Taibbi, "YouTube, Facebook Purges Are More Extensive Than You Think: Legitimate Journalists Are Again Being Caught in the Wash of Internet Cleanups," *Rolling Stone,* June 7, 2019, https://www.rollingstone.com/politics/politics-features/youtube-facebook-purges-journalists-845790/.

30. Higdon and Huff, *United States of Distraction.*

31. Lewis, *935 Lies,* 102.

32. Faye, "Governing the Grapevine," 1; Pickard, *America's Battle;* Crescimbene, La Longa, and Lanza, "Science of Rumors"; Stanford History Education Group, "Evaluating Information."

33. McGrew et al., "Can Students Evaluate"; Guess et al., "Less Than You Think."

34. Faye, "Governing the Grapevine"; Crescimbene, La Longa, and Lanza, "Science of Rumors."

35. Hobbs and McGee, "Teaching about Propaganda," 5.

36. R. Hobbs and McGee, "Teaching about Propaganda"; Institute for Propaganda Analysis, "We Say Au Revoir," 1.

37. Foner, *Give Me Liberty!*

38. Higdon and Huff, *United States of Distraction.*

39. Dai and Hao, "Transcending the Opposition"; Dickel and Schrape, "Renaissance of Techno-Utopianism."

40. Picon, "Robots and Architecture."

41. Levine, *Surveillance Valley.*

42. Mazzucato, *Entrepreneurial State;* Zuboff, *Age of Surveillance Capitalism.*

43. Sykes and Maroto, "Wealth of Inequalities"; Temin, *Vanishing Middle Class;* Anne Lise Stranden, "Why New Technology Makes Us Work More," *Science Nordic,* April 4, 2014, sciencenordic.com/why-new-technology-makes-us-work-more; Zuboff, *Age of Surveillance Capitalism;* Eubanks, *Automating Inequality.*

44. McNamee, *Zucked.*

45. Zuboff, *Age of Surveillance Capitalism.*

46. Noble, *Algorithms of Oppression;* Eubanks, *Automating Inequality.*

47. Lackner and Plebani, "Theranos Saga."

48. CNBC Staff, "Read Mark Zuckerberg's Full Remarks on Russian Ads That Impacted the 2016 Elections," September 21, 2017, https://www.cnbc.com /2017/09/21/zuckerbergs-full-remarks-on-russian-ads-that-impacted-2016-e-lection.html.

49. See chapter 5.

50. Mike Isaac, "Facebook Unveils Redesign as It Tries to Move Past Privacy Scandals," *New York Times,* April 30, 2019, https://www.nytimes.com/2019/04/30 /technology/facebook-private-communication-groups.html.

51. Jack Stubbs and Christopher Bing, "Special Report: How Iran Spreads Disinformation around the World," *Reuters,* November 30, 2018, https://www .reuters.com/article/us-cyber-iran-specialreport/special-report-how-iran-spreads-disinformation-around-the-world-idUSKCN1NZ1FT; see also chapter 4.

52. Seth Fiegerman, "Silicon Valley Throws Big Money at Clinton and Virtually Nothing at Trump," CNN, August 23, 2016, https://money.cnn.com/2016 /08/23/technology/hillary-clinton-tech-fundraisers/index.html; Jim Edwards,

"Social Media Is a Tool of the CIA, Seriously," CBS, July 11, 2011, https://www
.cbsnews.com/news/social-media-is-a-tool-of-the-cia-seriously/; Dustin Volz,
Joel Schectman, and Jack Stubbs, "Tech Firms Let Russia Probe Software Widely
Used by U.S. Government," Reuters, January 25, 2018, http://www.reuters.com
/article/us-usa-cyber-russia/tech-firms-let-russia-probe-software-widely-used-
by-u-s-government-idUSKBN1FE1DT; Angus West, "17 Disturbing Things Snowden Has Taught Us (So Far)," PRI, July 9, 2013, https://www.pri.org/stories/2013–
07–09/17-disturbing-things-snowden-has-taught-us-so-far; BBC Staff, "Edward
Snowden: Leaks That Exposed U.S. Spy Programme," BBC, January 17, 2014,
www.bbc.com/news/world-us-canada-23123964; "Obama's Legacy: The Most
Tech-Savvy President," EnGadget, January 1, 2017, https://www.engadget
.com/2017/01/21/obamas-legacy-the-most-tech-savvy-president/; Fiegerman,
"Silicon Valley"; MIT Technology Review Editors, "Obama's Technology Legacy:
The Past Eight Years Saw Some Wins, and More Than a Few Failures," *MIT Technology Review,* January 9, 2017, https://www.technologyreview.com/s/603316
/obamas-technology-legacy/; Bryan Rich, "Is the Obama-Led Boom In Silicon
Valley Over?," *Forbes,* March 7, 2017, https://www.forbes.com/sites/bryanrich
/2017/03/07/is-the-obama-led-boom-in-silicon-valley-over/#17f6cf3a1931; Ce-
cilia Kang and Juliet Eilperin, "Why Silicon Valley Is the New Revolving
Door for Obama Staffers," *Washington Post,* February 28, 2015, https://www
.washingtonpost.com/business/economy/as-obama-nears-close-of-his-tenure-
commitment-to-silicon-valley-is-clear/2015/02/27/3bee8088-bc8e-11e4-bdfa-
b8e8f594e6ee_story.html?utm_term=.57f390b3cc29; Nicholas Confessore and
Matthew Rosenberg, "Damage Control at Facebook: 6 Takeaways from the
Times's Investigation," *New York Times,* November 14, 2018, https://www
.nytimes.com/2018/11/14/technology/facebook-crisis-mark-zuckerberg-sheryl-
sandberg.html?action=click&module=Top%20Stories&pgtype=Homepage.

53. Natasha Bach, "President Obama Tried to Warn Mark Zuckerberg about
the Massive Threat of Election Hacking on Facebook," *Forbes,* September 25,
2017, fortune.com/2017/09/25/obama-warned-zuckerberg-about-russia-hack-
fake-news/; "The Facebook Dilemma, Part 1," *Frontline,* PBS, season 37, episode
8; Alyssa Newcomb, "A Timeline of Facebook's Privacy Issues—and Its Re-
sponses," NBC, March 24, 2018, https://www.nbcnews.com/tech/social-media
/timeline-facebook-s-privacy-issues-its-responses-n859651; Heather Kelly, "Facebook Says Cambridge Analytica May Have Had Data on 87 Million People,"
CNN, April 4, 2018, money.cnn.com/2018/04/04/technology/facebook-
cambridge-analytica-data-87-million/index.html; Troy Wolverton, "Sen.

Chuck Schumer Intervened on Facebook's Behalf This Summer, Telling a Prominent Democratic Critic of the Company to Back Off," *Business Insider,* November 14, 2018, https://www.businessinsider.com/chuck-schumer-facebook-mark-warner-2018-11.

54. David Pegg, "Facebook Labelled 'Digital Gangsters' by Report on Fake News," *Guardian,* February 17, 2019, https://www.theguardian.com/technology/2019/feb/18/facebook-fake-news-investigation-report-regulation-privacy-law-dcms.

55. Sridhar et al., "Improving Health Aid."

56. "YouTube Will Counter Conspiracy Video Misinformation by Adding Wikipedia Info," *TechSpot,* March 14, 2018, https://www.techspot.com/news/73708-youtube-counter-conspiracy-video-misinformation-adding-wikipedia-info.html; Elizabeth Dwoskin and Hamza Shaban, "Facebook Will Now Ask Users to Rank News Organizations They Trust," *Washington Post,* January 19, 2018, https://www.washingtonpost.com/news/the-switch/wp/2018/01/19/facebook-will-now-ask-its-users-to-rank-news-organizations-they-trust/?utm_term=.9ad3d7e7b11b; Sebastian Murdock, "Facebook to Shut Down 'Trending' News Section in Favor of Breaking News Test," *Huffington Post,* June 1, 2018, https://www.huffingtonpost.com/entry/facebook-to-shut-down-trending-news-section-in-favor-of-breaking-news-test_us_5b116135e4b02143b7cc00b7?5y; Staff, "CNN to Launch 'Anderson Cooper Full Circle' Show on Facebook," CNN, June 6, 2018, cnnpressroom.blogs.cnn.com/2018/06/06/cnn-to-launch-anderson-cooper-full-circle-show-on-facebook-watch/.

57. Nolan Higdon and Ben Boyington, "Has Media Literacy Been Hijacked?," Project Censored, March 19, 2019, https://www.projectcensored.org/has-media-literacy-been-hijacked/; Edmund Lee, "Veterans of the News Business Are Now Fighting Fakes," *New York Times,* January 16, 2019, https://www.nytimes.com/2019/01/16/business/media/media-steve-brill-fake-news.html.

58. "Our Advisory Board," NewsGuard, https://www.newsguardtech.com/our-advisory-board/.

59. Hallin, "Media, the War"

60. Higdon and Boyington, "Has Media Literacy Been Hijacked?"

61. Aufderheide, *Media Literacy,* 1.

62. "New Literacy," last updated May 18, 2017, University Libraries, University of Oklahoma, https://guides.ou.edu/newsliteracy.

63. Kahne, Lee, and Feezell, "Digital Media Literacy Education."

64. Druick, "Myth of Media Literacy."

65. Staff, "A New Resource for Educators: Digital Literacy Library," Facebook, August 2, 2018, https://newsroom.fb.com/news/2018/08/digitalliteracylibrary/; NAMLE, "Corporate Partners," n.d., accessed January 9, 2020, https://namle.net/corporate-partners/; Poynter Institute for Media Studies, "MediaWise: Teaching Teens to Sort Fact from Fiction Online," 2019, https://www.poynter.org/be-mediawise/.

66. Tim Walker, "Students Still Can't Tell Fact from Fiction on the Internet," National Education Association, January 6, 2020, neatoday.org/2020/01/06/students-still-cant-tell-fact-from-fiction-on-the-internet/.

67. Williamson, *Big Data in Education.*

68. Higdon and Huff, *United States of Distraction.*

69. C. O'Neil, *Weapons of Math Destruction;* Muller, *Tyranny of Metrics;* and Criado-Perez, *Invisible Women.*

70. Boettcher, *Technically Wrong;* Criado-Perez, *Invisible Women;* Noble, *Algorithms of Oppression.*

71. NAMLE, "Corporate Partners"; Poynter Institute for Media Studies, "MediaWise."

72. R. Hobbs, "Literacy," 141.

73. Higdon and Boyington, "Has Media Literacy Been Hijacked?"

74. Donoso et al., "Faraway, So Close," 200.

75. Kelly, Foucault, and Habermas, *Critique and Power;* Horkheimer, *Critical Theory;* Piccone, *Essential Frankfurt School Reader.*

76. Kelly, Foucault, and Habermas, *Critique and Power;* Hall et al., *Culture, Media, Language.*

77. Funk, Kellner, and Share, "Critical Media Literacy," 1.

78. Kellner and Share, "Critical Media Literacy"; Goldberg, "Responding to Fake News."

79. Kellner and Share, "Critical Media Literacy."

80. Kellner and Share, "Critical Media Literacy."

81. Kellner and Share, "Critical Media Literacy."

82. Prilleltensky, "Role of Power," 128.

83. Postman, *Technopoly.*

84. Zuboff, *Age of Surveillance Capitalism.*

85. Piven and Cloward, *Poor People's Movements,* 3-4.

86. Garcia, Seglem, and Share, "Transforming Teaching and Learning"; Morrell and Duncan-Andrade, "Popular Culture."

87. Kathy Frankovic, "Belief in Conspiracies Largely Depends on Political Identity," YouGov, December 27, 2016, https://today.yougov.com/news/2016/12/27/belief-conspiracies-largely-depends-political-iden/.

7. The Fake News Detection Kit

1. Copeland, *Idea of a Free Press*. The Thomas Jefferson letter quoted in the epigraph can be found at https://founders.archives.gov/documents/Jefferson/03-09-02-0209.
2. Kellner and Share, "Critical Media Literacy."
3. Ashley, Maksl, and Craft, "News Media Literacy," 98.
4. Nolan Higdon and Allison Butler, "5 Ways to Be a More Media Literate Citizen," *Along the Line* [podcast], episode 19, March 12, 2019, https://www.youtube.com/watch?v=Kwfcc2wGNJE&list=PLefnCMJ5W_iILomqv3wJKyKLyYolWtebw&index=21&t=3s.
5. Gabielkov et al., "Social Clicks."
6. Marquez, "How Accurate Are the Headlines?"; Bourgonje, Schneider, and Rehm, "From Clickbait."
7. Andy Lee Roth, "Five Ways to Flex Your Media Literacy Muscles," Project Censored, February 28, 2014, https://www. projectcensored.org/five-ways-flex-media-literacy-muscles/.
8. Higdon and Butler, "5 Ways."
9. Michael Arthur Caulfield, "Web Literacy for Student Fact-Checkers," 2017, https://digitalcommons.liberty.edu/cgi/viewcontent.cgi?article=1004&context=textbooks.
10. Walton, "Why Fallacies Appear," 159.
11. Ireland, "Fake News Alerts."
12. Browne and Keeley, *Asking the Right Questions*.
13. Jeff Share, Tessa Jolls, and Elizabeth Thoman, "5 Key Questions That Can Change the World: Lesson Plans for Media Literacy," in *CML MediaLit Kit: A Framework for Learning and Teaching in a Media Age* (Malibu, CA: Center for Media Literacy, 2007), https://medialiteracyweek.us/wp-content/uploads/2015/07/cml25lessons.pdf.
14. "Download an 'E.S.C.A.P.E. Junk News' Poster, Bookmark," Newseum, https://newseumed.org/download-escape-junk-news-poster-bookmark.
15. Allen, *Difference Matters*.

16. Peter Henshall and David Ingram, *The News Manual,* Online Edition, 2012, chapter 1,"What Is News?," https://www.thenewsmanual.net/Manuals Volume 1/volume1_01.html.

17. A. Knight, Geuze, and Gerlis, "Who Is a Journalist," 123.

18. "The 5 Principles of Ethical Journalism," Ethical Journalism Network, n.d., accessed January 10, 2020, https://ethicaljournalismnetwork.org/who-we-are/5-principles-of-journalism.

19. Onuf, *Jefferson's Empire,* 4.

20. Winston Churchill, speech in House of Commons, November 11, 1947.

Bibliography

Academic American Encyclopedia. Danbury, CT: Grolier Press, 1987.

Adornato, Anthony. *Mobile and Social Media Journalism: A Practical Guide.* Thousand Oaks, CA: Sage Publications, 2017.

Allcott, Hunt, and Matthew Gentzkow. "Social Media and Fake News in the 2016 Election." *Journal of Economic Perspectives* 31, no. 2 (2017): 211–36.

Allen, Brenda J. *Difference Matters: Communicating Social Identity.* Long Grove, IL: Waveland   Press, 2010.

Allen, T. S., and A. J. Moore. "Victory without Casualties: Russia's Information Operations." *Parameters* 48, no. 1 (2018): 59–71.

Amarasingam, Amarnath, ed. *The Stewart/Colbert Effect: Essays on the Real Impacts of Fake News.* Jefferson, NC: McFarland Press, 2014.

Ambrose, Stephen E. *Citizen Soldiers: The U.S. Army from the Normandy Beaches, to the Bulge, to the Surrender of Germany.* New York: Simon and Schuster, 2013.

Anderson, Carol. *White Rage: The Unspoken Truth of Our Racial Divide.* New York: Bloomsbury, 2016.

Anderson, C. W., Leonard Downie Jr., and Michael Schudson. *The News Media: What Everyone Needs to Know.* New York: Oxford University Press, 2016.

Applebaum, Anne. *Iron Curtain: The Crushing of Eastern Europe, 1944 to 1956.* New York: Anchor Books, 2012.

Araújo, Ana Cristina. "The Lisbon Earthquake of 1755: Public Distress and Political Propaganda." *E-Journal of Portuguese History* 2 (2006).

Ashley, Seth, Adam Maksl, and Stephanie Craft. "News Media Literacy and Political Engagement: What's the Connection?" *Journal of Media Literacy Education* 9, no. 1 (2017): 79–98.

Aufderheide, Patricia. *Media Literacy: A Report of the National Leadership Conference on Media Literacy.* Washington, DC: Aspen Institute, 1993.

Aysa-Lastra, María, and Lorenzo Cachón. *Immigrant Vulnerability and Resilience: Comparative Perspectives on Latin American Immigrants during the Great Recession.* Cham, Switzerland: Springer International, 2015.

Bailey, Thomas A. *Essays Diplomatic and Undiplomatic of Thomas A. Bailey.* New York: Ardent Media, 1969.

Bakir, Vian, and Andrew McStay. "Fake News and the Economy of Emotions: Problems, Causes, Solutions." *Digital Journalism* 6, no. 2 (2018): 154–75.

Bandurski, David. "China's Guerrilla War for the Web." *Far Eastern Economic Review,* July 7, 2008. http://chinamediaproject.org/2008/07/07/feer-chinas-guerrilla-war-for-the-web/.

Barclay, Donald. *Fake News, Propaganda, and Plain Old Lies: How to Find Trustworthy Information in the Digital Age.* New York: Rowman and Littlefield, 2018.

Bard, Mitchell T. "Propaganda, Persuasion, or Journalism? Fox News' Prime-Time Coverage of Health-Care Reform In 2009 and 2014." *Electronic News* 11, no. 2 (2017): 100–118.

Bartlett, Bruce. *The Truth Matters: A Citizen's Guide to Separating Facts from Lies and Stopping Fake News in Its Tracks.* New York: Ten Speed Press, 2017.

Batson, C. Daniel, Christopher L. Kennedy, Lesley-Anne Nord, E. L. Stocks, D'Yani A. Fleming, Christian M. Marzette, David A. Lishner, Robin E. Hayes, Leah M. Kolchinsky, and Tricia Zerger. "Anger at Unfairness: Is It Moral Outrage?" *European Journal of Social Psychology* 37, no. 6 (2007): 1272–85.

Baym, Geoffrey. "The Daily Show: Discursive Integration and the Reinvention of Political Journalism." *Political Communication* 22, no. 3 (2005). DOI: 10.1080/10584600591006492.

Bebić, Domagoj, and Marija Volarević. "Viral Journalism: The Rise of a New Form." *Medijska Istraživanja: Znanstveno-Stručni Časopis za Novinarstvo i Medije* 22, no. 2 (2016): 107–26.

Bellamy, Chris. *Absolute War: Soviet Russia in the Second World War.* New York: Alfred A. Knopf, 2007.

Benkler, Yochai, Robert Faris, and Hal Roberts. *Network Propaganda: Manipulation, Disinformation, and Radicalization in American Politics.* New York: Oxford University Press, 2018.

Berkhoff, Karel Cornelis. *Harvest of Despair: Life and Death in Ukraine under Nazi Rule.* Cambridge, MA: Harvard University Press, 2004.

Berlinger, Nancy, and Rachel L. Zacharias. "Resources for Teaching and Learning about Immigrant Health Care in Health Professions Education." *AMA Journal of Ethics* 21, no. 1 (2019): 50–57.

Bernhard, Nancy. *U.S. Television News and Cold War Propaganda, 1947–1960*. Cambridge: Cambridge University Press, 2003.

Berry, Jeffrey M., and Sarah Sobieraj. *The Outrage Industry: Political Opinion Media and the New Incivility*. New York: Oxford University Press, 2013.

Billington, Louis. "The Millerite Adventists in Great Britain, 1840–1850." *Journal of American Studies* 1, no. 2 (1967): 191–212.

Bliss, Sylvester. *Memoirs of William Miller*. Boston: Joshua V. Himes, 1853.

Blumer, Herbert. *Symbolic Interactionism: Perspective and Method*. Upper Saddle River, NJ: Prentice-Hall, 1969.

Boettcher, Sarah Wachter. *Technically Wrong: Sexist Apps, Biased Algorithms, and Other Threats of Toxic Tech*. New York: Norton, 2017.

Bolsover, Gillian, and Philip Howard. "Computational Propaganda and Political Big Data: Moving toward a More Critical Research Agenda." *Big Data* 5, no. 4 (2017): 273–76.

Bourgonje, Peter, Julian Moreno Schneider, and Georg Rehm. "From Clickbait to Fake News Detection: An Approach Based on Detecting the Stance of Headlines to Articles." In *Proceedings of the 2017 EMNLP Workshop: Natural Language Processing Meets Journalism*, edited by Octavian Popescu and Carlo Strapparava, 84–89. Stroudsburg, PA: Association for Computational Linguistics, 2017. DOI: 10.18653/v1/w17-4215.

Bradford, William. "Of Plymouth Plantation." In *The Mayflower Papers: Selected Writings of Colonial New England*, edited by Nathaniel Philbrick and Thomas Philbrick, 1–106. New York: Penguin, 2007.

Breakstone, Joel, Mark Smith, Sam Wineburg, Amie Rapaport, Jill Carle, Marshall Garland, and Anna Saavedra. "Students' Civic Online Reasoning: A National Portrait." November 14, 2019. Stanford History Education Group and Gibson Consulting, Stanford Digital Repository. https://purl.stanford.edu /gf151tb4868.

Brinkley, Alan. *The Publisher: Henry Luce and His American Century*. New York: Alfred Knopf, 2010.

Brinkley, Douglas. *Cronkite*. New York: Harper Collins, 2012.

Broniatowski, David A., Amelia M. Jamison, Sihua Qi, Lulwah Alkulaib, Tao Chen, Adrian Benton, Sandra C. Quinn, and Mark Dredze. "Weaponized Health Communication: Twitter Bots and Russian Trolls Amplify the Vaccine Debate." *American Journal of Public Health* 108, no. 10 (2018): 1378–84.

Browne, Neil, and Stuart Keeley. *Asking The Right Questions: A Guide To Critical Thinking.* Upper Saddle River, NJ: Pearson Education, 2018.

Brune, Lester H. *Chronological History of U.S. Foreign Relations: 1607-1932.* New York: Routledge, 2003.

Buenstorf, Guido, and Dirk Fornahl. "B2C—Bubble to Cluster: The Dot-Com Boom, Spin-Off Entrepreneurship, and Regional Agglomeration." *Journal of Evolutionary Economics* 19, no. 3 (2009): 349–78.

Bulger, Monica, and Patrick Davison. "The Promises, Challenges and Futures of Media Literacy." *Journal of Media Literacy Education* 10, no. 1 (2018): 1–21.

Bytwerk, Randall. *Julius Streicher: Nazi Editor of the Notorious Anti-Semitic Newspaper Der Sturmer.* New York: Cooper Square Press, 2001.

Calef, Robert. *More Wonders of the Invisible World.* London: Nathan Hillard, 1700.

Callender, James T. *The Prospect before Us.* Richmond, VA: Jones, Pleasants, and Lyon, 1800.

Cardaras, Mary. *Fear, Power, and Politics: The Recipe for War in Iraq after 9/11.* Lanham, MD: Lexington Books, 2013.

Carrasco, David. "Give Me Some Skin: The Charisma of the Aztec Warrior." *History of Religions* 35, no. 1 (1995): 1–26.

Cave, Alfred. *The Pequot War.* Amherst: University of Massachusetts Press, 1996.

Cheung, Chi-Kim. "Media Education across Four Asian Societies: Issues and Themes." *International Review of Education* 55, no. 1 (2009): 39–58.

Cohen, Stanley. *Folk Devils and Moral Panics: The Creation of the Mods and Rockers.* London: Granada, 1972.

Copeland, David A. *The Idea of a Free Press: The Enlightenment and Its Unruly Legacy.* Evanston, IL: Northwestern University Press, 2006.

Coulter, Ann. *Adios, America! The Left's Plan to Turn Our Country into a Third World Hellhole.* Washington, DC: Regnery, 2016.

Coward, John M. *The Newspaper Indian: Native American Identity in the Press, 1820-90.* Urbana: University of Illinois Press, 1999.

Cowie, Jefferson. *Stayin' Alive: The 1970s and the Last Days of the Working Class.* New York: New Press, 2010.

Crampton, R. J. *Eastern Europe in the Twentieth Century and After.* London: Routledge, 1997,

Creel, George. *How We Advertised America.* New York: Arno Press, 1972.

Crescimbene, Massimo, Federica La Longa, and Tiziana Lanza. "The Science of Rumors." *Annals of Geophysics* 55, no. 3 (2012): 421–25.

Criado-Perez, Caroline. *Invisible Women: Data Bias in a World Designed for Men.* New York: Abrams Press, 2019.

Dai, Yu-Xiao, and Su-Tong Hao. "Transcending the Opposition between Techno-Utopianism and Techno-Dystopianism." *Technology in Society* 53 (2018): 9–13.

Dain, Bruce R. *A Hideous Monster of the Mind: American Race Theory in the Early Republic.* Cambridge, MA: Harvard University Press, 2003.

D'Angelo, Paul, and Jim A. Kuypers, eds. *Doing News Framing Analysis: Empirical and Theoretical Perspectives.* New York: Routledge, 2010.

Davis, David Brion. *The Slave Power Conspiracy and the Paranoid Style.* Baton Rouge: Louisiana State University Press, 1969.

Davis, Nicholas T., and Johanna L. Dunaway. "Party Polarization, Media Choice, and Mass Partisan-Ideological Sorting." *Public Opinion Quarterly* 80, no. S1 (2016): 272–97.

Davis, Tracy C. "Operation Northwoods: The Pentagon's Scripts for Overthrowing Castro." *TDR/The Drama Review* 50, no. 1 (2006): 134–48.

De Baets, Antoon. "Taxonomy of Concepts Related to the Censorship of History." In *Government Secrecy: Research in Social Problems and Public Policy,* edited by Susan Maret, 53–65. Bingley, UK: Emerald Group, 2011.

Dick, Everett. *William Miller and the Advent Crisis.* Berrien Springs, MI: Andrews University Press, 1994.

Dickel, Sascha, and Jan-Felix Schrape. "The Renaissance of Techno-Utopianism as a Challenge for Responsible Innovation." *Journal of Responsible Innovation* 4, no. 2 (2017): 289–94.

Diggins, John Patrick. *Mussolini and Fascism: The View from America.* Princeton, NJ: Princeton University Press, 2015.

Dizard, Wilson P. *Inventing Public Diplomacy: The Story of the U.S. Information Agency.* Boulder, CO: Lynne Rienner, 2004.

Doherty, Martin A. *Nazi Wireless Propaganda: Lord Haw-Haw and British Public Opinion in the Second World War.* Edinburgh: Edinburgh University Press, 2000.

Donoso, Verónica, Valerie Verdoodt, Maarten Van Mechelen, and Lina Jasmontaite. "Faraway, So Close: Why the Digital Industry Needs Scholars and the Other Way Around." *Journal of Children and Media* 10, no. 2 (2016): 200–207.

Dorman, William A., and Mansour Farhang. *The U.S. Press and Iran: Foreign Policy and the Journalism of Deference.* Berkeley: University of California Press, 1988.

Druick, Zoë. "The Myth of Media Literacy." *International Journal of Communication* 10 (2016): 1125–44.

Duggan, Maeve, and Joanna Brenner. *The Demographics of Social Media Users,* 2012. Vol. 14. Washington, DC: Pew Research Center's Internet and American Life Project, 2013.

Dumas, Barry M. *Diving into the Bitstream: Information Technology Meets Society in a Digital World.* New York: Routledge, 2012.

Earl, Jennifer, and Katrina Kimport. *Digitally Enabled Social Change: Activism in the Internet Age.* Cambridge, MA: MIT Press, 2011.

Earley, Pete. *Comrade J: The Untold Secrets of Russia's Master Spy in America after the End of the Cold War.* London: Penguin Books, 2007.

Eisenstein, Elizabeth L. *The Printing Press as an Agent of Change.* Cambridge: Cambridge University Press, 1980.

Elliott, Robert N. "The Nat Turner Insurrection as Reported in the North Carolina Press." *North Carolina Historical Review* 38, no. 1 (1961): 1–18.

Esposito, Luigi. "White Fear and US Racism in the Era of Obama: The Relevance of Neoliberalism." *Theory in Action* 4, no. 3 (2011): 1–24.

Eubanks, Virginia. *Automating Inequality: How High-Tech Tools Profile, Police, and Punish the Poor.* New York: St. Martin's Press, 2018.

Farsetta, Diane, and Daniel Price. "Fake TV News: Widespread and Undisclosed." *Center for Media and Democracy* 6 (2006): 1–6.

Faye, Cathy. "Governing the Grapevine: The Study of Rumor during World War II." *History of Psychology* 10, no. 1 (2007): 1–21.

Fazio, Lisa K., Nadia M. Brashier, B. Keith Payne, and Elizabeth J. Marsh. "Knowledge Does Not Protect against Illusory Truth." *Journal of Experimental Psychology: General* 144, no. 5 (2015): 993–1002.

Fleming, Jennifer. "Media Literacy, News Literacy, or News Appreciation? A Case Study of the News Literacy Program at Stony Brook University." *Journalism and Mass Communication Educator* 69, no. 2 (2014): 146–65.

Fleming, Thomas. *The Illusion of Victory: America in World War I.* New York: Basic Books, 2003.

Foer, Franklin. *World without Mind: The Extensional Threat of Big Tech.* New York: Penguin Press, 2017.

Foner, Eric. *Give Me Liberty! An American History.* 4th ed. Vol. 1. New York: Norton, 2013.

Fried, Richard M. *The Russians Are Coming! The Russians Are Coming! Pageantry and Patriotism in Cold-War America.* New York: Oxford University Press, 1998.

Friendly, Fred W. *The Good Guys, the Bad Guys and the First Amendment: Free Speech vs. Fairness in Broadcasting.* New York: Random House, 2013.

Fuchs, Christian. *Digital Demagogue: Authoritarian Capitalism in the Age of Trump and Twitter.* London: Pluto Press, 2018.

Fuchs, Christian, Kees Boersma, Anders Albrechtslund, and Marisol Sandoval. *Internet and Surveillance: The Challenges of Web 2.0 and Social Media.* London: Routledge, 2013.

Funk, Steven, Douglas Kellner, and Jeff Share. "Critical Media Literacy as Transformative Pedagogy." In *Handbook of Research on Media Literacy in the Digital Age,* edited by Meida N. Yildiz and Jared Keengwe, 1–30. Hershey, PA: IGI Global, 2016.

Gabielkov, Maksym, Arthi Ramachandran, Augustin Chaintreau, and Arnaud Legout. "Social Clicks: What and Who Gets Read on Twitter?" *ACM SIGMETRICS Performance Evaluation Review* 44, no. 1 (2016): 179–92.

Garcia, Antero, Robyn Seglem, and Jeff Share. "Transforming Teaching and Learning through Critical Media Literacy Pedagogy." *Learning Landscapes* 6, no. 2 (2013): 109–24.

Geissler, Suzanne. *God and Sea Power: The Influence of Religion on Alfred Thayer Mahan.* Annapolis, MD: Naval Institute Press, 2015.

Gentzkow, Matthew, Edward L. Glaeser, and Claudia Goldin. "The Rise of the Fourth Estate: How Newspapers Became Informative and Why It Mattered." National Bureau of Economic Research, NBER Working Paper No. 10791, September 2004. https://www.nber.org/papers/w10791.

Germond, Jack, and Jules Witcover. *Whose Broad Stripes and Bright Stars: The Trivial Pursuit of the Presidency.* New York: Warner Books, 1989.

Gleijeses, Piero. *Shattered Hope: The Guatemalan Revolution and the United States, 1944–1954.* Princeton, NJ: Princeton University Press, 1992.

Goldberg, David. "Responding to Fake News: Is There an Alternative to Law and Regulation." *Southwestern Law Review* 47 (2017): 417–48.2Goodwin, Doris Kearns. *The Bully Pulpit: Theodore Roosevelt, William Howard Taft, and the Golden Age of Journalism.* New York: Simon and Schuster, 2013.

Goulden, Joseph C., and Peter Earnest. *The Dictionary of Espionage: Spyspeak into English.* New York: Dover Publications, 2012.

Gravel, Mike, Noam Chomsky, and Howard Zinn, eds. *The Pentagon Papers; Critical Essays; and an Index to Volumes 1–4.* Boston: Beacon Press, 1971.

Guess, Andrew, Jonathan Nagler, and Joshua Tucker. "Less Than You Think: Prevalence and Predictors of Fake News Dissemination on Facebook." *Science Advances* 5, no. 1 (2019). DOI: 10.1126/sciadv.aau4586.

Guilday, Peter. "The Sacred Congregation de Propaganda Fide (1622–1922)." *Catholic Historical Review* 6, no. 4 (1921): 478–94.

Guo, Lei, and Chris Vargo. "'Fake News' and Emerging Online Media Ecosystem: An Integrated Intermedia Agenda-Setting Analysis of the 2016 US Presidential Election." *Communication Research,* June 4, 2018, 1–23. DOI: 10.1177%2F0093650218777177.

Hadley, David P. *The Rising Clamor: The American Press, the Central Intelligence Agency, and the Cold War.* Lexington: University Press of Kentucky, 2019.

Hagedorn, Ann. *Savage Peace: Hope and Fear in America, 1919.* New York: Simon and Schuster, 2007.

Hall, Stuart, Dorothy Hobson, Andrew Lowe, and Paul Willis, eds. *Culture, Media, Language: Working Papers in Cultural Studies, 1972-79.* New York: Routledge, 2003.

Hallin, Daniel C. "The Media, the War in Vietnam, and Political Support: A Critique of the Thesis of an Oppositional Media." *Journal of Politics* 46, no. 1 (1984): 2–24.

Hallin, Daniel C. *The Uncensored War: The Media and Vietnam.* Los Angeles: University of California Press, 1986.

Halperin, Mark, and John Heilemann. *Double Down: Game Change, 2012.* New York: Penguin Press, 2013.

Hamm, Theodore. *The New Blue Media: How Michael Moore, Moveon. Org, Jon Stewart and Company Are Transforming Progressive Politics.* New York: New Press, 2008.

Hammond, William M. *Reporting Vietnam: Media and Military at War.* Lawrence: University Press of Kansas, 1998.

Harris, Bronwyn. "Xenophobia: A New Pathology for a New South Africa." In *Psychopathology and Social Prejudice,* edited by Derek Hook and Gillian Eagle, 169–84. Cape Town: University of Cape Town Press, 2002.

Hartman, John J. "A Psychoanalytic View of Racial Myths in a Nazi Propaganda Film: *Der Ewige Jude* (the Eternal Jew)." *Journal of Applied Psychoanalytic Studies* 2, no. 4 (2000): 329–46.

Hedges, Chris. *War Is a Force That Gives Us Meaning.* New York: Anchor, Books 2003.

Henderson, Timothy J. *A Glorious Defeat: Mexico and Its War with the United States.* New York: Macmillan, 2007.

Hendricks, John Allen, and Dan Schill. "The Social Media Election of 2016." In *The 2016 US Presidential Campaign,* edited by Robert Denton Jr., 121–50. New York: Palgrave Macmillan, 2017.

Herring, George C. *From Colony to Superpower: U.S. Foreign Relations since 1776.* New York: Oxford University Press, 2008.

Herring, George C., ed. *The Secret Diplomacy of the Vietnam War: The Negotiating Volumes of the Pentagon Papers.* Austin: University of Texas Press, 2014.

Heyer, Paul. *Communications and History: Theories of Media, Knowledge, and Civilization.* New York: Greenwood Press, 1988.

Higdon, Nolan, and Mickey Huff. *United States of Distraction: Media Manipulation in Post-truth America and What We Can Do about It.* New York: City Lights, 2019.

Hirschman, Charles, Samuel Preston, and Vu Manh Loi. "Vietnamese Casualties during the American War: A New Estimate." *Population and Development Review* 21, no. 4 (1995): 783–812.

Hitler, Adolf. *Mein Kampf.* Translated by James Vincent Murphy. London: Hurst and Blackett, 1939.

Hobbs, Renee. "Literacy: Understanding Media and How They Work." In *What Society Needs from Media in the Age of Digital Communication (Media vol. 21),* edited by Robert G. Picard, 131–60. Ramada: Formalpress, 2016.

Hobbs, Renee. "The Seven Great Debates in the Media Literacy Movement." *Journal of Communication* 48, no. 1 (1998): 16–32.

Hobbs, Renee. "Teaching and Learning in a Post-truth World." *Educational Leadership* 75, no. 3 (2017): 26–31.

Hobbs, Renee. "Teach the Conspiracies." *Knowledge Quest* 46, no. 1 (2017): 16–24.

Hobbs, Renee, and Richard Frost. "Measuring the Acquisition of Media-Literacy Skills." *Reading Research Quarterly* 38, no. 3 (2003): 330–55.

Hobbs, Renee, and Amy Jensen. "The Past, Present, and Future of Media Literacy Education." *Journal of Media Literacy Education* 1, no. 1 (2009): 1–12.

Hobbs, Renee, and Sandra McGee. "Teaching about Propaganda: An Examination of the Historical Roots of Media Literacy." *Journal of Media Literacy Education* 6, no. 2 (2014): 56–66.

Hobbs, Renee, Christian Seyferth-Zapf, and Silke Grafe. "Using Virtual Exchange to Advance Media Literacy Competencies through Analysis of Contemporary Propaganda." *Journal of Media Literacy Education* 10, no. 2 (2018): 152–68.

Hobbs, William R., and Margaret E. Roberts. "How Sudden Censorship Can Increase Access to Information." *American Political Science Review* 112, no. 3 (2018): 621–36.

Hogeland, William. *The Whiskey Rebellion: George Washington, Alexander Hamilton, and the Frontier Rebels Who Challenged America's Newfound Sovereignty*. New York: Simon and Schuster, 2010.

Holmes, Clive. "The Opinion of the Cambridge Association, 1 August 1692: A Neglected Text of the Salem Witch Trials." *New England Quarterly* 89, no. 4 (2016): 643–67.

Horkheimer, Max. *Critical Theory: Selected Essays*. New York: Continuum, 1982.

Horne, Benjamin D., and Sibel Adali. "This Just In: Fake News Packs a Lot in Title, Uses Simpler, Repetitive Content in Text Body, More Similar to Satire Than Real News." Paper presented at the Association for the Advancement of Artificial Intelligence's Eleventh International Conference on Web and Social Media, 2017. arXiv, March 2017. https://arxiv.org/pdf/1703.09398.pdf.

Howe, Russell Warren. *The Hunt for Tokyo Rose*. Lanham, MD: Rowman and Littlefield, 1993.

Hsia, R. Po-Chia. *Trent 1475: Stories of a Ritual Murder Trial*. New Haven, CT: Yale University Press, 1992.

Huddy, Leonie, Alexa Bankert, and Caitlin Davies. "Expressive versus Instrumental Partisanship in Multiparty European Systems." *Political Psychology* 39, no. 1 (2018): 173–99.

Hunt, Lynn, Thomas R. Martin, and Barbara H. Rosenwein. *The Making of the West: Peoples and Cultures*. New York: Bedford/St. Martin's Press, 2015.

Institute for Propaganda Analysis. "We Say Au Revoir." *Propaganda Analysis* 4, no. 13 (1942): 1–6.

Ireland, Sonnet. "Fake News Alerts: Teaching News Literacy Skills in a Meme World." *Reference Librarian* 59, no. 3 (2018): 122–28.

Ivanova, Galina Mikhailovna, Donald J. Raleigh, Galina Mikhailovna, and Carol A. Flath. *Labor Camp Socialism: The Gulag in the Soviet Totalitarian System*. New York: Routledge, 2015.

Jane, Emma A. *Misogyny Online: A Short and Brutish History*. London: Sage Publications, 2016.

Jansen, Marius B. *The Making of Modern Japan*. Cambridge, MA: Harvard University Press, 2002.

Jean, Susan. "'Warranted' Lynchings: Narratives of Mob Violence in White Southern Newspapers, 1880–1940." *American Nineteenth Century History* 6, no. 3 (2005): 351–72.

Jensen, Carl. *Censored 1996: The News That Didn't Make the News*. New York: Seven Stories Press, 1996.

Johnson, Nicholas. *Your Second Priority: A Former FCC Commissioner Speaks Out.* Morrisville, NC: Lulu, 2007.

Jordan, Laylon Wayne. *America's Mussolini: The United States and Italy, 1919–1936.* Charlottesville: University of Virginia, 1972.

Joseph, Gilbert M., and Greg Grandin, eds. *A Century of Revolution: Insurgent and Counterinsurgent Violence during Latin America's Long Cold War.* Durham, NC: Duke University Press, 2010.

Kahne, Joseph, Nam-Jin Lee, and Jessica Timpany Feezell. "Digital Media Literacy Education and Online Civic and Political Participation." *International Journal of Communication* 6, no. 1 (2012): 1–24.

Kaminski, Margot E., and Shane Witnov. "The Conforming Effect: First Amendment Implications of Surveillance, beyond Chilling Speech." *University of Richmond Law Review* 49, no. 465 (2014): 465–78.

Kazanjian, Howard, and Chris Enss. *The Trials of Annie Oakley.* Guilford, CT: Rowman and Littlefield, 2017.

Keenan, Jerry. *Encyclopedia of the Spanish-American and Philippine-American Wars.* Santa Barbara, CA: ABC-CLIO, 2001.

Kellner, Douglas. *The Persian Gulf TV War.* Boulder, CO: Westview Press, 1992.

Kellner, Douglas, and Jeff Share. "Critical Media Literacy: Crucial Policy Choices for a Twenty-First-Century Democracy." *Policy Futures in Education* 5, no. 1 (2007): 59–69.

Kellner, Douglas, and Jeff Share. "Critical Media Literacy, Democracy, and the Reconstruction of Education." In *Media Literacy: A Reader,* edited by Donaldo Pereira Macedo and Shirley R. Steinberg, 3–23. New York: Peter Lang, 2007.

Kelly, Michael, Michel Foucault, and Jürgen Habermas, eds. *Critique and Power: Recasting the Foucault/Habermas Debate.* Cambridge, MA: MIT University Press, 1994.

Kennett, Lee B. *For the Duration . . . : The United States Goes to War, Pearl Harbor, 1942.* New York: Charles Scribner's Sons, 1985.

Kim, Sei-Hill. "Spiral of Silence: Fear of Isolation and Willingness to Speak Out." In *International Encyclopedia of Media Effects,* March 8, 2017, 1–9. DOI: 10.1002/9781118783764.wbieme0037.

Kind-Kovács, Friederike, and Jessie Labov, eds. *Samizdat, Tamizdat, and Beyond: Transnational Media during and after Socialism.* New York: Berghahn Books, 2013.

Kindleberger, Charles P. *Manias, Panics and Crashes: A History of Financial Crises.* New York: John Wiley and Sons, 2005.

King, Gary, Jennifer Pan, and Margaret Roberts, "How the Chinese Government Fabricates Social Media Posts for Strategic Distraction, Not Engaged Argument." Harvard University, April 9, 2017. http://gking.harvard.edu/files/gking/files/50c.pdf?m=1464790150.

Kinsbruner, Jay. *Independence in Spanish America: Civil Wars, Revolutions, and Underdevelopment*. Albuquerque: University of New Mexico Press, 2000.

Kinzer, Stephen. *All the Shah's Men: An American Coup and the Roots of Middle East Terror*. Hoboken, NJ: John Wiley and Sons, 2003.

Kinzer, Stephen. *The Brothers: John Foster Dulles, Allen Dulles, and Their Secret World War*. New York: Times Books, 2013.

Kinzer, Stephen. *Overthrow: America's Century of Regime Change from Hawaii to Iraq*. New York: Macmillan, 2007.

Kinzer, Stephen. *The True Flag: Theodore Roosevelt, Mark Twain, and the Birth of American Empire*. New York: Henry Holt, 2018.

Kleinknecht, William. *The Man Who Sold the World: Ronald Reagan and the Betrayal of Main Street America*. New York: Nation Books, 2009.

Knight, Alan, Cherian Geuze, and Alex Gerlis. "Who Is a Journalist." *Journalism Studies* 9, no. 1 (2008): 117–31.

Knight, George R. *Joseph Bates: The Real Founder of Seventh-Day Adventism*. Hagerstown, MD: Review and Herald Publication Association, 2004.

Koppes, Clayton R., and Gregory D. Black. "Blacks, Loyalty, and Motion-Picture Propaganda in World War II." *Journal of American History* 73, no. 2 (1986): 383–406.

Kornbluh, Peter. *The Pinochet File: A Declassified Dossier on Atrocity and Accountability*. New York: New Press, 2013.

Kreimer, Seth F. "Censorship by Proxy: The First Amendment, Internet Intermediaries, and the Problem of the Weakest Link." *University of Pennsylvania Law Review* 155, no. 127 (2006): 11–80.

Krom, Cynthia L., and Stephanie Krom. "The Whiskey Tax of 1791 and the Consequent Insurrection: A Wicked and Happy Tumult." *Accounting Historians Journal* 40, no. 2 (2013): 91–113.

Kruschinski, Simon, and Andre Haller. "Restrictions on Data-Driven Political Micro-targeting in Germany." *Internet Policy Review* 6, no. 4 (2017). DOI: 10.14763/2017.4.780.

Lackner, Karl J., and Mario Plebani. "The Theranos Saga and the Consequences." *Clinical Chemistry and Laboratory Medicine (CCLM)* 56, no. 9 (2018): 1395–96.

Lange-Ionatamishvili, Elina, and Sanda Svetoka. "Strategic Communications and Social Media in the Russia Ukraine Conflict." In *Cyber War in Perspective: Russian Aggression against Ukraine*, edited by Kenneth Geers, chap. 12. Tallinn, Estonia: NATO Cooperative Cyber Defense Centre of Excellence, 2015. https://ccdcoe.org/uploads/2018/10/Ch12_CyberWarinPerspective_Lange_Svetoka.pdf.

Laurie, Clayton D. "'The Chinese Must Go': The United States Army and the Anti-Chinese Riots in Washington Territory, 1885-1886." *Pacific Northwest Quarterly* 81, no. 1 (1990): 22-29.

Laursen, John Christian. "David Hume and the Danish Debate about Freedom of the Press in the 1770s." *Journal of the History of Ideas* 59, no. 1 (1998): 167-72.

Lazer, David M J, Matthew A. Baum, Yochai Benkler, Adam J. Berinsky, Kelly M. Greenhill, Filippo Menczer, Miriam J. Metzger, et al. "The Science of Fake News." *Science* 359, no. 6380 (2018): 1094-96.

Leland, Anne. *American War and Military Operations Casualties: Lists and Statistics*. Washington, DC: Congressional Research Service, 2010.

Lepore, Jill. *These Truths: A History of the United States*. New York: Norton, 2018.

Levendusky, Matthew. *How Partisan Media Polarize America*. Chicago: University of Chicago Press, 2013.5Levine, Yasha. *Surveillance Valley: The Secret Military History of the Internet*. New York: Hachette Books, 2018.

Levitin, Daniel. *Weaponized Lies: How to Think Critically in the Post-truth Era*. New York: Dutton, 2016.

Lewis, Charles. *935 Lies: The Future of Truth and the Decline of America's Moral Integrity*. New York: Public Affairs, 2014.

Lightbody, Bradley. *The Second World War: Ambitions to Nemesis*. New York: Routledge, 2004.

Lin, Herbert. "A Virtual Necessity: Some Modest Steps toward Greater Cybersecurity." *Bulletin of the Atomic Scientists* 68, no. 5 (2012): 75-87.

Lippmann, Walter. *Public Opinion*. 1922. Reprint, New York: Routledge, 2017.

Lowry, Richard. *The Photographer and the President: Abraham Lincoln, Alexander Gardner, and the Images That Made a Presidency*. New York: Rizzoli Publications, 2015.

Lucas, Richard. *Axis Sally: The American Voice of Nazi Germany*. Philadelphia: Casemate, 2010.

Lutz, William. "Fourteen Years of Doublespeak." *English Journal* 77, no. 3 (1988): 40-42.

Lyman, Stanford M. "The 'Yellow Peril' Mystique: Origins and Vicissitudes of a Racist Discourse." *International Journal of Politics, Culture, and Society* 13, no. 4 (2000): 683-747.

Maddock, Jim, Kate Starbird, Haneen J. Al-Hassani, Daniel E. Sandoval, Mania Orand, and Robert M. Mason. "Characterizing Online Rumoring Behavior Using Multi-dimensional Signatures." In *Proceedings of the 18th ACM Conference on Computer Supported Cooperative Work and Social Computing,* 228-41. New York: ACM, 2015.

Major, Patrick, and Rana Mitter. "East Is East and West Is West? Towards a Comparative Sociocultural History of the Cold War." In *Across the Blocs: Exploring Comparative Cold War Cultural and Social History,* chap. 1. London: Taylor and Francis, 2004.

Marquez, F. T. "How Accurate Are the Headlines?" *Journal of Communication* 30, no. 3 (1980): 30-36.

Masaharu, Sato. "'Negro Propaganda Operations': Japan's Short-Wave Radio Broadcasts for World War II Black Americans." *Historical Journal of Film, Radio and Television* 19, no. 1 (1999): 5-26.

Mather, Cotton. *The Wonders of the Invisible World: Being an Account of the Tryals of Several Witches Lately Executed in New-England.* Whitefish, MT: Kessinger, 2003.

Mazzucato, Mariana. *The Entrepreneurial State: Debunking Public vs. Private Sector Myths.* New York: Anthem Press, 2013.

McClain, James L. *Japan: A Modern History.* New York: Norton, 2002.

McConnell, Michael. "Two-and-a-Half Cheers for Bush v. Gore," In *The Vote: Bush, Gore, and the Supreme Court,* edited by Cass Sunstein and Richard Epstein, 657-78. Chicago: University of Chicago Press, 2001.

McGillen, Petra S. "Techniques of 19th-Century Fake News Reporter Teach U.S. Why We Fall for It Today." The Conversation, April 5, 2017. https://theconversation.com/techniques-of-19th-century-fake-news-reporter-teach- us-why-we-fall-for-it-today-75583.

McGrew, Sarah, Joel Breakstone, Teresa Ortega, Mark Smith, and Sam Wineburg. "Can Students Evaluate Online Sources? Learning from Assessments of Civic Online Reasoning." *Theory and Research in Social Education* 46, no. 2 (2018): 165-93.

McIntyre, Lee. *Post-truth.* Cambridge, MA: MIT Press, 2018.

McLuhan, Marshall. *Gutenberg Galaxy: The Making of Typographic Man.* Toronto: University of Toronto Press, 1962.

McLuhan, Marshall. *Understanding Media.* New York: Mentor Press, 1964.

McLuhan, Marshall, and Quentin Fiore. *The Medium Is the Massage: An Inventory of Effects.* Produced by Jerome Agel. San Francisco: Hardwired, 1967.

McNamee, Roger. *Zucked: Waking Up to the Facebook Catastrophe.* New York: Penguin Press, 2019.

Mihailidis, Paul. "Civic Media Literacies: Re-imagining Engagement for Civic Intentionality." *Learning, Media and Technology* 43, no. 2 (2018): 152–64.

Mihailidis, Paul, and Samantha Viotty. "Spreadable Spectacle in Digital Culture: Civic Expression, Fake News, and the Role of Media Literacies in 'Post-fact' Society." *American Behavioral Scientist* 61, no. 4 (2017): 441–54.

Miller, William. *William Miller's Apology and Defence.* 1845. Reprint, Loma Linda, CA: Heritage Room, Loma Linda University, 1997.

Minnite, Lorraine C. *The Myth of Voter Fraud.* Ithaca, NY: Cornell University Press, 2017.

Morrell, Ernest, and Jeffrey Duncan-Andrade. "Popular Culture and Critical Media Pedagogy in Secondary Literacy Classrooms." *International Journal of Learning* 12, no. 9 (2006): 273–80.

Mott, Frank Luther. *American Journalism.* New York: Routledge, 2000.

Muller, Jerry. *The Tyranny of Metrics.* Princeton, NJ; Princeton University Press, 2018.

Myers, B. R. *The Cleanest Race: How North Koreans See Themselves and Why It Matters.* Brooklyn, NY: Melville House, 2010.

Nabi, Zubair. "Censorship Is Futile." arXiv, November 2014. https://firstmon-day.org/article/view/5525/4155.

Nevins, Allan. *Ordeal of the Union: Fruits of Manifest Destiny, 1847–1852.* New York: Charles Scribner's Sons, 1947.

Newton-Matza, Mitchell. *The Espionage and Sedition Acts: World War I and the Image of Civil Liberties.* New York: Routledge, 2017.

Noble, Safiya Umoja. *Algorithms of Oppression: How Search Engines Reinforce Racism.* New York: New York University Press, 2018.

Noelle-Neumann, Elisabeth. "The Spiral of Silence: A Theory of Public Opinion." *Journal of Communication* 24, no. 2 (1974): 43–51.

Odum, Howard Washington. *Race and Rumors of Race: Challenge to American Crisis.* Chapel Hill: University of North Carolina Press, 1943.

Olson, Lynne, and S. V. Cloud. *The Murrow Boys: Pioneers on the Front Lines of Broadcast Journalism.* Boston: Houghton Mifflin, 1996.

O'Neil, Cathy. *Weapons of Math Destruction: How Big Data Increases Inequality and Threatens Democracy.* New York: Broadway Books, 2016.

O'Neil, Patrick. *Post-communism and the Media in Eastern Europe*. London: Routledge, 1997.

Onuf, Peter S. *Jefferson's Empire: The Language of American Nationhood*. Charlottesville: University of Virginia Press, 2000.

Ovadya, Aviv. "What's Worse Than Fake News? The Distortion of Reality Itself." *New Perspectives Quarterly* 35, no. 2 (2018): 43–45.

Overholser, Geneva, and Kathleen Hall Jamieson. *The Press*. Institutions of American Democracy. New York: Oxford University Press, 2005.

Overy, Richard. *1939, Countdown to War*. New York: Viking Press, 2010.

Paddock, Troy. *A Call to Arms: Propaganda, Public Opinion, and Newspapers in the Great War*. Westport, CT: Greenwood, 2004.

Pariser, Eli. *The Filter Bubble: How the New Personalized Web Is Changing What We Read and How We Think*. London: Penguin, 2011.

Patterson, David S. *The Search for Negotiated Peace: Women's Activism and Citizen Diplomacy in World War I*. New York: Routledge, 2012.

Patterson, Graeme. *History and Communications: Harold Innis, Marshall McLuhan, and the Interpretation of History*. Toronto: University of Toronto Press, 1990.

Paxton, Robert. *The Anatomy of Fascism*. New York: Vintage Books, 2004.

Petersen, Anne Helen. "Towards an Industrial History of Celebrity Gossip: The *National Enquirer, People Magazine* and 'Personality Journalism' in the 1970s." *Celebrity Studies* 2, no. 2 (2011): 131–49.

Phillips, Peter. *Giants: The Global Power Elite*. New York: Seven Stories Press, 2018.

Piccone, Paul. *The Essential Frankfurt School Reader*. New York: Continuum, 1978.

Pickard, Victor. *America's Battle for Media Democracy*. Cambridge: Cambridge University Press, 2015.

Picon, Antoine. "Robots and Architecture: Experiments, Fiction, Epistemology." *Architectural Design* 84, no. 3 (2014): 54–59.

Piven, Frances Fox and Richard Cloward. *Poor People's Movements: How They Succeed, Why They Fail*. New York: Pantheon, 1977.

Ponder, Stephen. *Managing the Press: Origins of the Media Presidency, 1897–1933*. New York: Palgrave, 2000.

Porch, Douglas. "'No Bad Stories': The American Media-Military Relationship." *Naval War College Review* 55, no. 1 (2002): 85–107.

Postman, Neil. *Teaching as a Conserving Activity*. New York: Delacorte Press, 1979.

Postman, Neil. *Technopoly: The Surrender of Culture to Technology.* New York: Vintage Books, 1993.

Potolsky, Matthew. *The National Security Sublime: On the Aesthetics of Government Secrecy.* New York: Routledge, 2019.

Press, Bill. *Toxic Talk: How the Radical Right Has Poisoned America's Airwaves.* New York: St. Martin's Press, 2010.

Prilleltensky, Isaac. "The Role of Power In Wellness, Oppression, and Liberation: The Promise of Psychopolitical Validity." *Journal of Community Psychology* 36, no. 2 (2008): 116–36.

Quinn, Patrick J. *The Conning of America: The Great War and American Popular Literature.* Atlanta, GA: Rodopi, 2001.

Ratner, Lorman A., and Dwight L. Teeter Jr. *Fanatics and Fire-Eaters: Newspapers and the Coming of the Civil War.* Chicago: University of Illinois Press, 2010.

Ray, Thomas M. "'Not One Cent for Tribute': The Public Addresses and American Popular Reaction to the XYZ Affair, 1798–1799." *Journal of the Early Republic* 3, no. 4 (1983): 389–412.

Reilly, Tom. "Newspapers: U.S. Press." In *The United States and Mexico at War: Nineteenth-Century Expansion and Conflict,* edited by Donald Frazier, 294–96. New York: Macmillan, 1998.

Reilly, Tom. *War with Mexico! America's Reporters Cover the Battlefront.* Lawrence: University Press of Kansas, 2010.

Reinarman, Craig, and Harry G. Levine. "The Crack Attack: America's Latest Drug Scare, 1986- 1992." In *Images of Issues: Typifying Contemporary Social Problems,* edited by Joel Best, 147–86. New York: Routledge, 2017.

Reuth, Ralf Georg. *Goebbels.* New York: Harcourt Brace, 1993.

Rhodes, Anthony. *Propaganda: The Art of Persuasion: World War II.* New York: Chelsea House, 1976.

Roberts, Priscilla. "Paul D. Cravath, the First World War, and the Anglophile Internationalist Tradition." *Australian Journal of Politics and History* 51, no. 2 (2005): 194–215.

Roberts, Robert C. "The Vice of Pride." *Faith and Philosophy* 26, no. 2 (2009): 119–33.

Ronan, John. "'Young Goodman Brown' and the Mathers." *New England Quarterly* 85, no. 2 (2012): 253–80.

Rorabaugh, William J. *The Alcoholic Republic: An American Tradition.* New York: Oxford University Press, 1981.

Rosenheim, Shawn James. *The Cryptographic Imagination: Secret Writing from Edgar Poe to the Internet Parallax*. Baltimore: Johns Hopkins University Press, 1996.

Roskos-Ewoldsen, David R., Beverly Roskos-Ewoldsen, and Francesca R. Dillman Carpenter. "Media Priming: A Synthesis." In *Media Effects: Advances in Theory and Research*, edited by Jennings Bryant, Dolf Zillmann, and Mary Beth Oliver, 97–120. New York: McGraw-Hill, 2002.

Ross, Michael W., E. James Essien, and Isabel Torres. "Conspiracy Beliefs about the Origin of HIV/AIDS in Four Racial/Ethnic Groups." *Journal of Acquired Immune Deficiency Syndromes* 41, no. 3 (2006): 342–44.

Rudenstine, David. *The Day the Presses Stopped: A History of the Pentagon Papers Case*. Berkeley: University of California Press, 1998.

Russell, Jeffrey Burton. *Witchcraft in the Middle Ages*. Ithaca, NY: Cornell University Press, 1972.

Saldaña, Johnny. *The Coding Manual for Qualitative Researchers*. Thousand Oaks, CA: Sage Publications, 2015.

Schinkel, Willem. "Contexts of Anxiety: The Moral Panic over 'Senseless Violence' in the Netherlands." *Current Sociology* 56, no. 5 (2008): 735–56.

Schlesinger, Stephen, Stephen Kinzer, and John H. Coatsworth. *Bitter Fruit: The Story of the American Coup in Guatemala*. Cambridge, MA: David Rockefeller Center for Latin American Studies, 2005.

Schrag, Peter. *Not Fit for Our Society: Nativism and Immigration*. Berkeley: University of California Press, 2010.

Schulman, Bruce. *The Seventies: The Great Shift in American Culture, Society, and Politics*. New York: New Press, 2001.

Segal, Adam. *The Hacked World Order: How Nations Fight, Trade, Maneuver, and Manipulate in the Digital Age*. New York: PublicAffairs, 2017.

Service, Robert. *A History of Modern Russia, from Nicholas II to Putin*. Cambridge, MA: Harvard University Press, 2005.

Shaw, Daron. "Assessing the Impact of Campaigning in the 2016 US Presidential Election." *Zeitschrift für Politikberatung* 8, no. 1 (2017): 15–23.

Sheldon, Marcus. *Father Coughlin: The Tumultuous Life of the Priest of the Little Flower*. Boston: Little, Brown, 1973.

Sherman, Gabriel. *The Loudest Voice in the Room: How The Brilliant, Bombastic Rodger Ailes Built Fox News and Divided a Country*. New York: Random House, 2014.

Shu, Kai, and Huan Liu. *Detecting Fake News on Social Media*. Synthesis Lectures on Data Mining and Knowledge Discovery 11, no. 3. San Rafael, CA: Morgan and Claypool, 2019.2Silver, Peter. *Our Savage Neighbors: How Indian War Transformed Early America*. New York: Norton, 2009.

Simmonds, Alan G. V. *Britain and World War One*. New York: Routledge, 2013.

Skinner, B. F. *The Behavior of Organisms: An Experimental Analysis of Behavior*. New York: Appleton-Century-Crofts, 1938.

Skinner, Daniel. "'Keep Your Government Hands Off My Medicare!': An Analysis of Media Effects on Tea Party Health Care Politics." *New Political Science* 34, no. 4 (2012): 605–19.

Smith, Craig R. "The Alien and Sedition Crisis." In *Silencing the Opposition: How the US Government Suppressed Freedom of Expression during Major Crises*, edited by Craig R. Smith, 1–21. Albany, NY: SUNY Press, 2011.

Smith, Douglas J. *Managing White Supremacy: Race, Politics, and Citizenship in Jim Crow Virginia*. Chapel Hill: University of North Carolina Press, 2002.

Spencer, Mark G. "Democratic-Republican Societies." In *Conspiracy Theories in American History: An Encyclopedia*, edited by Peter Knight. Santa Barbara, CA: ABC-CLIO Press, 2003.

Sridhar, Devi, Josip Car, Mickey Chopra, Harry Campbell, Ngaire Woods, and Igor Rudan. "Improving Health Aid for a Better Planet: The Planning, Monitoring and Evaluation Tool (PLANET)." *Journal of Global Health* 5, no. 2 (2015). DOI: 10.7189/Jogh.05.020404.

Stamps, Judith. *Unthinking Modernity: Innis, McLuhan, and the Frankfurt School*. Montreal: McGill-Queens University Press, 2001.

Stein, Judith. *Pivotal Decade: How the United States Traded Factories for Finance in the Seventies*. New Haven, CT: Yale University Press, 2010.

Stephens, Mitchell. *A History of News: From the Drum to the Satellite*. New York: Viking Press, 1988.

Stephens, Niall P. "Toward a More Substantive Media Ecology: Postman's Metaphor versus Posthuman Futures." *International Journal of Communication* 8 (2014): 2027–45.

Stephens-Davidowitz, Seth. *Everybody Lies: Big Data, New Data, and What the Internet Can Tell Us about Who We Really Are*. New York: HarperCollins, 2017.

Steuter, Erin, and Deborah Wills. *At War with Metaphor: Media, Propaganda, and Racism in the War on Terror*. Lanham, MD: Lexington Books, 2009.

Strate, Lance. "Media Ecology." *Communication Research Trends* 23, no. 2 (2004): 1–48.

Straubhaar, Joseph, Robert LaRose, and Lucinda Davenport. *Media Now: Understanding Media, Culture, and Technology*. Boston: Cengage Learning, 2013.

Stroud, Natalie Jomini. "Polarization and Partisan Selective Exposure." *Journal of Communication* 60, no. 3 (2010): 556–76.

Suri, Jeremy. *Henry Kissinger and the American Century.* Cambridge, MA: Belknap Press of Harvard University Press, 2007.

Sweeney, Michael S. *Secrets of Victory: The Office of Censorship and the American Press and Radio in World War II.* Chapel Hill: University of North Carolina Press, 2001.

Sykes, Bryan L., and Michelle Maroto. "A Wealth of Inequalities: Mass Incarceration, Employment, and Racial Disparities in US Household Wealth, 1996 to 2011." *RSF: The Russell Sage Foundation Journal of the Social Sciences* 2, no. 6 (2016): 129–52.

Taibbi, Matt. *Hate Inc.: Why Today's Media Us Despise One Another.* New York: OR Books, 2019.

Talbot, David. *The Devil's Chessboard: Allen Dulles, the CIA, and the Rise of America's Secret Government.* New York: HarperCollins, 2015.

Tandoc, Edson C., Jr., and Joy Jenkins. "Out of Bounds? How Gawker's Outing a Married Man Fits into the Boundaries of Journalism." *New Media and Society* 20, no. 2 (2018): 581–98.

Tandoc, Edson C., Jr., Zheng Wei Lim, and Richard Ling. "Defining 'Fake News': A Typology of Scholarly Definitions." *Digital Journalism* 6, no. 2 (2018). DOI: 10.1080/21670811.2017.1360143.

Temin, Peter. *The Vanishing Middle Class: Prejudice and Power in a Dual Economy.* Cambridge, MA: MIT Press, 2018.

Terraine, John. *Mons: The Retreat to Victory.* London: Wordsworth Military Library, 1960.

Thacker, Toby. *Joseph Goebbels: Life and Death.* 2009. Reprint, New York: Palgrave Macmillan, 2010.

Thaler, David Stewart. "Was He Or Wasn't He?" *Menckeniana* 182 (2007): 1–9.

Tocqueville, Alexis de. *Democracy in America.* New York: Barnes and Noble, 2003.

Townend, Judith. "Freedom of Expression and the Chilling Effect." In *The Routledge Companion to Media and Human Rights,* edited by Howard Tumber and Silvio Waisbord, 73–82. New York: Routledge, 2017.

Trommler, Frank. "The Lusitania Effect: America's Mobilization against Germany in World War I." *German Studies Review* 32, no. 2 (2009): 241–66.

Tucker, Robert W. *Woodrow Wilson and the Great War: Reconsidering America's Neutrality, 1914–1917.* Charlottesville: University of Virginia Press, 2007.

Ubelaker, Douglas H. "North American Indian Population Size, AD 1500 to 1985." *American Journal of Physical Anthropology* 77, no. 3 (1988): 289–94.

Vaidhyanathan, Siva. *Anti-social Media: How Facebook Disconnects Us and Undermines Democracy.* New York: Oxford University Press, 2018.

Vaughn, Stephen L. *Encyclopedia of American Journalism.* New York: Routledge, 2007.

Vaughn, Stephen L. *Holding Fast the Inner Lines: Democracy, Nationalism, and the Committee on Public Information.* Chapel Hill: University of North Carolina Press, 1980.

Vida, István Kornél. "The 'Great Moon Hoax' of 1835." *Hungarian Journal of English and American Studies* 18, no. 1 (2012): 431–41.

Villanueva, Robert. "Gilded Freedom: U.S. Government Exclusion of Chinese Migrants, 1848–1882," *Hohonu* 14, no. 1 (2016): 70–77.

Volokh, Eugene. "Freedom for the Press as an Industry, or for the Press as a Technology: From the Framing to Today." *University of Pennsylvania Law Review* 160 (2011): 459–71.

Voorveld, Hilde A.M., Guda Van Noort, Daniël G. Muntinga, and Fred Bronner. "Engagement with Social Media and Social Media Advertising: The Differentiating Role of Platform Type." *Journal of Advertising* 47, no. 1 (2018): 38–54.

Vosoughi, Soroush, Deb Roy, and Sinan Aral. "The Spread of True and False News Online." *Science* 359, no. 6380 (2018): 1146–51.

Waller, Michael J. *Strategic Influence: Public Diplomacy, Counterpropaganda, and Political Warfare.* Washington, DC: Institute of World Politics Press, 2009.

Walton, Douglas. "Why Fallacies Appear to Be Better Arguments Than They Are." *InformalLogic* 30, no. 2 (2010): 159–84.

Ward, Ken. "Social Networks, the 2016 US Presidential Election, and Kantian Ethics: Applying the Categorical Imperative to Cambridge Analytica's Behavioral Microtargeting." *Journal of Media Ethics* 33, no. 3 (2018): 133–48.

Wendling, Mike. *Alt-Right: From 4chan to the White House.* London: Pluto Books, 2018.

Wever, Peter C., and Leo Van Bergen. "Death from 1918 Pandemic Influenza during the First World War: A Perspective from Personal and Anecdotal Evidence." *Influenza and Other Respiratory Viruses* 8, no. 5 (2014): 538–46.

Wiley, Terrence G. "A Brief History and Assessment of Language Rights in the United States." In *Language Policies in Education,* edited by James W. Tollefson, 73–102. New York: Routledge, 2012.

Williams, Rob. "Fighting Fake News in an Age of Digital Disorientation: Towards 'Real News,' Critical Media Literacy Education, and Independent

Journalism for 21st-Century Citizens." In *Critical Media Literacy and Fake News in Post-truth America,* edited by Christian Z. Goering and Paul L. Thomas, 53–65. Boston: Brill Sense, 2018.

Williamson, Ben. *Big Data in Education: The Digital Future of Learning, Policy, Practice.* Los Angeles: Sage Publications, 2017.

Winders, Richard Bruce. *Mr. Polk's Army: The American Military Experience in the Mexican War.* College Station: Texas A&M University Press, 2001.

Wingard, Jennifer. "Some of the People, All of the Time: Trump's Selective Inclusion." *Women's Studies in Communication* 40, no. 4 (2017): 330–33.

Wolin, Sheldon. *Democracy Incorporated: Managed Democracy and the Specter of Inverted Totalitarianism.* 2008. Reprint, Princeton, NJ: Princeton University Press, 2017.

Wright, Lawrence. *The Terror Years, from Al-Qaeda to the Islamic State.* New York: Vintage Books, 2016.

Wu, Tim. *Attention Merchants: The Epic Scramble to Get inside Our Heads.* New York: Vintage, 2016.

Yildiz, Meida N., and Jared Keengwe, eds. *Handbook of Research on Media Literacy in the Digital Age.* Hershey, PA: IGI Global, 2016.

Young, Kevin. *Bunk: The Rise of Hoaxes, Humbug, Plagiarists, Phonies, Post-facts, and Fake News.* Prince Frederick: HighBridge, 2017.

Zaitchick, Alexander. *The Gilded Rage: A Wild Ride through Donald Trump's America.* New York: Skyhorse, 2016.

Zembylas, Michalinos. "The Politics of Shame in Intercultural Education." *Education, Citizenship and Social Justice* 3, no. 3 (2008): 263–80.

Zhou, Xinyi, Reza Zafarani, Kai Shu, and Huan Liu. "Fake News: Fundamental Theories, Detection Strategies and Challenges." In *Proceedings of the Twelfth ACM International Conference on Web Search and Data Mining,* 836–37. New York: ACM, 2019.

Zinn, Howard. *A People's History of the United States.* 3rd ed. New York: Harper-Collins, 2005. Published online at History Is a Weapon, 2010. http://www .historyisaweapon.com/zinnapeopleshistory.html.

Zuboff, Shoshana. *The Age of Surveillance Capitalism: The Fight for the Future at the New Frontier of Power.* New York: Profile Books, 2019.

Index

Acosta, Jim, 1, 196
Action Coalition for Media Education (ACME), 145
Adams, John Quincy, 33–34, 128
African Americans: fake news about, 36, 57, 79, 82, 108, 110, 155; and slave revolts, 31, 32, 36; and slavery, 15, 37
AIDS, 82
Ailes, Roger, 61–62, 174, 224
Air America, 64
algorithms, 24, 94, 101–102, 105, 109, 133, 138, 141, 158
Allende, Salvador, 85
"Allen-Scott Report," 84
Al-Qaeda, 87
Alsop, Joseph, 83
Alt-Right, 109–112, 159
Amazon, 39, 96, 98, 100, 115
Amerikadeutscher Volksbund (German American Bund), 77
Apple, 95, 98, 100, 115, 129, 137; Siri, 100, 133
Árbenz-Guzmán, Jacobo, 85
"astroturfing," 58

Association of Community Organizations for Reform Now (ACORN), 108, 150, 161
Atwater, Lee, 56–57, 61

Baker, James, 59
Baltimore Sun, 39
Bannon, Steve, 107, 112
Barstow, David, 89
Beck, Glenn, 62
Bee, Samantha, 54
Behar, Joy, 52
Bernays, Edward, 40, 70
Bernstein, Carl, 83–84, 86
bin Laden, Osama, 87
"birther conspiracy," 58–59
Bissonnette, Alexandre, 112
Black, Manafort & Stone (BMS), 56–57
Blackshirts, 77
Blair, Jayson, 46, 155
Bohemian Grove, California, 109
"brain-hacking," 102, 141
Breitbart, 107–110, 112, 121
Brexit, 91, 116
Brooks Brothers' Riot (Docker's Rebellion), 58

Buckley, William, 130
Buffalo Commercial, 4
Bureau of International Information Programs, 117
Bureau of Motion Pictures (BMP), 80
Bush, George H.W., 59- 61
Bush, George W., 52, 56–58, 62, 63
Butler, Allison, 145–146
BuzzFeed, 67

Cambridge Analytica, 114
Carlson, Tucker, 51, 52
Carnegie, Andrew, 37
Carter, Jimmy, 82
Carter, Page, 90
CBS, 40, 43, 50, 83
censorship: and blacklisting, 44; by government, 34, 74, 76, 79, 84, 91, 127–128; by industry, 128–129; opposition to, 146; self-, 111, 130
Central Intelligence Agency, 63, 64, 83–86, 89, 90, 122
Chegg, 137
Chicago Tribune, 39, 78, 89
China/Chinese, 17, 25, 28, 40, 114, 115, 117, 121, 126, 128
Christianity, 4, 26, 68
Church Committee, 86
Churchill, Winston, 158
Clapper, James, 122
Clinton, Bill, 58, 67, 107, 126
Clinton, Hillary, 4, 65, 67, 116, 122, 125, 126
CNBC, 61
CNN, 1, 51–52, 54, 90, 107, 122, 135
Colbert, Stephen, 51
Cold War, 12, 44, 48, 69, 80, 82–84, 86, 115, 128, 129
Columbus, Christopher, 17, 28, 29
Comcast, 50
Comey, James, 126

Committee on Public Information (CPI), 70, 72
Communication Act of 1934, 46, 130–131
Communications Decency Act (1996), 95
computational journalism, 100
Computational Propaganda Research Project, 7
conspiracies, 32, 58, 59, 74, 77, 89, 106, 142
Conway, Kellyanne, 120
Coors Brewing Company, 61
Coughlin, Father Charles, 42–43
Creel, George, 70
Cronkite, Walter, 15, 45, 84
Crossfire (CNN), 51

data collection, 9, 12, 56, 94–104, 114–119, 123–124, 133–135, 137–141, 150
deepfake videos, 104
democracy: practice of, 4, 20–25, 52–58, 62–66, 83, 90–92, 107–108, 122–125; system of, 7, 15, 118, 157
Democratic Party, 37, 58, 62, 64
Disney Corporation, 50
doublespeak, 49
doxing, 112
Dropbox, 115
Drudge, Matt, 106
Drudge Report, 107, 109
Drug Enforcement Administration (DEA), 57
Druick, Zoe, 137
Duterte, Rodrigo, 119, 120, 122, 134

Edison. *See* Theranos
Edwards, John, 62
Eisenhower, Dwight D., 41, 84, 106
Ellsberg, Daniel, 46

Enlightenment, 15, 18
Espionage Act of 1917, 72

Facebook. *See* social media
Fairness Doctrine, 42, 43, 46, 130–131
"false flag" operation, 75, 85, 90
fascism, 42, 77, 78, 79
Federal Bureau of Investigation (FBI), 90, 126
Federal Communications Commission (FCC), 19, 40, 42, 44, 70, 130
feminism, 74, 110, 113, 155
Ford, Gerald, 78
Ford Motor Company, 137
Foreign Intelligence Surveillance Act (FISA), 90
Fox News Channel, 22, 47–49, 51–54, 61–66, 89, 112, 136
France, 15, 16, 33, 34, 115, 126, 128
Francis (pope), 119, 120
Franco, Francisco, 41
Franken, Al, 64
Frankfurt School, 8, 139, 140
Fulbright, William, 86

Gamergate, 112
Gawker, 39
Germany, 17, 42, 67, 70–78, 80, 90, 108, 115
Glass, Stephen, 46, 155
Global Positioning System (GPS), 99, 132
Goebbels, Paul Joseph, 73
Google, 92, 95, 96, 98, 99, 100, 105, 115, 118, 126, 133, 137, 138
Gore, Al, 95
Gould, Jay, 37, 39
Great Britain, 1, 18, 27, 43, 63, 69, 73, 126, 134
Greenwald, Glenn, 90
Guantanamo Bay, 85

Gutenberg, Johann, 17
Guzmán, Juan Jacobo Árbenz, 85–86

hackers/hacking, 24, 114, 117
Hagel, Chuck, 108
Hamilton, Alexander, 33
Hannity, Sean, 2, 43, 49, 50, 62, 65–66
Hearst, William Randolph, 37; Hearst newspapers, 38, 40
Hedges, Christopher, 36, 63
Himmler, Heinrich, 75
Hitler, Adolf, 41–42, 73, 75, 77, 80, 81, 85
Hobbes, Thomas, 74
Hobbs, Renee, 7, 138
Holmes, Elizabeth, 133, 134
Homeland Security, 118
Horton, Willie, 57
Houston, Texas, 117
Huns, 71, 73
Hussein, Saddam, 63, 87

IBM, 137
Illuminati, 109
immigrants, 34, 40, 63, 74, 80, 90, 108, 112, 115, 122
incels, 112
indigenous peoples in Americas, 16, 28–30; Pequots, 29, 30
INFEKTION, 82, 90
"infocalypse," 126
"infotainment," 50, 52
InfoWars, 2, 109, 110, 112, 123, 129
Institute for Propaganda Analysis (IPA), 131
Internet Research Agency (IRA), 115
internet trolls, 116
Iran, 84, 85, 117
Iraq, 47, 60, 63, 64, 87, 88, 126
Islam, 87, 110, 117, 112; Islamophobia, 58, 108, 111, 112, 122; Muslims, 59, 85, 108, 112, 117, 121–122

Islamic State of Iraq and Syria (ISIS), 87
Italy, 18, 63, 77–78

Japan/Japanese, 28, 78–80
Jefferson, Thomas, 18, 33, 34, 144, 157
Jensen, Carl, 21
Jews/Judaism, 4, 42, 73–75, 77
Johnson, Lyndon Baines (LBJ), 45, 84
Johnson, Nicholas, 19
Jolls, Tessa, 152
Jones, Alex, 109
"junk food news," 21

Kellner, Douglas, 140
Kerry, John, 107
Khashoggi, Jamal, 24
Kitchener, Lord Horatio, 69–70, 146
Korea, North, 17, 115, 117, 121
Korea, South, 19
Ku Klux Klan, 111, 112

Levin, Mark, 43
Lewinsky, Monica, 47, 107
Limbaugh, Rush, 43, 46
LinkedIn, 98
Lippmann, Walter, 68, 70, 73
Lügenpresse (lying press), 67, 74, 81, 90
Lusitania, 70, 71
Lynch, Jessica, 87, 88
lynching, 110

MacArthur, General Douglas, 41
Maddow, Rachael, 64–65
Maher, Bill, 63
Manafort, Paul, 56
Mather, Cotton, 31
McCain, John, 58, 107
McCarthy, Joseph, 43–44
McConnell, Mitch, 65
media literacy, 2–3, 8, 14, 140, 142, 153
Mexico, 37, 47, 63

Microsoft, 95, 98, 103, 115, 137
microtargeting, 99, 114, 118–119, 141
Miller, Judith, 63, 155
Miller, William, 26, 27; Millerism, 27;
    Millerites, 26–27, 35, 47
moral outrage, 69, 70, 88, 91, 152
moral panic, 10, 27, 30, 31, 36, 43, 44,
    48, 69–71, 107, 153
Morning Herald (New York), 35
Mosaddegh, Mohammad, 84, 85
MSNBC, 47, 51, 54, 64–65, 90, 120
Murdoch, Rupert, 61–62
Murphy Brown, 1
Murrow, Edward R., 41
Muslims. See Islam
Mussolini, Benito, 41, 42, 77–78

NASDAQ, 96
National Association for Media
    Literacy Education (NAMLE), 2,
    138, 139
National Association for the Advance-
    ment of Colored People (NAACP),
    79, 108
National Enquirer, 39
National Park Service (NPS), 120
National Public Radio (NPR), 89
National Security Agency (NSA), 90,
    115
Nazism, 67, 68, 73–77, 90, 110–111
NBC, 40, 43, 60, 61, 83, 126
neoliberalism, 138, 155
Netflix, 98
Newseum, 154
NewsGuard, 135–136
Newsweek, 83, 85
New York, 4, 27, 32, 39, 77
New York Herald-Tribune, 83
New York Packet, 15
New York Times, 45, 46, 54, 59, 63, 78,
    83–85, 89, 123, 148

New York Tribune, 78
New York Weekly Journal, 17
Nickelodeon, 137, 138
Nielsen Corporation, 98
Nixon, Richard: presidency of, 61;
    Watergate scandal, 86
Noble, Safiya Umoja, 105
North Atlantic Treaty Organization
    (NATO), 82, 116
Novak, Bob, 63

Oakley, Annie, 38
Obama, Barack, 43, 58–59, 62, 103,
    107–108, 111, 117, 119–122, 126
O'Brien, Conan, 51
Office of War Information (OWI), 79,
    80, 131
Olbermann, Keith, 54, 150
Omnicom Public Relations Group,
    60
Operation Mockingbird, 83, 88, 90
Operation Northwoods, 85
O'Reilly, Bill, 47, 54, 62, 150, 155
Orwell, George, 49
Ovadya, Aviv, 126

papacy, 119, 120
Parscale, Brad, 119
partisanship, 12, 32–33, 43, 46, 50–52,
    54, 55, 105, 120, 148, 153
PayPal, 137
Pearl Harbor, Hawaii, 78, 80
pedophiles/pedophilia, 125, 142
Pelosi, Nancy, 104
Pennsylvania, 18, 27, 33, 53
penny press, 34–36, 43, 48, 52
Pentagon, 45, 46, 60, 63, 88–89
Pew Research Center, 55
Philippines, 56, 119, 126, 134
Pirro, Jeanine, 49
Pizzagate, 107, 142

Plame, Valerie, 63
Plato, 100
Poe, Edgar Allan, 35
polarization, 32, 54, 106, 121
PolitiFact, 148, 149
Postman, Neil, 52, 141
POWs, 79
pranks, 7, 43, 103
Pravda, 81
Prius, runaway, 52–53
privacy, 141. See also data collection
"Private Snafu" series, 42
Project Censored, 146, 152
propaganda, defined, 68
Public Broadcasting Service (PBS), 51
Pulitzer, Joseph, 37
Pulitzer Prize, 89, 90
push-polling, 56, 58

race/racism, 35, 36, 47, 57, 58, 78, 105,
    107–108, 110, 111, 116, 138
radio, 40–43, 81–82, 109, 111, 141
RAND Corporation, 45
Reagan, Ronald, 56, 61, 95, 106
Reddit, 92, 110, 113
Remington, Frederic, 38
Republican Party, 10, 44, 53, 56–65,
    83, 107–108, 116, 120, 126, 152
Rockefeller, John D., 37
Rodgers, Elliot, 112
Roosevelt, Eleanor, 110
Roosevelt, Franklin Delano (FDR), 42,
    79–80, 83
Roosevelt, Theodore, 39, 59
Roth, Andy Lee, 146
rumors, 3, 27, 32, 36, 41, 42, 47, 131
Russia, 6, 65, 91, 113, 115–117

Sabah, Saud al-, 60
Sacra Congregatio de Propaganda
    Fide, 68

Salem witch trials, 31, 47
Samsung, 100
Sanders, Bernie, 65, 116
satirical fake news: *Clickhole,* 51; *The Colbert Report,* 51; *The Daily Show,* 52–53, 120; *The Onion,* 51; *Red Eye,* 52, 54–55
Sayoc, Cesar, 122
scams, 47, 53, 150
scapegoating, 38, 40
Shapiro, Ben, 112
Share, Jeff, 140, 152
Sherrod, Shirley, 108
Shillue, Tom, 52
Shultz, Ed, 64
Sinclair, Upton, 56
Skinner, B. F., 101
Skype, 98
Slate, 6
Smith-Mundt Act, 82, 86, 89
Snell, George, 21–22
Snopes, 93, 94, 148, 149
Snowden, Edward, 115
socialism, 59, 72, 78, 80
social media, 2–4, 99–102, 104–105, 117–122, 134–137, 145–146; Facebook, 93, 98–102, 104, 105, 114–116, 118–120, 122, 129, 133–135, 137–139, 145; Friendster, 101; MySpace, 101; Snapchat, 98, 101
Sony, 117, 137
Soros, George, 92
spaghetti tree hoax, 43
Spicer, Sean, 120
Spotify, 98–99, 129
Stewart, Jon, 51–55
Sulzberger, Arthur Hays, 54, 83
Sun (New York), 82
Sun Reporter (San Francisco), 35
Sunstein, Cass, 89
surveillance capitalism, 97, 133, 137

Tableau software, 93
Taibbi, Matt, 53
Tarbell, Ida, 72
techno-utopianism, 131–140, 142
Television News Inc. (TVN), 61
terrorism, 86–89, 95–96, 108, 121, 129–130
Tesla, 133
Theranos; 133
Tillman, Pat, 88
Time Warner, 50
Tocqueville, Alexis de, 15
trolls, internet, 116
Truman, Harry, 56, 82
Trump, Donald, 1, 5, 49, 59, 65, 67, 90, 92–93, 103, 107, 109, 114, 116, 119–123, 126, 134, 142, 145

Uber, 99, 137
Union of Soviet Socialist Republics (USSR), 80–82, 129
United Newsreel, 79
US Department of Homeland Security, 118
US military: Army, 88; Marines, 87, 119; Navy, 45, 47, 88

Vanderbilt, Cornelius, 37
Verizon, 115
Viacom, 50
Video News Releases (VNRs), 4, 62
Vietnam / Vietnamese, 11, 44–48, 136
Voice of America (VOA), 79, 82

Warner, Marc, 134
Warren, Elizabeth, 65
Washington Post, 24, 39, 44–46, 60, 63, 85, 88–89
Watergate scandal, 86
weapons of mass destruction (WMDs), 63–64, 126

Welch, Edgar Maddison, 125, 142
Whitaker, Clem, 55
White House Office of Information and Regulatory Affairs (OIRA), 89
Wikipedia, 99, 121, 135
Williams, Brian, 47, 155
Williamson, Ben, 137
Wilson, Joseph, 63
Woodrow, Wilson, 71-72

xenophobia, 39, 40, 90, 107, 108, 116

Yahoo, 98, 115
yellow journalism, 38
YouTube, 98, 110, 118, 125, 129, 135

Zinn, Howard, 29
Zuboff, Shoshana, 97, 100, 133
Zuckerberg, Mark, 104, 105, 133, 134

Founded in 1893,
UNIVERSITY OF CALIFORNIA PRESS
publishes bold, progressive books and journals
on topics in the arts, humanities, social sciences,
and natural sciences—with a focus on social
justice issues—that inspire thought and action
among readers worldwide.

The UC PRESS FOUNDATION
raises funds to uphold the press's vital role
as an independent, nonprofit publisher, and
receives philanthropic support from a wide
range of individuals and institutions—and from
committed readers like you. To learn more, visit
ucpress.edu/supportus.

Made in the USA
Monee, IL
23 January 2024

52232972R00143